Summer Food

Summer Food

JUDITH OLNEY

NEW YORK 1978 Atheneum

DRAWINGS BY JUDITH OLNEY

Library of Congress Cataloging in Publication Data

Olney, Judith.
Summer food.
Includes index.
1. Cookery. I. Title.
TX652.O544 1978 641.5 77-15870
ISBN 0-689-10882-6

Published simultaneously in Canada by McClelland & Stewart Ltd.
Manufactured by American Book–Stratford Press,
Saddle Brook, New Jersey
Designed by Kathleen Carey
First Edition

For Richard

Now with constant song the cicadas rend the thickets;
now the spotted lizard lurks in her cool retreat:
if thou art wise, lay thee down now and steep thyself in a
bowl of summer-time. . . .

VIRGIL

Acknowledgments

I wish to thank the following students, assistants and friends for their help: Linda Austin, Brenda Brodie, Bob Fowler, Harvey Gunter, Charles Haynes, Ruth Klingel, Terry McNairy, Happy Procter, Harriet Skinner, Betty Wahler, Gail Weinerth, and especially, José Wilson.

My deepest gratitude is to my husband, James, for his gentle and supportive care.

Contents

PREFACE: ON SUMMER FOOD 3

FIRST COURSES (*Hors d'oeuvre, Eggs, Soups, Terrines*) 19

VEGETABLES AND SALADS 60

MAIN COURSES (*Pastas, Fish, Poultry, Meats*) 110

DESSERTS 175

PRESERVING SUMMER 226

APPENDIX (*Mail Order Sources*) 246

INDEX 252

Summer Food

Preface: On Summer Food

COOKING in summer (and I include in that period all time from spring's quickening of nature through the last languorous days of September) should provide one with particular aesthetic pleasure. Fresh produce, small green gardens, beds of herbs, dappled sunlight playing through trees and onto picnic spreads, fruits and flowers in overflowing abundance—all combine to suggest an approach to summer cooking based on unity, harmony and radiance.

The unified meal is a necessity due to the fact that summer meals, like summer appetites, are often small and light—often a main dish and a salad. The sign of a creative intelligence moving upon the elements is the blurring of rigid boundaries concerning what constitutes salad, what determines a main course. Throughout this book you will find vegetables that could be salads that could be main courses; main courses that could be first courses; salads that might as well be vegetables. A unified meal will combine two or more dishes into harmonious accord, but it will take into account that faded summer palates need the awakening whimsy, the unexpected, the surprise of an old familiar recipe in a new guise, a different pattern of presentation or organization.

The aesthetic harmony of summer meals depends upon attention paid to colors, temperatures and flavors. The very palette of summer suggests those hues most pleasing in its foods, and over and over again in the recipes to follow, colors group themselves: green and white; green and lavender; peach, green and white; red, yellow and green. Summer's food is brighter, more intense than winter's, not only in color but also in flavor (we have no need of hot, bland comfort). Instead dishes shade into luke or cool to stand against the climate.

Radiant food, with light refracted from the hidden recessed depths of cool, trembling gel especially pleases in the summer (though the same dish appears cold, overformal, uninviting in winter). The bright, open candor of raw salads, unsauced vegetables, lightly garnished meats stands directly opposed to our winter need for succulence and heat to be retained, enwrapped in solacing gratins and golden crusts. The shining glazes on bread and fruit tarts, the brilliance of crystalline ices, the last-minute misting of salads and crudités to ensure their luster, all contribute to the conscious use of light and radiance.

Although this book contains many brief, easy recipes, it also assumes that a serious cook will need and desire to do serious cooking in summer, and it assumes that even if there is no opportunity to grow fresh produce, the good cook will at least search out the best that is offered.

As I wrote this book through a long, hot, home-based summer, I continually thought of food and occasions from past seasons, and so these pages reflect and sometimes record those evocative memories of childhood when sweet corn and homemade ice cream were all one needed to survive happily; of travels away from home to exotic lands; and especially of pleasant hazy days in the spinning sun and nights gathered around table at the Provençal home of the person to whom this book is dedicated.

A Note on Recipes and Ingredients

Recipes in this book have all been tested in classes and for home use. Temperatures and cooking times of necessity are based on a single stove's capabilities, and therefore one should take into account the fast or slow temperament of one's own oven.

All cream referred to is meant to be whipping cream.

All butter is meant to be unsalted.

All references to fresh and specific herbs are given as ideal. Make intelligent substitutions when necessary.

On Summer Menus (some general thoughts)

1. Consider weather (a rainy, cool May night—a wilting August noon), time of day, the possible heat a meal could generate, carefully.

2. With thoughtful planning, there is no need to have more than one cooked-that-day dish in any meal.

3. Turn off heat five to ten minutes early when baking. The dish will continue to cook in dying heat.

4. Bringing dishes to table in their cooking vessels and opening them under people's noses often has a stimulating effect on the gastric juices of guests.

5. When feeding guests garlic (as in bourride, aïoli, etc.) remember that it is a soporific and, as such, calls for drastic countermeasures to keep guests from becoming heavy-laden. A bright salad, anything whimsical, an icy, acid dessert will refresh their spirits.

6. The nicest summer meals (and the most ice-breaking) are those that call for a shared physical experience, with everyone making his own vinaigrette and dipping and sucking artichoke leaves, or eating warm asparagus with the fingers, or tearing off huge chunks of bread from a communal loaf. (There are many such participation dishes in this book.)

7. A more formal summer's menu, where there are many (though light) courses, should be a psychological continuum of sensuous sights, aromas, tastes, textures and temperatures. It should be carefully considered, then constructed much as a writer of fiction might write a short story. That is, first some exposition/hors d'oeuvre—a detail or two that will start the action and give the reader/eater the necessary knowledge of events to follow. Then some first course rising action—a complication wherein the senses quicken and expectations liven. Then the climax, the *raison d'être* of the story/meal, the point at which all things converge and beyond which it is not possible to go. What is left can only be the *dénouement*—the unknotting, untangling "and they lived happily ever after" that salad/cheese/dessert provides.

Some Participation Dishes:

Artichokes with Gremolata
Delicacies in Grape Leaves
Tabbouleh Rolled in Bibb Lettuce
Lobster à l'Américaine
Le Grand Aïoli
Bourride
Making and consuming ice cream

Picnic Food:

A Picnic Loaf
Olive Quiche
Sausage in Herbed Brioche
Toasted Pan Bagnat
Pressed Lemon Chicken
Boned, Roasted Chicken with Country Pâté
Cold Neapolitan Potato Cake with Sausage
Stuffed Pizza
Lemon Terrine
Raspberry Pâté

Elegant Showpieces:

Three-Layered Fish Terrine
Molded Chicken Liver Mousse
Fresh Morel Sausage
Molded Spring Vegetables in Herbed Jelly
A Macédoine of Grated Vegetables
Shrimp Mousse with Sauce Américaine
Scallop Mousse with Watercress Sauce
Peach Cake
Chilled Chocolate Framboise Cakes
Eggs in an Orange Nest

A Large, Rustic Dinner Party:

Red and Green Soufflé Cakes
Leg of Lamb in a Crust
Thin Onion Tart
Rough and Wild Greens with Grilled Chapons and Walnut Sauce
Grape Bread with Fruit and Cheese

A Large, Formal Dinner Party:

Small Cold Paupiettes of Salmon
A Rapid Roast of Beef (hot and minus sauce)
Celery and Watercress Purée
Peach Cakes with Raspberry Purée

An Italian Party:

Artichokes, Mushrooms and Olives Sott'olio
Focaccia, Grissini
Rolled, Stuffed Omelets with Chicken Livers and Basil
Chocolate and Vanilla Pudding with Poached Pears

A Flowered Luncheon:

Flowered Green Frittata
Frittata Niçoise
Shrimp and Zucchini Fritters
Filigreed Bread
Peaches Aswim in Rose Petals
Flemish Tart

Some Dishes Low in Calories:

Flower Garden Soup
Flowered Green Frittata
Eggs Baked in Peppers
Rolled, Stuffed Nasturtium Leaves
Herbed Cheese
Ratatouille Terrine
Molded Spring Vegetables in Herbed Jelly
An Oriental Salad Plate
Herbed and Jellied Chicken
Café Brûlot and Cream
Champagne Jelly with Raspberries
Cantaloupe and Cassis
Granités

Fast, Easy Dishes:

Quick Baked Eggs
Lettuce and Asparagus Stew
Grated Corn Pudding
Fresh Vegetable Stew with Herbed Dumplings
Sautéed Vegetables with Persillade
Tabbouleh Rolled in Bibb Lettuce
Crab and Onions in a Crumb Crust

Lobster à l'Américaine
Kathleen Taylor's Stewed Flounder
Chicken and Cucumbers
Crisp Sage and Liver
Raspberry Pâté
Quick Jam Tart
Sautéed Figs
Breaded Peach Pudding

GRILLS:

Delicacies in Grape Leaves
Grilled Zucchini Salad with Herb Flowers
Grilled Pepper Salad
Shrimp Brochettes with Lemon and Dill Sauce
Mackerel Brochettes with Saffron Sauce
Grilled, Smoked Fish with Braised Celery
Grilled Steak and Vegetables à l'Orientale
Breast of Lamb Riblets with Artichokes and Mustard Cream

ONE DISH MEALS:

Green Bean Soup with Swirled Pistou
Purée of Shrimp with Watercress Cream
Delicacies in Grape Leaves
Molded Risotto alla Primavera
Rigatoni with Eggplant and Basil
Grilled Smoked Fish with Braised Celery
Le Grand Aïoli
Bourride

On Summer Bread

I first started baking bread when I lived, for two years, in a land of continual summer. Deep in sub-tropic Liberian bush country, two rugged hours from the main supply center, one either made one's own bread or did without, a situation that provided an excellent education in the art of baking.

Week after week I experimented with flour, water, yeast and salt—the only elements needed in honest bread—and I learned from Africa's climatic extremes. While it was certainly always hot, the seasons divided into hot-dry and hot-rainy. In dry season, dough would rise and billow from the bowl in record time, over-fermenting itself and baking off in pale, dumpy loaves. In rainy season, the dough sulked under its protective towel and loaves were often damp, ropy specimens. No sooner had I mastered bread-making in the face of Africa's elemental peculiarities than we moved to an English winter in which all dough seemed to sit like a lumpen, grudging rock, heavy and unmoving in its bowl. But that is another story.

Today, when bread-making has become such an instinctive part of hands and being, every loaf turns out perfectly. However, in classes, when students bring me their obligatory loaf after a bread demonstration, I see again the flaws that used to plague me so. Those students who persist in weekly baking soon develop the feel and experience necessary to remedy any faults, and this continuous experimentation is the only way to evolve the intuitive rapport with basic ingredients that allows bread-making to become an easy joy.

The bread I bake in summer is quite different from its winter version. Winter calls for solid, flavorful *pain au levain* that adapts itself readily to crumbs for gratins and thick slices for peasant soups. Then a longer preparation and baking time is no bother, and the yeasty beer *levain,* put to ferment two or three days before bread is baked, adds its aroma to a kitchen full of heat and baking fragrance.

Summer loaves, to my way of thinking, should be light, crisp, and easily broken apart at table. A flat or filigreed loaf best fulfills these demands. It is less dense than thicker, more conventional shapes, and the multi-segmented surface provides expansive area for crusting. Because its baking time is shorter, the crust that does develop is exceedingly crisp. The bread can, literally, be broken at table an hour out of the oven with no fear of resultant indigestion.

The following recipe yields the amount of dough necessary to build large and spectacular loaves. The sesame seed is added to increase the wheaty "grain-ness" of the bread. It must be pulverized so that the seed becomes only a flavoring element that is not specifically recognizable as sesame. Use a mortar and pestle to crush the seed.

Summer Bread

2⅔ cups warm but not hot water
1½ packages dry yeast
or
a generous ounce fresh yeast
Unbleached flour (at least 6½ cups)
3 teaspoons salt
¼ cup toasted sesame seed, ground to a powder
1 egg yolk, for glaze

A plant mister

Place water in a large mixing bowl. Add yeast and stir until dissolved.

Add 5 cups of flour, the salt and sesame seed and, mixing with the hand, continue adding flour until the dough is firm enough to turn out on a floured surface.

As the dough is kneaded, continue adding flour by sprinkling it on the working surface. It is foolish to give precise amounts of flour in any bread recipe as flours vary drastically in their protein strengths and their ability to absorb water. Here, however, is what you should aim for. Continue adding flour until the dough no longer sticks to and pulls away on your hand as you knead. Stop adding flour as soon as this point is reached so that you work with a soft dough. The dough itself will firm during kneading. Too much flour only binds into a hard, difficult to work mass. A soft dough rises faster and shapes more easily. *Keep dough as soft as possible.*

Knead hard for 10 to 12 minutes. Plant your right foot forward and rock your weight heavily onto it and into the heels of your hands. Push, fold over; push, fold over. Dough which is underkneaded, poked at by someone unwilling to take off rings, or twiddled delicately with the fingers, will not form the elastic network of strong proteinaceous gluten that it needs to become a sturdy loaf. Correct kneading will probably leave you winded. *Knead vigorously.* (The correct level at which to perform kitchen work is one on which you can rest the flat of your hands without bending your back or your elbows. An inch over or under will give you backache or strain the upper arms.)

Place the dough in a bowl and cover with a towel. Leave to rise until double in bulk. In the summer, this can be as short a time as 40 minutes, though it usually takes longer. If the dough overripens and, in effect, over-extends itself, it will have a toneless, cottony appearance and feel flabby to the touch. A faintly sour fruit smell can develop. (It is particularly important that the later second rising does not reach this stage or the baked loaf will have a loose, honeycombed crumb.)

If the day is cool and rainy and the dough seems sluggish, nudge it by placing the bowl in a briefly warmed, then turned off oven. Dough that is underripe will bake off in undersized loaves. The crumb will be close-textured and streaked with damp, bound 'ropes' of dough. The bread will ferment and mold quickly.

When the dough has risen, lightly oil a large baking sheet (preferably of cast-iron), and form the dough in baking shape upon it. There is no need to officially punch down. Manipulate the dough as much as necessary to gain an interesting design or texture. When formed, cover the loaf loosely with a towel and let rise until there appears to be almost a full-volumed (though white) loaf. A good 85% of the rising will have taken place at this point, with only minimal further expansion to come in the oven. *Let rise twice, once in bowl, once on baking sheet.*

Beat the egg yolk with a tablespoon of water to form a light glaze. Brush over the loaf and place in a preheated 400° oven. Spray everything generously with a plant mister—the oven sides and bottom, the loaf itself, and the baking tray. Repeat three or four more times in the first 20 minutes of baking. At the end of 20 minutes, lower heat to 350° and bake another 25 minutes. Turn the oven off and allow the bread to remain for 10 more minutes. Remove from oven and let loaf rest on a cake rack or at a tilt so steam doesn't soften the undercrust. Eat with unsalted butter.

(These directions are specifically for loaves formed in the following patterns.)

THREE FILIGREED DESIGNS

Push and press the dough into basic broad shapes (see below) directly on the baking sheet. Cut slashes with a sharp knife and tuck into shape with the fingers. Use the largest rectangular pan you have for the first two breads. The butterfly pattern, for instance, will be a good twenty inches across at the top. The round loaf can be baked on a pizza pan. The holes should be large enough that there is no danger of their closing over when the dough expands.

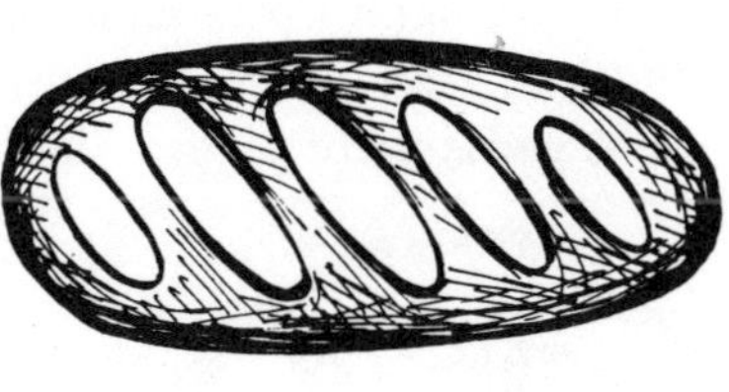

A Grape Loaf

A nice loaf to feed a crowd, for it breaks apart into small, easily halved rolls. Divide once-risen dough into 30 round grape balls, a stem, a leaf and a tendril. Form into a bunch on the oiled baking sheet. Allow the grapes just to touch but do not crowd them. Moisten with water and glue stem, tendril and leaf to the bunch. Let rise, glaze with egg yolk and water, and bake.

Pretzel Bread

Make one recipe bread dough (page 11), substituting ⅓ cup plain malt for the sesame seed. After the dough has risen once, form it into a rope 6 feet long and coil it into pretzel shape on an oiled baking sheet. Glaze with egg yolk and water and sprinkle with coarse sea salt. Let rise and bake. A particularly flavorful loaf.

A Picnic Loaf

1 recipe bread dough *(see page 11)*
10 ounces Gruyère cheese
4 eggs in the shell
1 pound Polish sausage (kielbasa) cut in four and pricked

Let the dough rise once in the bowl. Divide in two and make a thin, flat circle of dough (around 14 inches in diameter) on the oiled baking sheet. Place the cheese in the middle in a neat, round, 6-inch-wide heap. (Grate or cut it into shape.) Cover cheese with half the remaining dough, sealing on the lid with a small amount of water. Space the eggs evenly around the edge with a section of sausage between each egg. Form the remaining dough into narrow, rounded strips and use them in a criss-cross pattern to bind eggs and sausage to the bread base. Moisten ends to help them stick. Let rise, glaze, and bake, allowing an extra 5 minutes in the oven. The eggs will cook, the sausage render its flavorful juices, and the cheese melt succulently into the bread. Serve cut into pie wedges. The loaf will provide all that is necessary for a picnic but the wine.

FOCACCIA

There are many varieties of *focaccia*, basically a peasant bread, in Italy. A small portion of dough, reserved from a large batch, is flavored, formed into a flat round, and put to bake with the more traditional loaves as an adult snack or children's treat. There are chestnut flour *focaccia*, cheese *focaccia* and, during holidays, several types of sweetened *focaccia*. But of most interest in the summer are those flavored with fresh herbs and olives. Because the flavoring agents are strikingly obvious, perhaps even insistent, the loaves should accompany only those dishes rough enough in character to hold their own. The scattering of coarse salt is a welcome touch in a land where the majority of bread is flatly unsalted. It is little bother to make all three of the following varieties at once if the flavoring ingredients are prepared in advance.

Focaccia with White Wine and Olives

2 teaspoons dry yeast
½ cup warm but not hot water
½ cup dry white wine
⅓ cup pitted black Niçoise olives, chopped coarse
1 teaspoon oil from olives
Approximately 2½ cups unbleached flour
Egg yolk and water glaze
Coarse sea salt

Dissolve yeast in lukewarm water and wine. Add olives and olive oil (no need for salt as the olives will provide it), then work in flour, following usual kneading procedure. Leave to double in bulk. Roll out into a circle about 1 inch thick. Place on oiled baking sheet and make a series of indentations in the dough with a finger. Brush with egg yolk glaze and in the center, place a spiky flower of cut olive petals to decoratively identify the flavor. Sprinkle with a small handful of sea salt, let rise 20 minutes, and bake at 375° for about 45 minutes.

Ligurian Focaccia with Marjoram

1 cup warm but not hot water
2 teaspoons dry yeast
1 tablespoon olive oil
¼ cup minced marjoram leaves and knots, preferably fresh
Approximately 2½ cups unbleached flour
Egg yolk and water glaze
Coarse sea salt

Prepare in the same manner as Olive Focaccia. After the loaf is glazed, impress upon it a pretty sprig of marjoram.

Focaccia with Sage

Prepare in the same manner as the preceding recipe, substituting 35 large leaves of sage, preferably fresh, as the flavoring herb. Strip the leaves back from their center ribs and chop roughly. Decorate with a spray of small leaves after glazing.

Almond Grissini (Breadsticks)

Make ½ batch of regular bread dough (see page 11), but substitute ¼ cup ground roasted almonds for the sesame seed. Divide dough into 16 to 18 parts. Roll each section into a fat stick about 17 or 18 inches long. Work the dough back and forth under your palms on a flat and floured surface. Place lengthwise on a lightly oiled baking sheet. Bake at 375° for about 30 minutes. Turn each stick until it is uniformly brown on all sides. These *grissini* are meant to be chewy rather than totally dry. Serve massed in a basket.

First Courses

(HORS D'OEUVRE, EGGS, SOUPS, TERRINES)

THINKING on hors d'oeuvre brings to mind foods seen and savored in strange markets, walk-about-and-munch-on foods purchased in the streets of foreign cities during summer trips abroad. The bready pretzels at a Munich railway station, each slit in two and generously spread with creamery butter. The ubiquitous fruit stands of Italy, with their beds of crushed ice and watermelon slices. The bags of chewy tripe in certain sections of Rome, and roasted *ceci* to be munched like peanuts by the handful. The crisp, deep-fried pizzas of Naples; the *socca* stands of Genoa and Provence where flat, oiled cakes of chick-pea flour brown over grills.

The pleasure of double markets in Morocco—the indigenous native *souks* redolent of spices, green and red peppers, baskets of bread balanced on veiled heads, and heaps of honey-dipped pastries alight with flies, over against the small French markets (always nearby wherever the French have established ties) with thin wild asparagus and *cèpes* gathered from the inland hills. The main street of Tunis where one can buy *brik*, that crisp pastry enfolding a soft egg that drips down the chin when first bitten into. The markets of West Africa, produced so plentifully in certain seasons, so sparsely at "hungry time." The women in their colorful *lappas;* tethered chickens; the small heaps of smoked monkey legs, monkey arms, monkey heads; huge butterpear avocados ("No," you argue, "five cent–five cent is far too much to pay for one"); great knuckled hearts of palm trees all in a pile; the small roasting-fires where, for 3 cents you are given an ear of corn sprinkled with cayenne, moistened with palm oil and roasted to a char.

The last jellied eel stand in London, with people huddled about eating the gelatinous delicacy (for Britishers are too staid to actually walk, food in mouth, about the streets).

The neat row of chipolata sausages at a Provençal fête, each impaled on a thin skewer, half-robed in barding fat and with a sprig of fresh rosemary tied over the open edge, ready for grilling. The long stretch of the Toulon market, beginning at the port where fishing boats line the wharf with fresh rockfish for bouillabaisse, small whitings for friture . . . on up a gentle, tree-lined hill, past mounds of fruits, vegetables, to the *chichi-frégi* (fried frill) stand where thick cruller batter is pressed in long, serpentine strand into deep fat and fried. (For one franc the lady snips off an eight-inch portion, rolls it in abundant sugar and hands you the delicious, indigestible bit.) Further on the pizza and *pissaladière* stands, plump rounds of dough baked with onion and anchovy toppings, or mushrooms, or a thick spread of tomato paste, mussels, and shrimp. And the olive stands with a dozen different varieties waiting to be ladled from their briny casks into twisted paper cones and eaten on a summer's day.

Roasted Ceci (Chickpeas)

MAKES 4 CUPS

1 clove garlic, crushed
3 tablespoons olive oil
1 pound chickpeas
Table sea salt or *kosher salt*

Place the flat side of a knife blade over the garlic and press down. Put crushed clove in 3 tablespoons oil and leave to steep. Cover chickpeas generously with salted water and bring to a boil. Boil 2 minutes, turn off heat, and leave for 1 hour. Drain and pat dry. Place peas in an uncrowded baking pan.

Remove garlic and pour oil over the peas, making sure each is lightly moistened. Sprinkle with salt and bake at 350° for about 40 minutes, giving the *ceci* frequent shakes to turn and brown evenly all sides. Blot any extra oil away and resalt. Serve as a light hors d'oeuvre with radishes (left, in the French manner, with an inch of greenery attached) and Niçoise olives enhanced by the addition of fresh herb sprigs.

Green Olive Paste

MAKES 1½ CUPS

About 12 ounces ripe pitted green olives, well drained
1 large garlic clove
2 tablespoons diced red pepper (or canned pimento)
2 tablespoons white wine vinegar (or more, to taste)
Pepper

Cover the olives with water and bring to a boil in a small pan. Drain, and when perfectly dry, purée olives and garlic in mortar, blender, or food processor. Stir in the red pepper, add vinegar and grind on pepper to taste. Refrigerate at least 2 days before serving. A piquant spread for thin toast.

Brik

SERVES 1

2 leaves phyllo pastry
1 tablespoon melted unsalted butter
2 tablespoons cooked, dry, chopped spinach
1 medium egg
Salt and pepper
Peanut oil for frying

Trim phyllo leaves into rounds 8 inches in diameter. (Keep them moist under a lightly dampened dish towel.) Brush melted butter over one round, top with another and butter it, also. Tilt a dinner plate up by placing a spoon under one edge. Drape the phyllo so that the half point rests cupped in the lower curve of the plate. Place spinach in the center, indent it with a spoon, and carefully break in the egg. (The yolk will rest on the spinach.) Season and fold the lower phyllo half up, pressing the open edges together. Fry in a large pan containing a good inch of hot oil. The frying time should be just long enough to lightly brown the pastry on either side. The egg white should set, the yolk be still slightly runny so that it bursts when bitten into. Remove from the oil with a slotted spoon and drain on paper towels. May be kept warm in a low oven until more are finished, but is best when consumed immediately.

Toulonnais Pizzas

SERVES 6

Make 1 recipe of Marjoram Focaccia (see page 17), keeping the dough particularly soft. Divide dough into 6 portions and roll each into a 5-inch circle. Brush with olive oil and spread lightly with a thick homemade purée of tomatoes. Top with either:

Onions, anchovies, olives (Slice a large onion thin. Cook slowly in 1 tablespoon of olive oil until lightly browned. Add to pizzas and top each with 2 anchovy filets and 2 or 3 Niçoise olives.)

or mushrooms (Slice 10 medium mushrooms. Sauté in olive oil until mushrooms give, then reabsorb, their juices. Divide among pizzas, season with salt and pepper, and top each with 1 tablespoon of grated parmesan and Gruyère cheese mixed.)

or seafood (Dip a half pound each of mussels and shrimp in oil before placing on tomato sauce. Sprinkle lightly with cheese.)

Let pizzas rise for 30 minutes. Bake at 350° for about 35 minutes.

Toasted Pan Bagnat

SERVES 1

1 large kaiser roll
3 tablespoons olive oil
1 large garlic clove, crushed
2 or 3 sprigs fresh oregano (optional)
4 cherry tomatoes, halved
2 tablespoons green pepper, diced
2 scallions, chopped thin
3 anchovy filets, drained and dried
Capers
Salt and pepper

Slice a small cap from the roll. Dig out crumbs from the roll and also remove them from the cap so only a thin shell is left.

Heat 2 tablespoons oil with garlic and oregano, mashing down on the herb so that it will impart its volatile fragrance. Let oil steep off heat for 5 minutes, then remove garlic and oregano. Brush the interior of the roll and cap with oil, and place on a baking sheet to toast at 300° until crisp and golden (about 20 minutes).

Fill roll with cherry tomatoes, green peppers, scallions, anchovy filets and a few capers. Season well with salt and pepper and moisten the filling with another tablespoon of olive oil. Recap. Eat within 2 hours of assembly.

Another idea for crisped rolls:

Substitute butter for olive oil and toast the rolls. Fill with a mixture of scrambled eggs and asparagus. Cut the asparagus tips 1½ inches long. Slice the remaining edible stalk fine, sauté in butter and mix with the eggs before scrambling them.

Parboil the tips until just tender. Fill the rolls and let a cluster of asparagus tips sprout from the center. These rolls will be capless, of course.

Sausage in Herbed Brioche

SERVES 12 TO 15 AS AN APPETIZER

FOR THE BRIOCHE

1 ounce dry or compressed yeast
4 tablespoons warm milk
2 cups unbleached flour
1 teaspoon salt
3 medium eggs at room temperature
⅓ cup fine-chopped herbs (chives, parsley thyme, oregano)
5 tablespoons softened unsalted butter

FOR THE SAUSAGE

Approximately 1 pound Polish sausage (kielbasa)
1 egg
Flour

Dissolve yeast in milk. Put the flour and salt into a large bowl and make a well in the middle. Break in eggs, add the herbs and yeast and work ingredients into a dough. (The easiest way is to let a heavy mixer, with flat blade attached, beat the dough for about 6 minutes.) By hand, slap the dough down on a lightly floured surface, knead, pick up, and slap down again vigorously until it feels smooth and elastic and the protein has developed enough to toughen the consistency.

Add the softened butter and work well, another 2 minutes by machine, longer by hand. Cover dough and let rise for 1 hour in a warm, but not hot, place.

To assemble loaf, butter the longest cookie sheet that will fit in your oven. Cut the looped sausage into 2 or 3 pieces so that it can be arranged in a straight line. Beat 1 egg with a fork and use half of it to moisten the sausage. Roll sausage in a generous amount of flour. The coating formed will help the dough to adhere during baking.

Remove dough from the bowl and, without punching down any more than necessary, press and stretch it along the length of the baking sheet in a 6-inch wide strip. Lay sausage down the middle and fold up the dough to enclose it. Make sure the dough is sealed well. Mix remaining egg with 1 teaspoon of water and brush over the loaf to glaze. Let rise 30 minutes.

Bake in a preheated 400° oven for 20 minutes. Turn the heat down to 375° and continue baking for another 20 to 25 minutes or until the top is a rich, golden brown.

For convenience: the loaf may be made a day or two ahead, then cooled, wrapped and refrigerated. Reheat before serving. Freezes well. Good picnic fare.

Herbed Cheese

SERVES 6

1½ pounds cottage cheese
⅓ cup cream, lightly whipped
1 clove garlic, ground to a purée
½ teaspoon salt
⅓ cup fine-chopped fresh herbs (parsley, tarragon, lemon thyme, summer savory, chervil, but mostly chives)
1 egg white

Cheesecloth for the molds

This ingredient volume will either produce 1 large or 6 individual cheeses. Use a large *coeur à la crème* mold or make small molds by cutting down 6 plastic half-gallon milk containers to about 3 inches in height. Puncture 10 holes in the bottom of each with a skewer or nail. (Waxed cottage cheese containers and the like can also be used.)

Force the cottage cheese through a sieve with a pestle or large metal spoon. Add cream, garlic, salt and herbs. Whip the egg white until stiff and fold into the cheese.

Line each mold with a double layer of cheesecloth which will both help the cheese keep its shape and add a delicate mesh pattern to the surface. Spoon in the cheese, making sure the mixture firmly fills the entire mold by tapping it on a counter to settle the contents. Fold cheesecloth ends over the top of the cheese. Set molds on a platter and refrigerate for 48 hours. (Drain the platter off as it fills.) The cheese will firm and become redolent of garlic and herbs.

To serve, turn out on a platter or individual plates and peel off the cloth. The cheese is handsome when matted on one or two large green leaves. Press a small decorative sprig of tarragon or savory in the middle. Each person grinds on fresh pepper and adds salt to taste. Fresh bread and unsalted butter should also be on table.

Stuffed Tomato Tart with Pesto

SERVES 8

2 large onions, chopped fine
4 tablespoons unsalted butter
8 ounces firm mushrooms, cleaned and chopped fine
2 tablespoons chopped parsley
Salt and pepper
½ cup grated Parmesan cheese
7 or 8 firm, medium-small tomatoes
Butter

A prebaked 11-inch pie shell (a round quiche dish makes a perfect mold) (page 200)

A generous batch of thin Pesto Sauce (see page 28)

FOR GARNISH
Basil sprigs

Cook the onions in the melted butter until just soft. Do not allow to brown. Add mushrooms, turn up the heat, and sauté until the mushrooms have given off their juices then reabsorbed them and appear dry. Add parsley, seasoning, and half the grated cheese.

Cut the tomatoes in two, crosswise. Core and clean out seeds and juice so only shells remain. Stuff tomatoes with the mushroom mixture. Sprinkle remaining grated cheese on top and place a small shaving of butter on each half.

Place tomatoes in a lightly oiled pan and bake at 400° for 12 to 15 minutes. Arrange the tomatoes in the pie shell and place under a broiler briefly to brown the tops.

Let cool to room temperature then dribble the pesto sauce decoratively over all. Place small basil sprigs here and there in the open places between the tomatoes.

Pesto Sauce

MAKES ABOUT 1 CUP

3 large garlic cloves
2 tablespoons pine nuts
1 cup packed basil leaves
2 or 3 sprigs summer savory (optional)
½ cup Parmesan cheese freshly grated
Olive oil
Salt

In a mortar or heavy bowl, pound the garlic into a smooth purée. Add pine nuts and continue pounding to an even paste. Add herbs (stripped of stems or ribs) and mash to a purée. Mix in spoons of cheese and enough oil until a sauce of good body results. Pesto is usually required to be of mayonnaise consistency. Taste for salt.

Note: to make machine Pesto, place garlic, nuts, herbs, and 2 tablespoons oil in blender or food processor. When puréed, continue alternate additions of oil and cheese to build the sauce. Machine Pesto is always somewhat lighter than handmade.

Asparagus Quiche

SERVES 8 TO 10

2½ pounds asparagus
2 tablespoons butter
2 tablespoons olive oil
4 eggs, lightly beaten
1 cup whipping cream
1 tablespoon fine-chopped parsley
Salt, pepper, nutmeg

A half-baked, 10- or 11-inch pie shell (see page 200)

Break the asparagus stems at their tender point and discard the woody bottoms. Cut 2½-inch long tips from the stalks. Slice the stalks thin and sauté in butter and oil until just tender. Mix asparagus stems, eggs, cream, parsley, salt, pepper and a scraping or two of nutmeg. Pour into the half-baked shell and bake at 350° for 25 to 30 minutes or until set.

Cook the asparagus tips in boiling salted water. When just tender, drain immediately and refresh under cold water. Dry. Arrange around the edge of the baked quiche, with all tips pointed toward the center.

Mushroom Quiche

SERVES 8 TO 10

1 medium onion, chopped
4 ounces unsalted butter
8 ounces firm mushroom caps and stems, chopped
4 eggs, lightly beaten
1 cup whipping cream
⅓ cup grated Parmesan or *Gruyère cheese*
Salt, pepper, nutmeg

A half-baked, 10- or 11-inch pie shell (page 200)

FOR GARNISH

13 perfect, firm mushroom caps about 2 inches in diameter

Cook onion gently in butter until soft. Add mushrooms, turn up heat, and cook rapidly until the mushrooms have rendered water, then reabsorbed it again and the mixture appears dry. Mix mushrooms, eggs, cream, cheese and seasoning, stirring with a fork until smooth. Pour into the quiche shell and bake at 350° for about 30 minutes or until set.

Flute the mushroom caps or at least carve 5 or 6 swirls into each. (Use a small, sharp knife to strip out thin, delicate surface peels. Do not just cut the mushroom or it could break apart during cooking.) Sauté the decorated caps, cut side down, in oil or butter until cooked and golden. Drain and pat dry. Place one in the center of the baked quiche and the others around the edge.

Olive Quiche

SERVES 8 TO 10

2 cups ripe green olives
1 cup ripe black olives
7 ounces large, pimento-stuffed Spanish olives

A half-baked 10-inch pie shell (see page 200)

1 small onion, grated
4 eggs
1 cup whipping cream
1 teaspoon salt
Pepper

Remove flesh from the ripe green and black olives by turning it off the pits in spiral fashion, just as one turns a long orange peel from an orange. Use a small sharp knife. Chop olives well and gently press out excess fluids.

Bring the whole Spanish olives to a boil in fresh water. Drain and bring again to a boil in fresh water. This will remove any offensive brininess. Slice olives thin and set aside.

Place ripe, chopped olives in the bottom of the pie shell. Distribute grated onion over the olives. Stir the eggs, cream and seasonings until well blended and pour into the shell. Place thin slices of Spanish olives in concentric circles over the entire top. Bake at 350° for about 30 minutes or until set in the center.

Serve no warmer than room temperature. Tart is best with the slightest chill on it. Good picnic fare.

Red and Green Soufflé Cakes

Although either of these cakes stands nicely by itself and serves 6, full presentation demands two soufflés of the same size—one green from spinach and zucchini, the other red with tomato sauce. After baking and cooling, the soufflés are sliced in wedges and the two colors are mixed into two cakes of alternating red and green portions which provide a pretty presentation for cold buffet or picnic. Two identical spring-form pans speed the baking, but one soufflé can be made and then another later in the same mold with no ill effect. Season with a generous hand.

SERVES 12

FOR THE GREEN CAKE

10 ounces spinach
2 small zucchini
1 tablespoon unsalted butter
1 tablespoon fine-chopped chives and marjoram mixed

FOR THE RED CAKE

1 cup homemade Tomato Sauce (see page 39)
1 clove garlic, pressed
½ cup Parmesan cheese, freshly grated

FOR EACH CAKE (MAKE THIS RECIPE TWICE)

2 tablespoons unsalted butter
2 tablespoons flour
1 cup whipping cream
8 eggs, separated, at room temperature
Salt and pepper

For the green cake, wash and rib the spinach. Cook uncovered in a large pot of boiling, salted water. When it is just cooked and still bright green, drain and refresh under cold water. Squeeze out all possible moisture. (Both coloring agents must be exceedingly dry.) Rub the spinach through a sieve. The resulting fine purée will color the cake.

Wash zucchini, trim the ends and grate. Salt and leave to water out in a large bowl for 30 minutes. Squeeze out all moisture. Sauté briefly in 1 tablespoon of butter.

To make the green cake, prepare a thick white sauce by melting the butter, stirring in the flour and cooking briefly. Do not allow to brown. Add the cream and whisk over heat until very thick. Cool slightly, then beat in the egg yolks, spinach, herbs, zucchini, salt and pepper.

Whisk the egg whites (preferably by hand in a copper bowl) until they form firm peaks, and fold into the yolk mixture. Pour into a buttered 9- or 10-inch spring-form pan and bake at 350° for about 30 minutes or until firm to the touch and golden. Remove from oven and cool. (The cake will fall a bit.)

For the red cake, cook and reduce the tomato sauce to ¾ cup of thick, dry sauce.

Make the basic white sauce mixture in the same manner as for the green soufflé. Add the tomato sauce, the pressed garlic clove, the egg yolks, and half the cheese. Season and fold in the beaten whites. Pour into a buttered mold and sprinkle the top with remaining cheese. Bake about 28 minutes.

To assemble, allow both cakes to cool, then cut each into 6 wedges. Remove every other wedge of green and substitute red and vice versa.

For convenience: prepare the coloring, flavoring agents a day ahead. Bake cakes 2 to 3 hours before needed. They should be eaten luke or just slightly chilled.

Chive Blossom Omelet

SERVES 4

6 eggs, separated, at room temperature
1 tablespoon whipping cream
1 tablespoon water
⅓ cup fine-chopped fines herbes (*parsley, chives, chervil, tarragon*)
Salt and pepper
1 stick unsalted butter
8 to 10 chive blossoms, pulled from the stem and into small petals.

Beat the egg yolks lightly with cream and water. Add the finely chopped herbs and seasoning. Whisk the whites to firm peaks and gently fold into the yolks.

Heat 4 tablespoons butter to a sizzle in a large frying pan or, for prettier presentation, an oval copper gratin dish. Pour in the eggs and gently shake the pan over medium heat. When the omelet is set and a dark golden brown on the bottom, gently lift one side over on top of the other with two spatulas. The omelet may crack a bit but it is still handsome. Melt and pour the remaining 4 tablespoons of butter over the omelet and sprinkle with the chive blossom petals. (A whole flower would prove offensively aggressive to the taste.) Serve at once directly from the pan.

The following frittatas are best eaten warm or cool but not hot. I make them in two large, 15-inch paella pans and garnish the edges with a frieze of salad greenery. Guests are served a slice from each frittata and the raw garnishes are combined on a separate salad plate and dressed with herbed vinaigrette. If you make both omelets, count on their serving 8 to 10 people. Smaller versions, using perhaps 6 eggs in a

9-inch frying pan, are also pretty but not large enough to support a garnishing border. Count 2½ to 3 eggs per person.

A Flowered Green Frittata

SERVES 4 TO 5

FOR A 12-TO 15-INCH PAN

3 medium zucchini, sliced thin and lightly sautéed in butter
2 cloves garlic, chopped
1 teaspoon marjoram
½ cup fine-chopped raw greens (fresh herbs, spinach, watercress)
12 eggs, lightly beaten
Salt and pepper
½ cup grated Gruyère cheese
6 tablespoons unsalted butter

FOR GARNISH

Raw spinach, watercress and either violets, borage flowers or *chive blossoms*

Preheat broiler. Start frittata on top of stove.

Mix zucchini, garlic, greens, eggs and seasoning. Melt 4 tablespoons of the butter in a large pan and when sizzling, pour in the eggs. Shake pan gently and smooth out the eggs as they begin to set. When the bottom is firm and the top still runny, sprinkle with the grated cheese, dot with remaining 2 tablespoons of butter, and transfer pan under broiler until the eggs are golden. Do not overcook. The whole process should take slightly less than 2 minutes. Garnish with a border of small, raw spinach leaves and watercress. Sprinkle the lavender flowers over the center. (Violets are most effective. If using chive blossoms, separate the petals from the central head.)

Frittata Niçoise

SERVES 4 TO 5

1 cup cooked, diced string beans
1 cup cooked, diced potatoes
2 cloves garlic minced
Salt and pepper
1 tablespoon mixed oregano and thyme
12 eggs, lightly beaten
6 tablespoons olive oil

FOR GARNISH
Anchovies, Niçoise olives, cherry tomato halves, Bibb lettuce

Use a 12- to 15-inch pan. Preheat broiler. Start frittata on top of stove. Mix beans, potatoes, garlic, seasoning, herbs and eggs. Heat 4 tablespoons of the olive oil in a large pan and, when sizzling, pour in the eggs. Shake the pan gently, smoothing and spreading eggs as they begin to set. When the bottom is just firm and the top still runny, make a free-form garnish of anchovy fillets, cherry tomato halves (cut side down) and black olives on top. Sprinkle 2 tablespoons of olive oil over all and place dish under broiler until eggs are golden and the tomatoes lightly broiled. Encircle the frittata with small lettuce leaves.

Roulade with Spinach and Sorrel

SERVES 6 TO 8

10 ounces spinach
A medium bowl of sorrel leaves
1 stick unsalted butter
Salt and pepper
4 eggs, separated
½ cup grated Parmesan cheese
1½ cups whipping cream

Wash and rib spinach. Cook uncovered in boiling, salted water until just tender. Drain, refresh under cold water, and squeeze the mass completely dry.

Wash sorrel in two changes of water. Rib and shake dry. Cut into thin shreds (chiffonnade). Melt 4 tablespoons of the butter in a saucepan and cook sorrel over medium heat until it melts into a purée. Purée spinach and sorrel together in blender or food processor until smooth. Season well and set aside.

Oil a cookie sheet or jelly roll pan. Cover with 2 lengths of kitchen parchment and oil the paper well.

Whisk egg whites to firm peaks. Briefly whisk the yolks and 1 tablespoon cream, then fold yolks into whites. Don't worry about a perfect blending. Pour eggs out onto the baking sheet and smooth into a rectangle approximately 10 x 14 inches. Bake in a preheated 350° oven for about 12 minutes or until golden and dry to the touch.

Dribble half the cream, half the cheese, and 2 tablespoons melted butter over the eggs. Spread on the spinach purée and, holding the paper edge and using it to push and firm, roll up the eggs lengthwise. Trim both ends neatly and transfer the roulade to a long gratin dish or oven-proof serving platter. Pour remaining cream over eggs, top with grated cheese and thin scrapings of the remaining butter. (The roulade can be refrigerated at this point for up to 4 hours.) Bake in a preheated 350° oven until bubbling and flecked with brown. The cream will thicken and be absorbed into the hungry eggs, resulting in a moist and succulent roulade.

Scrambled Eggs with Sorrel and Croûtons

The loose, creamy consistency of these eggs may be a surprising curiosity to those familiar only with the lumpy, dry coagulum that is frequently served up as scrambled eggs.

It would be wrong to assume the eggs are not cooked because they are slightly runny, and once they are eaten, the superior delicacy of this method should be readily apparent.

SERVES 4 TO 6

4 slices firm bread, preferably homemade
1½ sticks unsalted butter
½ pound sorrel
1 dozen eggs
1 garlic clove, peeled
Salt and pepper
Chopped chives

Remove crusts and slice the bread into small croûtons. Melt 4 tablespoons of the butter in a frying pan, add croûtons and allow them to absorb butter on all sides until coated. Keep turning the squares as they brown (a simple flip of the pan is the most expedient method). (Good croûtons should be golden on every side and should contain as much butter as they can hold without becoming greasy. There should be no additional melted butter swimming in the pan.) Turn the finished croûtons into 3 layers of paper toweling, roll them up, and keep warm.

Wash sorrel well in at least two changes of water. Rib it, shake dry, and place in a saucepan with 4 tablespoons melted butter. Over medium heat, allow sorrel to melt down into a purée. Stir constantly and, when smooth, set aside in a warm spot.

Break eggs into a bowl. Spear a garlic clove onto a fork (an old Escoffier trick that imparts the barest tint of flavoring) and beat the eggs. Discard garlic. Pass eggs through a sieve to strain out *chalaza* (that small bit of condensed protein "string" that binds yolk to white) and any stray shell that would hinder a custard-smooth scramble. Add salt and pepper.

Melt the remaining 4 tablespoons butter in a heavy pan; add eggs and whisk continuously over very low heat. The eggs will take a good while to thicken and at no time should the heat be high enough to cause coagulation. (If you start scraping egg from sides and bottom of the pan, lower heat immediately.) The eggs should gradually evolve into a thick custard with no hint of curded scramble about them. When thickened but still moist, add the sorrel and remove from heat. The buttery sorrel will stop the cooking of the eggs. Sprinkle with croûtons and chopped chives and serve directly from the cooking vessel.

Basque Pipérade with Basil

SERVES 3 TO 4

1 large onion, chopped medium
2 cloves garlic, minced
1 stick unsalted butter
1 large green pepper, chopped medium
4 tomatoes, peeled, seeded, squeezed dry
1 tablespoon chopped parsley
1 teaspoon thyme and oregano mixed
Salt and pepper
9 eggs
A handful of basil leaves

Stew onion and garlic in 2 tablespoons of the butter until soft and transparent. Add pepper, tomatoes, herbs and seasoning, and let mixture simmer for about 15 minutes. It should form a thick, dry stew of chunky vegetables rather than a sauce.

Melt 4 tablespoons butter in a heavy pan. Season eggs, then leisurely scramble them following the procedures in the preceding recipe. Melt remaining 2 tablespoons butter, and just as eggs appear done, stir in the butter and the vegetable mixture. Tear basil leaves over the surface and serve at once directly from the cooking utensil.

For convenience: cook the vegetable addition a day or so before, or keep a supply frozen for emergency use. A sprinkling of croûtons would further expand this dish.

Eggs Baked in Peppers

For a variation on the Pipérade theme.

SERVES 6

3 large, round peppers (green or red)
1 dozen eggs
Salt and pepper
3 tablespoons unsalted butter
1½ cups Tomato Sauce (see below)

Select well-shaped peppers that will sit upright. Halve them crosswise, remove seeds and cut off stem but do not leave a hole. Parboil peppers in simmering, salted water until just tender. Drain, reserving the water, and dry.

Break 2 eggs into each half. Season and add a scraping of butter. Place peppers in a small baking pan, pour in 1 inch of the hot water used for poaching, and bake briefly at 375° until just set. Ribbon with tomato sauce.

A Standard Tomato Sauce

MAKES APPROXIMATELY 2 CUPS

1 large onion, chopped
1 clove garlic, minced
2 tablespoons unsalted butter
One 28-ounce can tomatoes or
6 medium-sized fresh tomatoes
A small pinch sugar
1 teaspoon minced parsley
Oregano and thyme to taste (optional)
Salt and pepper

Simmer the onion and garlic in butter until soft. If using canned tomatoes, drain them of most of their juice. Peel fresh tomatoes by dipping them briefly in boiling water. Peel off skin, cut crosswise and squeeze out seeds. Chop either canned or fresh tomatoes. When onion is transparent, add tomatoes, sugar, herbs and seasoning and cook over low heat for 30 minutes. Stir frequently to guard against scorch. Can be used as is or puréed. Add oregano or thyme to the sauce for a provincial flavoring, but if it is to be used in a delicate setting, omit the more vulgar herbs.

Quick Baked Eggs

A frothy dish of little substance befitting a light breakfast or lunch.

SERVES 1

2 eggs at room temperature
Unsalted butter
Salt and pepper
3 tablespoons whipping cream
1 teaspoon fine-chopped fines herbes (*chives, parsley, chervil, tarragon*)

Butter a small ramekin. Separate the eggs. Beat whites until firm and pile into the dish. Make two rounded indentions in the whites and lay the yolks in carefully. Sprinkle with salt and pepper. Pour cream over the whites and strew herbs and butter shavings over the yolks. Place dish in a preheated 350° oven until the yolks are just set and the whites are crested with gold. Serve with a large, buttery croûton.

Eggs with Cressed Mayonnaise

SERVES 6 TO 12

1 dozen eggs
1 large bunch fresh watercress
Homemade Mayonnaise (see page 145)
Whipping cream, as needed

Hard-boil the eggs. To peel them easily, run cold water over the eggs, roll each one back and forth under the palm until a light network of cracks is apparent, and shell immediately. Cut a thin slice off the larger ends so the eggs will sit upright, and place in a dish that just holds them. Cool.

Parboil the leaves and tender stalks of watercress until bright green, then refresh under cold water. Squeeze dry and purée. When cool, add purée to the mayonnaise. This should thin the dressing to the point where it can be poured over the eggs as a coating sauce. If it seems a bit thick, add a small amount of cream to lighten consistency. Coat eggs and serve cool.

To Make an Egg as big as twenty

"Part the yolks from the whites, strain them both separate through a sieve, tie the yolks up in a bladder in the form of a ball. Boil them hard, then put this ball into another bladder, and the whites round it; tie it up oval fashion and boil it. These are used for grand sallads. This is very pretty for a ragoo, boil five or six yolks together, and lay in the middle of the ragoo of eggs; and so you may make them of any size you please"

MRS. HANNAH GLASSE, *The Art of Cookery Made Plain and Easy*,
LONDON, 1747

Note: If you care to try this, turn bladders inside out and soak in lightly vinegared water for 1 hour before use. Dry both sides thoroughly before filling. Turn the ball frequently as it cooks. The egg yolks and whites can be seasoned to taste with salt, pepper, and herbs.

Lovage Soup

Though there are many herb flavors in this soup, only one will predominate, bending the broth toward the parsley-celery-anise essence that is lovage. If you have none of this most useful herb, try the soup with generous amounts of chopped celery leaves and stalks, parsley (leaves, stems and scraped roots) and anise seeds.

SERVES 4 TO 6

FOR THE HERB STOCK

2 or 3 generous stalks each of: thyme, parsley, tarragon, summer savory, a bunch of chives, all tied together.
4 cups water
2 medium all-purpose potatoes, peeled and diced
½ teaspoon salt

FOR THE SOUP

3 tablespoons unsalted butter
1 small onion, chopped
2 medium stalks lovage including leaves, chopped
1 egg yolk
½ cup whipping cream
Pepper

Carefully wash and dry the herbs. Place in a saucepan and bear down on them with a pestle or heavy spoon, mashing and bruising the leaves to release the volatile oils. Add 4 cups of water, the potatoes and salt. Simmer for 5 minutes, then turn off heat and steep for 10 minutes.

In a frying pan, melt the butter; add onion and a small ladle of the herb stock. Cook until onion is translucent. Add lovage, stirring until the leaves look a dark, wilted green. Add onions and lovage to the stock and bring the whole to a simmer. Cook just until the potatoes are purée soft. Remove the herb bundle.

Pass soup through a sieve, pressing down on the residue until the potatoes, onions and a bit of lovage green have passed through.

Beat egg yolk and cream together in a large bowl. Whisk the hot broth slowly into the egg, then return soup to the stove to thicken slightly over low heat. Do not allow to boil. Add pepper and taste for seasoning.

Flower Garden Soup

A light soup, oriental in character, with a small garden floating on top. The egg-white garden base acts as insulation, keeping the soup hot. There are two presentations possible. Use either a large tureen or enameled pot and float the entire garden, or make individual gardens in eight soup bowls. (To do this, preheat oven to 300°. Place bowls on a large baking tray and ladle in vegetables and broth. Heap egg whites on top and place tray in oven for one minute. Arrange flowers over the whites and serve.) The kelp, bonito and mushrooms are commonly available in exotic food sections of large supermarkets.

SERVES 8

FOR THE FLOWERS

8 radishes
1 carrot, scraped
1 bunch scallions
A leafy celery heart
8 toothpicks

FOR THE SOUP

5 dried oriental mushrooms
A few snow peas
1 carrot
A 3-inch length of lemon zest, cut in thin strips
1 large cooked chicken breast or
8 large, peeled, deveined shrimp
A handful of spinach leaves, washed, ribbed, and shredded

FOR THE BROTH

2 square inches of dried kelp
2 ounces dried, pre-flaked bonito
3 egg whites at room temperature
Salt or soy sauce

For the garden garnish, trim radishes into flowers. Ridge the large end of the carrot with a vegetable stripper or small knife. Cut 16 thin flower slices. Trim scallion whites to 2½-inch lengths. Leaving the bottom intact, make small incisions around the edge until scallion resembles a broom. Cut 8 long strips of celery, each with a leaf or two. Put radishes, carrots, scallions and celery in ice water. Select 8 thin scallion greens, insert toothpicks into their tubing to form green stems, and trim the ends. Slice remaining scallions thin.

Prepare soup ingredients. Soak mushrooms in 2 quarts cool water for 20 minutes. String snow peas. (Parboil briefly in salted water if they seem tough.) Slice carrot into thin rounds. Remove skin and bones from chicken, cut flesh into thin strips.

To make broth, rinse kelp in cold water and pat dry. Place the kelp and the mushroom water in an uncovered saucepan and bring to boil. Immediately remove kelp and stir in the flaked bonito. Cover pan, leave for 4 minutes, then pour off the clear broth.

Immediately before the soup is to be finished, whisk the egg whites and a pinch of salt to firm peaks.

Bring broth to a boil. Add all soup ingredients and boil for 30 seconds.

Remove from heat. Taste for seasoning and add salt or soy sauce to taste. Pile egg whites on top, cover (if using a large tureen), and leave to poach for 30 seconds. Spear radishes with scallion stems. Decorate egg surface with carrot, radish and scallion flowers, celery twigs and sliced green scallions.

For convenience: prepare garnishes and broth the night before and refrigerate. Whisk whites as soup is heating to a boil.

The following three swirled soups are rich, delicious and attractive, with variegated shades of red, white, pink and green intertwined and flowing together.

Potato Soup with Tomato and Basil

SERVES 4

3 large tomatoes
2 carrots, scraped and sliced thin
Pinch sugar
Salt and pepper
2 cups homemade chicken stock
4 medium potatoes, peeled and diced
1 large onion, sliced
1 clove garlic, crushed
1 cup whipping cream
Basil leaves

To make a tomato purée, stem tomatoes, cut in half crosswise, squeeze out most of the seeds and reserve the juice. Chop the tomatoes fine and place in a pan with carrots, sugar, and seasoning. Simmer until carrots are soft, adding a bit of reserved tomato juice if necessary to keep the pulp from sticking. Pass through a sieve and chill.

Put stock, potatoes, onion and garlic in a sauce pan. Simmer until potatoes are tender and the onion soft. Purée in blender or food processor. Add cream, season to taste, and chill.

Swirl the tomato purée into the chilled potato soup. Sprinkle with finely torn basil leaves.

Green Bean Soup with Swirled Pesto

SERVES 4

FOR THE SOUP

1 small onion, chopped
2 tablespoons olive oil
2 cups homemade chicken stock
1½ pounds tender green beans
1 cup whipping cream
Salt and pepper

Pesto Sauce (see page 28)

Cook the onion in olive oil and 2 tablespoons of stock until just tender. String the beans.

Bring a pot of salted water to a boil and throw in the beans. Cover pot and boil beans rapidly until almost fork tender. Drain.

Bring stock to a simmer; add the beans and onions. Simmer gently for 5 minutes then purée in a blender or food processor. Add the cream, taste for seasoning and set aside. The soup should be quite thick.

Prepare pesto sauce, mixing spoons of cheese and oil into the paste until a sauce results that is the same density as the soup.

Reheat soup to warm but not hot. Ladle into 4 bowls and spoon the pesto into the middle of each. Using a spoon handle, lightly stir the pesto into feathery swirls, dark green against the paler beans.

Purée of Shrimp with Watercress Cream

SERVES 4

1 bunch watercress
Approximately ⅓ cup whipping cream
1 pound peeled, deveined shrimp
1 small onion
2 medium tomatoes, peeled and seeded
1 ¾ cups milk
½ teaspoon salt
Pepper and cayenne
6 tablespoons unsalted butter

Parboil the leaves and tender watercress stems in salted water for 30 seconds. Drain, refresh under cold water, and squeeze dry. Place cress and cream in a blender and whip until thickened. Set aside.

Purée shrimp and onion together in blender or food processor. Chop tomatoes and squeeze out excess moisture. Bring milk to a simmer, stirring as it heats to avoid a skin. Add shrimp, onion, tomatoes and seasoning to taste. Simmer for 4 minutes. Off heat, stir in butter.

To serve, swirl the watercress cream into the shrimp. If necessary, add a bit more cream to the cress to make it swirlable.

Iced Seafood Consommé

SERVES 6

FOR THE STOCK

3 pounds fish heads and bones
The sliced white of a leek
1 carrot, sliced
3 lemon slices
Bay leaf
Thyme and parsley sprigs
Salt
4½ cups water
1½ cups dry white wine

FOR THE CLARIFICATION

2 egg whites and shells
½ pound skinless fillet of flounder, minced
The shredded green of a leek
A few parsley leaves and stems
3 mushrooms, sliced

FOR THE GARNISH

12 large, cooked shrimp, halved lengthwise
3 perfect mushrooms, sliced
Chervil or parsley leaves
6 lemon slices

Rinse off the fish trimmings. Combine all stock ingredients in a pot and heat on a medium burner. Just before the liquid breaks into a boil, scum will float to the surface. Spoon it off, immediately regulate the stock to a simmer, and cook, covered, for 30 minutes. Strain through a fine sieve and cool to room temperature.

To clarify, whisk the egg whites and crumbled shells lightly. Mix with the minced fish, leek greens, parsley and mushrooms. Whisk in the stock and return to the heat. Stirring constantly, bring the stock slowly to a simmer. Cover and simmer for 20 minutes. Let sit off the heat for 15 minutes.

Line a sieve with a clean kitchen towel which has been dampened and wrung out. Place sieve over a deep bowl, pour in the stock and let the liquid drip through of its own accord. (Do not let the sieve touch and taint the clear stock below.) If not perfectly transparent, let broth filter through the frothy debris again.

Chill the consommé until jelled. To serve, place 2 shrimp, a few slices of mushroom, an herb leaf and a lemon slice in the bottoms of 6 soup plates. (The most effective plate is plain glass or simple white.) Shirr the jelled soup with a fork until it glitters, then spoon into the plates. The garnish will appear serene in the pellucid depths.

A Perfect Poached Fish

There is nothing more handsome for an elegant first course than a cold, poached fish—particularly a speckled trout or salmon. Here are some general poaching principles.

1. Make a flavorful poaching *fumet* with:

1 large onion, chopped
Several leek greens, chopped
3 large carrots, sliced
1 celery stalk, chopped
2 pounds fish bones and heads
2 cups good quality dry white wine
Several lemon slices
Several parsley sprigs
3 or 4 thyme sprigs
1 small bay leaf
A 2-inch length of orange zest
1 teaspoon salt
A few peppercorns

Place all ingredients in a stainless pot. Cover with water and cook at a lazy boil for 30 minutes. Strain, pressing all liquid from the debris. Add 3 cups cold water.

2. Place fish on the rack of the poacher (*poissonière*). Pour the fumet over the fish and immediately add enough cold water to cover.

3. Heat the fish slowly. Just as the simmer breaks, regulate heat so there is no movement to the stock. It is difficult to specify poaching times, but I frequently find the standard 10 minutes per inch insufficient for larger fish. If the liquid is kept at a low steam and never breaks into a simmer, the timing might go as follows:

For a fish 1 inch thick (at the thickest point)—10 minutes
2 inches thick—22 minutes
3 inches thick—34 minutes
4 inches thick—46 minutes

4. Turn off heat and add 3 cups cold water to the broth. As soon as the liquid cools to room temperature, lift out the fish rack and allow fish to sit and firm for a good hour before garnishing. (The fish can remain overnight in its broth, then be taken out the next day for an hour's firming.)

Through mode of garnishing and choice of accompanying sauce, a fish may be made to complement any second course. For a rustic meal, choose a simple twisted lemon garnish, plain or herbed mayonnaise, or a sauce of blended pesto and mayonnaise. A light fish and salad meal would call for a delicate herb and flower garnish and should have a sauce very different in composition from the salad's dressing. An aspic-glazed cucumber garnish is particularly striking for a sumptuous cold buffet as both slices and aspic protect the fish from drying if it is to be held for some time. The open-fleshed design is most effective with salmon and a piping of green mayonnaise.

On Mousseline Forcemeats

Forcemeat (literally raw flesh and egg puréed fine enough to be forced through a sieve) is a particularly agreeable addition to summer recipes, for it provides rich though airy substance in a variety of situations. After the puréed flesh has chilled, it is expanded with loosely whipped cream and put to poach or bake in a *bain marie*. The forcemeat swells slightly and the final result is a luxurious texture floating somewhere between mousse and soufflé.

In the following two recipes, forcemeats are used to build cold terrines that are almost weightless when compared to their heavier brothers composed entirely from chopped meats. The forcemeats of shrimp and scallops on pages 128 and 130 provide hot main courses, again so light that they can be offered on the warmest summer's day. Some general rules concerning forcemeats:

1. The meat to be puréed must be impeccably fresh. If it has suffered even a brief freeze, the mixture will water and crack during cooking and the final texture will be grainy.

2. Although forcemeats can be made from chicken, veal or game, in this book they are built from fish and seafood, the flesh of which is especially easy to purée. The food processor makes light work of (and is perhaps most valuable for) this task. A fish purée can be effected almost as fast with the use of mortar and pestle, however. The final sieving allows any bits of skin or connective tissue that could flaw a uniform texture to be filtered out.

3. A forcemeat purée can be held overnight *before* its cream addition, which is a great boon to the summer cook.

4. The cream addition should be ice cold when it is added. Lighten the purée first with thin cream, then refrigerate it while the remaining cream is being whipped (preferably over ice to keep its chill). The consistency of the whipped cream is most important. In classes, I always refer to it as sludge—perhaps not a pretty image but a graphic one. The cream should thicken but not become so firm that it cannot move heavily in the bowl. Stiffer cream will dry a forcemeat or, if truly overwhipped, break down and actually separate during cooking.

Three-layered Fish Terrine

This pretty cold terrine is a complicated dish, but its elegant appearance, its delectable admixture of three distinct yet melding flavors, and the fact that it must be done a day ahead, mitigate the effort. Be sure the flounder is perfectly fresh.

SERVES 10

FOR THE FORCEMEAT

1½ pounds fillet of flounder (weight should be calculated after both skin and bones are removed)
3 eggs
1½ teaspoons salt
Pepper
2½ cups chilled whipping cream

Cut the fillet into small pieces and pound the flesh with the eggs, until it can be passed through a sieve. (A food processor will make short work of this. The more traditional way would be to pound the fish in a heavy bowl or mortar with a pestle.) Press the resulting mixture through a sieve. Use either a drum sieve (*tamis*) and an oval scraper (*corne*), or a large, sturdy sieve placed over a bowl and a wooden pestle or large spoon to pass the flesh. This necessary step rids the forcemeat of any membranous filaments that might mar the final texture.

Season the mixture well. Pack it into a small bowl and cover tightly with plastic wrap. Refrigerate forcemeat for at least 1½ hours. Place cream in freezer to chill for 15 minutes before use.

TO COLOR AND FLAVOR THE RED LAYER

One 28-ounce can tomatoes, well drained
1 egg yolk
1 cup peeled shrimp, in large dice
Pinch cayenne

Squeeze as much juice from the tomatoes as possible. Place them in a small pan over low flame and let them dry slowly. Stir frequently until the pulp shows no trace of moisture. When cool, stir in the egg yolk, shrimp, and cayenne. Chill.

TO COLOR AND FLAVOR THE GREEN LAYER

10 ounces fresh spinach
2 tablespoons minced parsley
⅓ cup shelled, natural pistachios

Wash and rib spinach. Salt lightly and cook it, uncovered, in the water clinging to its leaves. When just cooked and still green, refresh under cold, running water. Squeeze spinach as dry as possible. If necessary, place in a small pan over heat to evaporate juices. When dry, purée spinach and parsley together in blender or food processor.

Peel the pistachio nuts by placing them in boiling water for 1 minute. Strain, place in a kitchen towel, and rub. The brown, outer peeling will slip off easily. Chop coarsely and add to spinach.

FOR THE WHITE LAYER

1 small diced truffle

or

5 large mushrooms, chopped medium

If using mushrooms, sauté briefly in a small amount of unsalted butter until mushrooms have given off, then reabsorbed their liquid and are perfectly dry.

To assemble the three layers: generously butter an 8- to 10-cup terrine or loaf pan. Cut a piece of aluminum foil or kitchen parchment to fit the bottom and butter it also.

Work rapidly. Stir 1 cup of chilled cream into the forcemeat. Whip the remaining 1½ cups until thickened but not firm. Fold into the forcemeat. Divide mixture into three parts, one slightly larger than the others. Add mushrooms to the largest third. Add spinach to one part, the tomato mixture to the last.

Spoon spinach layer into the mold and level it. Add white layer next, then the tomato layer. Tap mold on a counter to settle the contents. Cover the top lightly with aluminum foil and place in a *bain marie* (a larger pan containing a water level that will come halfway up the terrine's side.) Bake in a preheated 350° oven for 1 hour. At no time should the water in the *bain marie* boil or break bubbles.

When finished, remove from *bain marie* and let cool to room temperature. Tip the dish and drain off any buttery juices. Put 2 layers of aluminum foil over the fish and weight with another terrine of the same size or three 1-pound cans. Refrigerate 12 to 24 hours.

To serve, remove weights and foil and run a knife around the mold's edge. Turn the terrine out onto a pretty serving dish and peel off bottom paper. Slice two or three servings from one end and lay them out to display the tiered pattern. Decorate the platter with lemon halves. Serve with a small boat of Homemade Mayonnaise (see page 145) highly flavored with lemon and colored with tomato purée, if a sauce is desired.

For convenience: the terrine can be composed over two days. Make the forcemeat and flavoring elements on the first day. Add cream and build the loaf on the second day.

Terrine of Salmon with Eggs and Almonds

SERVES 10

½ cup whole, skinless almonds
1 cup very fine-minced parsley, chives, (lemon thyme, optional)
Unsalted butter for mold
10 ounces fresh salmon
10 ounces fresh trout or bluefish
2 eggs
1⅔ cups whipping cream, chilled
1 teaspoon salt
Pepper
5 small eggs, hardboiled

Blanch almonds for 5 minutes in salted water. Drain and dry.

Mince parsley and chives exceedingly fine. The herbs must be impeccably dry in order to be properly chopped.

Generously butter a 9-cup terrine or loaf pan. Cut a piece of kitchen parchment or brown paper to fit the bottom and butter it, also.

To make the forcemeat, remove all skin and bone structure from both fish. (Around 4 ounces should measure out in debris, leaving a pound of flesh for the forcemeat.) Purée fish and eggs together in a blender or food processor, or pound them together with a pestle in a heavy bowl. Press purée through a sieve to strain out any connective, membranous filaments. Place forcemeat in a small bowl, smooth plastic wrap over the top, and refrigerate for at least 1½ hours.

Stir ⅔ cup cream into the purée to lighten the mixture. Season well. Whip 1 cup cream until loosely thickened but not firm, and fold into the forcemeat. Remove approximately ⅓ of the mixture to a small bowl and stir in the chopped herbs. Add almonds to the larger portion.

Frost the terrine's sides and bottom with the green purée, reserving some to top the loaf at the end. Smooth in half of the almond portion. Lay the eggs in a row down the middle, and cover with remaining almond forcemeat. Smooth green purée over the top. Give the mold a good tap on a towel-covered counter to settle its contents. Cover lightly with aluminum foil and place terrine in a *bain marie* (a larger container holding water halfway up the mold's height). Bake in a preheated 350° oven for 1 hour. Cool to room temperature. Tip the mold to drain off any juices, then cover with 2 layers of heavy foil and weight with three 1-pound cans. Refrigerate for 12 to 24 hours.

To serve, run a knife around the edge, dip the bottom briefly in hot water, and turn out. Peel off the paper. Serve with lemon wedges, Homemade Mayonnaise (see page 145), thin toast, and unsalted butter.

Small Fish à l'Orientale

This dish lends itself to a particularly pretty presentation. The fish can be attractive placed side by side in a rectangular dish, the sauce spread down the middle, but even nicer is a circular arrangement in a large *paella* pan. Ideally, the fish should weigh slightly less than a half pound each so that they can be kept whole. If it is necessary to buy larger fish, I trim off heads rather than sacrifice presentation. The garnish neatly covers the loss.

SERVES 8

FOR THE FONDUE

3 tablespoons olive oil
10 medium tomatoes, peeled, seeded, chopped
or
Two 28-ounce cans tomatoes, drained and chopped
2 cloves garlic, minced
¼ teaspoon powdered saffron
¼ cup chopped fennel greens
or
2 tablespoons dried fennel weed
1 tablespoon chopped thyme and chives
1 teaspoon coriander seeds
Pinch cumin
Salt and pepper

8 small fish (red or black mullet, trout) gutted and trimmed
Flour
Olive oil
⅓ cup pine nuts
5 lemons
⅓ cup currants, plumped in hot water for 20 minutes
Chopped parsley for garnish

Place all the fondue ingredients in a pan and gently stew for 35 to 40 minutes or until the tomatoes appear quite dry. Stir frequently.

Pat the fish dry, roll them in flour, and shake off the excess. Over relatively high heat, fry the fish briefly in oil until both sides are lightly browned. Fry in two or three batches so as not to overcrowd the pan.

Put a generous layer of oil in a bake-and-serve dish. (If dish is round, arrange the fish with tails toward the center.) Pour a ribbon of fondue over the bodies of the fish, leaving head and tails exposed. Place in a preheated 350° oven for 10 minutes. Sauté the pine nuts in a small amount of oil until lightly browned. Cut the lemons into zigzag halves.

When fish comes from the oven, sprinkle pine nuts over the tomato fondue. Place lemon halves between fish heads. Place one section in the center and squeeze the remaining half over the fish. Sprinkle with the currants and some chopped parsley. Refrigerate until chilled. Take from refrigerator shortly before serving so the congealed oil will liquify. To serve, simply scoop a lemon half and a fish with its covering sauce onto each plate.

Molded Chicken Liver Mousse

A delicious mousse in hot weather. Mace, a frigorific substance, acts as a natural cooling element. (Taste a bit on the tongue and feel the chill.)

SERVES 20

1 pound chicken livers
3 sticks soft, unsalted butter
1 medium onion, minced
1 clove garlic, minced
Salt and pepper
¼ teaspoon mace
⅔ cup whipping cream, well chilled

3 small, perfect savoy cabbage leaves
Paprika

Sort over the livers, removing any connective membranes or portions that appear green. Pat dry with paper toweling.

Melt 3 tablespoons butter in a large frying pan. Cook onion and garlic over low heat until transparently soft but not browned. Turn up heat, add livers, and stir constantly until they are brown on the outside but still retain a delicate pink interior. Remove from heat, spoon out

2 tablespoons of liquid, and season the livers with salt, pepper and mace. Purée livers in blender or food processor and add the remaining softened butter. Whip cream until thickened but not firm and stir into mousse. Pack into a bowl and press plastic wrap directly onto the surface. Refrigerate until firm.

Arrange 3 small cabbage leaves on a tray and mold mousse into a large rose on top. Using a pastry spatula (frequently dipped in hot water), make a central, coned core, then form individual leaves until the flower is complete. Besprinkle with paprika and refrigerate until needed. Store any leftovers in a crock and pour melted butter over the top to coat and preserve. Will keep for 3 or 4 days. (The recipe can be halved or doubled easily and, of course, it is not necessary to mold the mousse.)

Vegetables and Salads

Artichokes, Mushrooms and Olives Sott'olio

Sott'olio (literally, under oil) is a common Italian antipasto. Most vegetables can be cooked in this manner, but the following combination frequently turns up in restaurants, and I have seen large preserving jars spectacularly layered with these three ingredients in the central Florence market. The mushroom used (called *faggio* in Florentine dialect) is *funghi porcini* or "pig" mushroom. It is the same *Boletus edulis* which the French call *cèpe*.

SERVES 6 TO 8

8 artichokes
½ lemon
⅔ cup olive oil
½ pound firm white mushrooms, no larger than a half dollar, wiped clean and trimmed
A handful black Niçoise olives
Pepper

FOR THE BROTH

3 cups water
¼ cup white wine vinegar
1 bay leaf
Several thyme and parsley sprigs
1 teaspoon bruised coriander seeds
4 lemon slices
½ teaspoon salt

Break off the artichoke stems. Start snapping off leaves around the base, breaking and tearing each one back so as to leave the small, edible portion of each attached to the base. Continue working in this manner until you reach the tender, pale green leaves around the choke. Using a stainless steel knife, cut the artichoke across, ½ inch above the rim of the white heart. Cut the base into quarters. Rub all cut sides with a lemon half to prevent discoloration.

Dig out the furry choke, trim the top leaves and cut any dark green portions of the leaf ends that remain attached to the base. What is left should be entirely edible. Drop the quarters in a bowl containing ⅔ cup olive oil. Rub all the sections in this oil as they are finished. Reserve oil.

Place broth ingredients in a saucepan and simmer for 5 minutes. Add the artichokes and cook until a knife point easily penetrates the stem end. Lift quarters from the pan with a slotted spoon and leave to drain and cool. Add the mushrooms. Cook for 3 or 4 minutes until they are tender. Skim out with a spoon and add to the artichokes. Reduce broth to 1 cup and strain.

Arrange mushrooms and artichokes in a rustic serving dish. Sprinkle on a handful of black olives. Add the reserved ⅔ cup oil to the reduced broth and pour it over the dish. Add pepper and more salt to taste. Refrigerate, covered, for several days if need be.

Serve portions with plenty of oil dressing into which fresh bread can be dipped.

Artichokes with Gremolata

Gremolata, the parsley-garlic-lemon blend usually thrown into osso bucco at the last moment, is equally refreshing in other guises. Here it accompanies artichokes. As an hors d'oeuvre, think in terms of half a large artichoke per person. A whole artichoke will yield a substantial luncheon dish.

SERVES 8 AS AN HORS D'OEUVRE OR 4 AS A MAIN COURSE

4 large artichokes
1½ cups olive oil
Salt and pepper
Grated rind of 3 lemons
A large handful of parsley
4 garlic cloves, peeled
Lemon juice

Break the stem neatly off an artichoke. Remove the few small leaves at the base and cut the artichoke through the middle from top to stem with a stainless steel knife. Rub all exposed cuts with half a lemon to avoid discoloration. Dig out the bristly choke and all its surrounding purple leaves. Pour olive oil over each finished half to provide further protection from discoloring. When all are finished, place the halves in a roasting pan, cut side up. Season crevices with salt and pepper.

Chop together the lemon rind, parsley and garlic to a fine and fragrant mash. Divide among the artichokes and work it between leaves and into the crevices left from the chokes. Spoon oil over artichokes and bottom of dish.

Bake in a preheated 350° oven for about 45 minutes, basting twice during this time. When tender, the heart end should be easily pierced with a knife point.

Let cool 30 minutes before serving. Squeeze some lemon juice over the top of each artichoke, and make sure each person gets a portion of the oil as dressing. Serve with bread and unsalted butter.

Asparagus Fritters

SERVES 4 TO 6

1½ cups thin sliced asparagus
2 tablespoons whipping cream
1 egg, slightly beaten
1 tablespoon flour
¼ teaspoon salt
Pepper
Clarified butter for frying (see below)

Parboil asparagus briefly in salted, boiling water. Taste a slice and when slightly tender but still bright green, drain and refresh under cold water. Shake the asparagus in a pan over heat to dry it thoroughly and allow to cool.

Mix cream and egg into the flour. Add asparagus and seasoning. Fry by tablespoons in clarified butter. These are very delicate, in the manner of corn fritters, and are intended as family fare.

To clarify butter: Place 1 pound of unsalted butter in a small dish and let it melt in an oven's dying heat or over a very low burner. Cool and place dish in refrigerator. When the clear, oily butter on top has solidified, run a knife around the edge and turn butter out. The creamy whey on the bottom is to be discarded. Rinse the butter pat off under cold water and freeze it for future use. There is no sense in having to make clarified butter every time it is needed.

ASPARAGUS

Ripe 'Sparagrass
  Fit for Lad or Lass
To make their Water pass
O, 'tis pretty Picking
  With a tender Chicken

JONATHAN SWIFT

Asparagus Sauce

MAKES 1 ½ CUPS

1 large bunch asparagus
4 tablespoons unsalted butter
4 scallions
Salt and pepper
Small pinch sugar
6 tablespoons whipping cream

If the asparagus is small, break the stalks at their tender point. If large, peel the asparagus. Cut into 1-inch-long pieces and parboil, uncovered in boiling, salted water until just tender but still bright green. Drain and refresh under cold water.

Melt butter in a frying pan. Add asparagus, the fine-sliced whites and an inch of green scallions, seasoning, and a small pinch of sugar. (Ferdinand Point maintained that a small pinch was what could be held between thumb and forefinger. A large pinch uses a thumb and two fingers.) Stew gently for 3 minutes, then purée in blender or food processor. Add the cream, taste for seasoning, and keep warm until needed. Delicious over tender chicken suprêmes or, to gild the lily, over steamed asparagus.

Lettuce and Asparagus Stew

SERVES 4

3 small bunches scallions
1 ½ pounds asparagus
1 firm Boston lettuce
5 tablespoons unsalted butter
Salt and pepper
1 tablespoon fines herbes (*parsley, chives, tarragon, chervil*)
4 slices buttered toast

Trim scallions and slice thin the white and pale green parts.

Break the asparagus at its tender point and cut stalks into 2 or 3 pieces.

Give the lettuce core a hard knock on the edge of a counter and twist it out. Rinse lettuce, discarding any blighted outer leaves. Dry and cut into thin strips (*chiffonnade*).

Melt butter and gently stew the scallions until they start to become tender. Add the asparagus and scatter the lettuce over all. Season, cover the pan, and turn up heat to medium high. Shake the pan from time to time, and in 4 or 5 minutes, the asparagus should be just cooked, and the lettuce will have melted down into the onions forming a homely but delicious stew. Stir in the *fines herbes* and serve out on buttered toast.

Fresh Sautéed Beans with Savory

SERVES 4

2 pounds beans (fava, lima, black-eyed peas or *crowder peas)*
1 clove garlic, crushed
1/3 cup olive oil
Salt and pepper
1 tablespoon fresh savory, chopped

Hull the beans. If they are not in their first youth, parboil them for 1 minute in boiling, salted water. Drain and dry over low heat.

Heat the garlic clove in oil. Discard garlic and sauté the beans until just tender. Taste to ascertain this point. Season and add savory. Delicious with lamb.

Grated Beets and Greens

SERVES 6

6 medium beets and their greens
Juice of 1 lemon
Salt and pepper
1 tablespoon lemon thyme or *plain thyme*
6 tablespoons unsalted butter, cut in small pieces

Rinse the beets and cut off and reserve the leaves. Cover with cold, salted water and bring to a boil in a covered pan. Cook for 25 minutes.

Wash and rib the beet greens. When the beets are cooked, strain them from the water and immediately toss in the greens. Cook, uncovered, until tender. Drain and refresh under cold water.

Place the beets in cold water and peel off the outer skin. Cut beets into large julienne (matchsticks), the largest blade of the Mouli-julienne being the most helpful tool for this step. (The beets will still be somewhat firm at this point.)

Squeeze water from the greens and chop fine. Scatter beets and greens in a small gratin dish. Add lemon juice, salt, pepper and thyme. Disperse butter over the top and bake in a 350° oven for 15 minutes.

Celery and Watercress Purée

Most recipes for delicate purées of vegetables too watery or with not enough starch to hold their form after puréeing, call for an addition of rice or potato to provide substantive body. In so doing, the base vegetable's flavor cannot help but be attenuated. The following method for dehydration, though more tedious in execution, allows vegetables to maintain their vital, unadulterated essence.

SERVES 8

2 bunches celery
1 bunch watercress
Approximately 1 stick unsalted butter
Salt and pepper

Divide celery into stalks, and rinse them well. Cut into ½-inch slices and boil in salted water until tender. Add the leaves and tender stalks of watercress and, when they turn bright green, drain pan contents and refresh under cold water. Dry briefly over heat to evaporate any liquid.

Purée celery and watercress together in blender or food processor. Press through a sieve. Everything but the small celery strings should pass.

Put the mixture in a saucepan and place a double sheet of paper towels over the purée and up one edge of the pan. Tip the pan so the purée slides into the toweling. Press gently on the paper-covered mass and water will immediately seep through the towels. Lift off the paper, which will be heavy with water, and repeat the process with fresh towels until the mass is relatively dry.

To serve, place over gentle heat and build the purée back up with chunks of butter. You will use at least a stick, perhaps more, but don't allow a pure butter flavor to overshadow the fragile vegetables. Season and taste carefully.

For convenience: cook, purée, strain and dry the night before. Reheat and add butter just before serving. Purées scorch easily, so tend the fire. This dish is particularly fine with good beef.

Gratin of Chard

SERVES 4 TO 6

1 pound chard
½ cup olive oil plus 2 tablespoons
1 cup grated Gruyère and Parmesan cheese, mixed
Salt and pepper
1 tablespoon flour

Wash and rib the chard. Slice ribs thin and parboil for 2 minutes in boiling, salted water. Add the leaves and, when they are tender, drain and refresh chard under cold water. Squeeze the mass to extract liquids and dry briefly over heat.

Give chard a rough chop, then simmer briefly in ½ cup olive oil until it turns a dark green. Mix in ¾ cup of cheese, season well, and place in a small gratin dish. Mix flour with the remaining ¼ cup of cheese and scatter over the top. Dribble 2 tablespoons olive oil over the cheese and bake at 350° until the top is crusted and golden.

Paupiettes of Chard

The following delicate preparation should not come up against anything too strident on the same plate. It would form a nice accompaniment for a simple, lightly sauced suprême of chicken or make a good addition to an all-vegetable lunch. Or let it stand on its own as a separate small course in the French manner.

SERVES 4

15 large, perfect chard leaves and ribs
2 large leeks, trimmed
1 small head Boston lettuce
2 or 3 sorrel leaves
6 tablespoons unsalted butter
1 egg
½ cup whipping cream
½ cup finely grated Parmesan cheese
Salt, pepper, nutmeg

Carefully soak and wash the chard in two waters to rid its sculpted surface of sand. Peel off the outer layer of the leeks, slit them to within 1 inch of the root and gently spread the leaves under running water to rinse out any dirt. Wash lettuce and sorrel.

The chard leaves must be flexible enough to roll up so, with a paring knife, slice off the bottom of the thick rib. Start removing the rib from about the center of the leaf down. Reserve the ribs. Bring a saucepan of water to a boil and, holding them with tongs, parboil each leaf until it is bright green and limp. Spread the leaves out, back rib side up, on paper toweling. Choose the 8 best leaves for the paupiettes.

Slice the chard ribs and the leeks into thin julienne (matchsticks). Cut the lettuce, sorrel and remaining chard leaves into fine *chiffonnade* shred.

Melt 4 tablespoons butter in a frying pan, add ⅓ cup water and gently stew the chard stalks, leeks, and leafy *chiffonnade.*

Mix egg, cream, Parmesan and seasoning. When the greens are cooked (the water should be evaporated by this time), add them to the thick cream.

Spread an eighth of the mixture down the center of each paupiette leaf. Fold the long edges over the filling and roll up. Place in a well-buttered gratin dish. Add ½ cup water and place a cold shaving of butter on each paupiette. Bake at 350° for 25 to 30 minutes. Baste two or three times during this period. Serve with a spoonful of the buttery juices.

Grated Corn Pudding

SERVES 6

8 ears freshly picked corn
3 eggs
⅔ cup whipping cream
½ teaspoon salt
Pepper
Pinch sugar

Grate the corn into a large bowl. Place the gratings in a fine strainer and allow 5 tablespoons of the starchy milk to drain away so that about 1 cup of pulp remains. Mix corn, eggs, cream, salt, pepper and sugar. Pour into a lightly buttered gratin dish and bake 25 to 30 minutes. The pudding should be firm to the touch in the middle and golden at the edges.

Stuffed Cucumbers with Tomato Cream

SERVES 6

3 medium-large cucumbers
3 large tomatoes
½ cup whipping cream
Salt and pepper
3 tablespoons unsalted butter
½ cup firm bread crumbs

Peel cucumbers, slice them in half lengthwise, and scoop out the seeds with an apple corer or small spoon. Parboil in boiling, salted water until just tender. Lift out and drain on absorbent toweling.

Place tomatoes in the boiling water for 1 minute. Peel them, cut in half crosswise, and squeeze out seeds and juice. Squeeze the pulp until it is exceedingly dry and give the tomatoes a rough chop. Mix chopped tomatoes with cream and seasoning, and fill the cucumber hollows. Melt butter, stir in the bread crumbs and spoon them over the tomato stuffing. Bake cucumbers in a 350° oven for 20 minutes or until crumbs brown.

Dilled Cucumber Custard

SERVES 4 TO 6

4 large cucumbers
Salt
4 large eggs, lightly beaten
1 cup whipping cream
1½ teaspoons fine-chopped dill
Pepper

FOR GARNISH
Chopped parsley and dill

Peel, slice and seed the cucumbers. Grate them and sprinkle with 1 teaspoon salt. Leave to disgorge water for ½ hour. Press and squeeze cucumbers until very dry. Add eggs, cream, dill and pepper and mix well. Taste for seasoning, adding more salt if necessary.

Butter an 8-cup soufflé or charlotte mold. Place a round of buttered kitchen parchment paper in the bottom and fill with custard. Bake in a *bain marie* (a larger container holding water halfway up the mold) at 350° for 1 hour, or until firm in the center. Leave to set for 5 minutes before running a knife around the edge and unmolding. Sprinkle with a mixture of fine-chopped parsley and dill.

Eggplant Soufflés

SERVES 4

2 eggplants, approximately 1 pound each
4 tablespoons unsalted butter
4 tablespoons flour
2 cloves garlic, minced
⅔ cup grated Parmesan cheese
Salt and pepper
1 teaspoon oregano and thyme, mixed
5 eggs, separated and at room temperature
Chopped parsley
Tomato sauce (*see page 39*)

Cut the eggplants in two, lengthwise. Trim the stem ends. Cut out the flesh with a small, stainless knife until there remains only a thin-skinned shell. Cut the flesh into 1-inch cubes, sprinkle with salt, and leave to water out for 20 minutes. Squeeze the pulp by handfuls until a goodly quantity of moisture is passed. Purée the flesh in a blender or food processor.

Melt 4 tablespoons butter in a small, heavy pan. Stir in flour and cook gently for 1 minute, stirring constantly. Add eggplant purée and stir another minute. Off heat, add garlic, half the cheese, seasoning, herbs and the 5 egg yolks.

Whisk the egg whites until firm peaks are formed. Fold into the purée and fill the eggplant shells about two thirds full. Sprinkle the tops with the remaining cheese, place in a lightly oiled baking dish, and bake at 350° for 25 minutes.

Garnish with parsley and ribbon with tomato sauce. Serve hot or luke as an accompaniment to lamb.

Ratatouille Terrine

This recipe calls for transformation of classic ratatouille ingredients into a new medium—a firm, sliceable terrine. The working time is less than for the traditional long stew, and though this terrine cannot better the original, it does provide an interesting variation on a sometimes common dish.

SERVES 10 AS A FIRST COURSE OR SIDE DISH

One 1½-pound eggplant
2 medium-large zucchini, rinsed and dried
1 large onion, chopped
3 large garlic cloves, minced
Approximately 1 tablespoon olive oil
2 large sweet peppers, preferably red, chopped
1 egg plus 2 egg yolks
2 crustless slices fresh bread
1 teaspoon fresh thyme and oregano, mixed
2 tablespoons chopped parsley
Salt and pepper
Large pinch cayenne

Tomato Sauce (see page 39)

Lightly oil a 9- or 10-cup terrine or loaf pan.

Cut 6 long strips of eggplant skin, trimming them into neat ½-inch-wide lengths, and place, purple side down, in three decorative X's on the bottom of the mold. Continue peeling eggplant, cut into cubes and salt. Leave to disgorge water for 45 minutes. Cut the zucchini into medium dice. Salt and leave to drain.

Put the onion and garlic to stew in the smallest amount of olive oil necessary. When semi-soft, add the peppers.

Squeeze out all possible water from the zucchini and add them briefly to the onions and peppers. When the zucchini turns bright green remove mixture from heat.

Wring out the eggplant, squeezing firmly by hand until the mass is as dry as possible. Purée in blender or food processor.

Mix together the eggplant purée, sautéed vegetables, eggs, the bread broken into crumbs, herbs and seasoning. Pack into the terrine, being careful not to disarrange the design on the bottom. Bake at 350° for 1 hour and 10 minutes.

Leave to cool. Place a strong layer of aluminum foil over the top and weight down with two or three 1-pound cans. Press firmly and tip mold to drain off any juices. Refrigerate until needed.

To unmold, run a knife around the edge and shake down sharply over a serving platter. Serve in slices and ribbon with tomato sauce.

For convenience: make a day or two ahead. Keeps well.

A brisk, late spring day in southern Illinois. We (relatives and friends) have gathered for a day of mushroom hunting, and our hostess drives us across the Iowa border and deep into Illinois countryside. She has found, after considerable searching, the perfect hunting grounds—a long stretch of abandoned, overgrown apple orchard bordering gently wooded hills.

The car bumps along a deeply rutted tractor path to the wood's edge and we pile out, each of us with a paper bag to hold bounty and a thick sandwich to ward off later hunger. What we are exclusively searching for are morels, those hollow, globose, sponge-like mushrooms so highly prized in Europe, so highly priced when purchased dried, and so freely plentiful in late spring. We pair off and separate, each team staking out a claim of territorial rights.

Initially we have trouble spotting them, for their pale, buff-yellow heads blend into the forest mat of fallen leaves, but then they start to show themselves. At first there is a single cap, and when nearby leaves are overturned, several others are found clustered by. We spot a different variety, a darker, taller, cylindrical species, the *Morchella deliciosa* that is the most succulent of all. Gradually we realize the whole woods is covered and stand amazed at nature's multiplicity. They are at the bases of oak and apple trees, halfway up hillsides amongst trilliums and dutchmen's britches, some grouping, encircling, others standing bravely alone. Soon a voracious zeal overcomes us. We must pick more and more mushrooms, more than anyone else. We become stealthy, furtive, possessed. We track and overlap the others and misdirect each other away from abundant patches, sending people back over previously worked ground. When our two bags are full, we greedily stuff pockets, sandwich wrappers. Later we learn everyone has felt this same collective passion, and when we finally gather again, five hours later, a good two bushels of morels stand accumulated between us.

The rest of the day is spent cleaning and preserving. There are quantities of sand and small bugs to be dealt with in the honeycombed caps. We trim off the bottoms, leaving only esculent portions. Some mushrooms are put to soak in several waters for dinner, others are cleaned then instantly frozen, still others are pierced with a needle and strung up to dry.

Our evening meal consists of a comparative tasting: morels stewed in cream and butter; morels fried in garlic oil and seasoned with herbs; morels scrambled in eggs; morels stuffed in a roasted chicken. The rest we equitably divide.

Fresh Morel Sausage

The following densely textured composition is perhaps an unusual treatment for morels, but they show nicely in this guise. If you don't have fresh morels, dried ones will do. (These can be ordered from Maison Glass, see addresses page 250.) Soak them for thirty minutes in lukewarm water. Cut in two, then wash in several more waters to remove any sand from the spongy holes.

If no morels of any kind are available, firm fresh mushrooms may be substituted, but at some loss of character. Note that for the sauce you need mushroom liquid. If using dried morels, reserve the brown soaking water.

SERVES 5

FOR THE SAUSAGES

5 beef casings (see addresses page 250)
4 cups chopped morels or *mushrooms*
2 tablespoons butter
1 tablespoon fine-chopped chives
½ teaspoon mixed, dried herbs
1½ teaspoons salt
¼ teaspoon freshly ground pepper
2 large cloves garlic, minced
10 eggs
¼ cup fine-chopped parsley

String

Soak the casings in cool water for ½ hour. Rinse well and dry. Turn casings inside out so the smooth, unmembranous surface forms the interior. Tie a string about 1 inch from one end on all five casings. Set aside.

Carefully clean the fresh morels or mushrooms and chop thoroughly. (Morels should be trimmed, halved and washed in several grit-ridding waters.) Place them in a pan with the butter and sauté over medium heat. As the mushrooms water out, pull off the juices with a bulb baster or spoon and reserve for the sauce. When they have cooked and cooled, gently squeeze extra moisture out and hold it also for the sauce.

Mix mushrooms, herbs, seasoning, garlic and eggs in a bowl, blending until smooth. Fill the casings. Bunch the open end around a funnel and ladle in the filling, allowing about ¾ cup for each sausage. Leave ½ inch of empty leeway at the top so the eggs can expand, but press out any air bubbles so no deforming pockets will emerge during cooking. Tie another string at the top.

In a pan of water, simmer the sausages, covered, for 30 minutes. Do not boil. At the end of this time, remove them and leave to firm for 5 minutes.

Cut off both knots with scissors and slit the casing. Gently turn the plump little creatures out onto a plate, smoothest side up. Coat with sauce (see below) and sprinkle with chopped parsley.

FOR THE SAUCE

Approximately 1 cup reserved mushroom cooking liquid
Juice of ½ lemon
⅓ cup white wine
1¼ sticks cold unsalted butter, cut in small chunks
Salt and pepper

(If using soaking liquid from dried morels, measure 2 cups and make sure they contain no grit.) Place mushroom liquid, lemon juice, and wine in a small, heavy pan. Reduce the liquid over brisk heat until only 4 or 5 tablespoons of thick glaze remain. Lower heat and remove pan to cool slightly. Whisking constantly, add the butter, a few pieces at a time. Take pan on and off the heat so the butter is in no danger of melting but instead builds and mounts into a rich, gravy-like essence of mushroom.

For convenience: the sausages can be made a day in advance or early in the morning of a dinner party. They can be cooked, then left in their casings and gently reheated in hot water before the meal. The sauce should be composed only when needed.

Provençal Mushroom Gratin

SERVES 4 TO 6

1 pound large, firm mushrooms
Salt and pepper
¼ cup chopped parsley
3 large garlic cloves
⅓ cup fine dry bread crumbs
½ cup olive oil

Clean and trim the mushrooms. (Rubbing with a damp, salt-sprinkled cloth is an effective cleanser if they are not too dirty.) Remove stems. Place some caps in pleasing pattern in a small gratin dish to see how many will be needed for a top layer. Remove and reserve. Chop the stems and remaining caps fine and put them at the bottom of the gratin dish. Place the full caps on top. Season with salt and pepper. Purée the parsley, garlic and bread crumbs together in a blender or food processor. Spread over mushrooms and dribble oil over the top. Salt. Bake at 350° for 35 minutes. A warm, lukewarm or cool complement to red meat.

Delicacies in Grape Leaves

A plate of these packages, accompanied by small black olives and a generous chunk of bread, makes a delightful lunch as each diner opens and reveals the vegetable surprise within the charred and fragrant leaves. For a larger meal, the fillings could also include ground lamb or beef, or a simple chop might grill along with the packages.

If grape leaves are impossible to come by, wrap the vegetables in aluminum foil and a pleasing gratin will form over the surface. Unwrap the delicacies and arrange on dinner plates rather than leaving guests to pick off the less than esthetic coverings.

SERVES 4

4 small, firm tomatoes
2 medium onions
3 small green peppers
8 medium-large, firm clean mushrooms caps
1 large zucchini
1 small, long eggplant
Approximately 30 large grape leaves with long stems
2 cups cooked rice or *couscous*
Parsley, minced fine
Mint, minced fine
Olive oil
Lemon juice and wedges
Salt and pepper
1½ cups bread crumbs
⅓ cup pine nuts or *sliced almonds*
⅓ cup raisins plumped in hot water
Cinnamon
Cumin seeds, pulverized

Save all centers from hollowed vegetables to use in fillings.

Stem 2 tomatoes and cut in half. Hollow to make cups. Seed and chop the other 2 tomatoes.

Cut onions in half and dig out the centers with a small knife. There should remain a shell only 2 or 3 layers thick. Chop the scooped-out portions.

Make 4 half-pepper cups. Chop the remaining pepper fine.

Cut both zucchini and eggplant into 4 sections. Hollow each to a shell ⅜-inch thick.

Bring a large pot of salted water to a boil. Add the grape leaves and parboil until limp and olive green (less than 1 minute). Strain out and add onion, green pepper, eggplant and zucchini shells in turn, cooking until each is tender but still slightly crisp. Test with a fork.

Fill tomatoes with: rice and onion, highly colored with fine-minced parsley and mint, olive oil, lemon juice and seasoning.

Fill onions with: rice, raisins, parsley, touch of cinnamon, seasoning and oil.

Fill peppers with: 4 mushrooms, chopped and sautéed in oil, bread crumbs, rice, pulverized cumin, parsley and seasoning.

Fill mushroom caps with: mainly chopped nuts bound with rice, oil and lemon juice.

Fill zucchini with: onions sautéed in olive oil, tomato pulp, bread crumbs and seasoning.

Fill eggplant with: everything that remains, chopped fine, sautéed in oil, flavored with cumin, bread crumbs to bind, and seasoning.

Wrap vegetables in dry grape leaves. Trim stem ends into sharp points and use to needle the leaves together. (Use thin string and more than one leaf on larger packages.) Grill until charred on all sides. Serve with lemon wedges and a small pitcher of olive oil as dressing. Place a large bowl on table in which to discard leaves.

Thin Onion Tart

SERVES 6 TO 8

3 tablespoons butter
2½ pounds yellow or white Bermuda onions, sliced thin
1 teaspoon salt
Pepper
½ cup whipping cream
¼ cup grated Gruyère cheese
Rough Puff Pastry (see page 199)

FOR GARNISH
Parsley, minced fine

Melt the butter in a sauté pan, add onions and seasoning and cook, covered, over very gentle heat for 1 hour. Stir frequently and make sure the onions are in no danger of browning. There should be a gradual toning into succulent gold by the end of cooking time. Strain onions, pressing out and reserving all juice, and set aside. Reduce juices and cream together to about ½ cup of sauce and stir the onions back in. Taste for seasoning.

Prepare a round or rectangular tart crust. Roll out the dough to a 12-inch circle or a 15- x 8-inch rectangle. Cut a long strip of dough, moisten one side, and place around the crust's edge as a border. Prick the dough and bake at 375° until crisp and brown.

Smooth onions over crust, sprinkle cheese on top and place briefly under a broiler to brown. Rim the edge with fine-minced parsley. Absolutely delicious with red meat or as an addition to a rustic buffet, but slightly too sweet to stand on its own as a separate course.

For convenience: cook onions a day or two ahead. Warm gently before spreading on crust.

Polenta Tart

SERVES 8

FOR THE TOPPING

2 medium onions, chopped
2 cloves garlic, minced
3 tablespoons olive oil
1 green pepper, chopped
6 or 7 medium tomatoes, peeled, seeded, chopped
or
One 28-ounce can tomatoes, well drained
Pinch sugar
2 tablespoons chopped fresh parsley, oregano and thyme, mixed
Salt and pepper

FOR THE POLENTA BASE

3½ cups water
1 teaspoon salt
1 cup yellow cornmeal
2 eggs

⅓ cup grated Parmesan cheese
Olive oil

Make a thick, chunky tomato sauce. Put the onions and garlic to cook in the oil until soft. Add green pepper, tomatoes, sugar, herbs and seasoning. Simmer for about 30 minutes. Stir frequently and make sure the mixture is quite dry. Set aside.

Bring water and 1 teaspoon salt to a good boil. Pour in the cornmeal in a slow stream, stirring all the time. At no point should the water stop simmering. Continue stirring for about 15 minutes. When dry and of a mass, cool slightly, stir in the eggs, and spread the polenta in a buttered 10-inch pie pan. Pat and smooth the mixture with wet fingers until it forms a thin, rimmed pie shell. Place the tomato topping in the shell. Sprinkle with Parmesan cheese and dribble 2 tablespoons olive oil over the surface. Bake in a preheated 350° oven for 45 minutes. Serve just warm with grilled lamb chops.

For convenience: can be made a day ahead as it reheats nicely.

Garlic Potatoes

A good summer potato dish in that it is lightly crisp but still farinaceous enough when required to stand alongside a roast.

SERVES 4 TO 5

4 medium-large all-purpose potatoes
6 tablespoons unsalted butter
1 large clove garlic, pressed
Salt and pepper

Peel potatoes and cut them on the broad side into large slices no thicker than ⅛-inch. (A mandoline or slaw slicer does the job best.) Put slices in a bowl and cover with cold water. Let them sit and render starch for 45 minutes, then rinse and dry thoroughly.

Butter a combination serving-roasting dish (I use a 16-inch copper gratin) and place the potatoes loosely in the dish and around the sides. Melt the 6 tablespoons of butter, press in the garlic and let steep for 5 minutes. Dribble butter over potatoes, turning the slices so that most are covered with a thin film. Add salt and pepper. (At this point, the potatoes can sit, refrigerated and covered with plastic wrap, for an hour or two.)

Bake in a 375° oven for about 50 minutes or until the potatoes are uniformly browned.

Shredded Turnip Gratin

Another lightly starchy meat accompaniment:

SERVES 4

1½ pounds fresh, tender turnips
Salt
8 tablespoons unsalted butter
⅔ cup whipping cream
Pepper
⅓ cup firm breadcrumbs

Cut a thick peel from the turnips. Shred the turnips or grate them through the medium blade of a Mouli-julienne. Give the gratings a good salting and leave them to water out for 30 minutes. Place a large sieve over the sink and repeatedly squeeze the turnips over it until the mass feels dry and weightless.

Melt 4 tablespoons butter in a frying pan and, stirring frequently, cook the turnips over low heat for 10 minutes. Place in a buttered gratin dish, suffuse with cream, and pepper generously. Melt remaining 4 tablespoons butter, stir in breadcrumbs and cook until lightly browned. Sprinkle crumbs over the turnips and bake at 375° for 30 minutes or until a pleasingly golden gratin has formed.

Fresh Vegetable Stew with Herbed Dumplings

SERVES 4 TO 5

FOR THE DUMPLINGS

3 tablespoons unsalted butter
3 eggs
½ teaspoon salt
⅔ cup flour
1 tablespoon fine-chopped parsley and chives, mixed

FOR THE STEW

1½ cups pearl onions, peeled
2 sticks unsalted butter
½ teaspoon salt
2 cups tender green peas
1½ cups zucchini, sliced thin
1 tablespoon chopped parsley, chives, thyme, mixed
Fresh-ground black pepper

To make dumplings, cream the butter; stir in eggs, salt, flour and herbs, mixing until smooth, and set aside.

In a dish that can serve for both cooking and table presentation, parboil the onions in 1½ cups water. When just tender, add butter and salt. When butter is melted and the water boiling, throw in peas, zucchini and herbs. Just as the liquid returns to a boil, drop the dough by spoonfuls over the vegetables, regulate to a simmer and cook, covered, for about 12 minutes. Ladle broth, vegetables and dumplings into soup plates and grind fresh pepper over the surface. A homespun but tasty dish.

Sautéed Vegetables with Persillade

The following vegetables and amounts are not mandatory and could include substitutions such as sliced, tender asparagus, zucchini, broccoli or parboiled pearl onions. There should, however, be no more than five or six component parts to the dish so that individual flavors are not lost in an anonymous hodgepodge.

SERVES 4

4 tender celery stalks, trimmed and washed
The white and pale green parts of 6 scallions
5 artichoke hearts (see page 103 for turning method)
A large handful of tender, stringless green beans parboiled for 5 minutes in salted water
12 small, firm mushrooms, wiped clean, trimmed
¼ cup olive oil

FOR THE PERSILLADE

1 large garlic clove and a small handful of parsley chopped together to a fine mince

Salt and pepper
Juice of ½ lemon

Slice celery and scallions thin. Cut artichokes (with a stainless knife) into thin slice, and halve the beans. If mushrooms are small, leave whole; if large, cut in halves or quarters.

Heat the oil in a sauté pan. Add beans first and stir-fry over brisk heat in the Chinese manner. Add artichokes, celery, scallions and mushrooms last. Shake and stir the vegetables quickly, gently, briefly until all are tender-crisp. Immediately stir in the *persillade* and seasoning. Squeeze on the lemon juice, filtering it through the fingers so no seeds intrude, and serve immediately.

Cymling (Patty pan) Squash in Sour Cream

SERVES 6 TO 8

2 large and 2 small cymling squash
6 tablespoons unsalted butter
Pepper
1 tablespoon lemon juice
1 teaspoon chopped dill
⅔ cup sour cream
Parsley, minced fine

Cymling squash is white, scalloped summer squash, the very form of which begs to be used in presentation. Cut a rounded top off the two large squash at the stem end. Dig out all seeds with a spoon; remove and reserve squash flesh until only hollowed containers are left. (Be careful not to cut through the tender skin.)

Take the 2 small squash and the extra flesh and either grate it or put through the medium blade of a Mouli-julienne. Sprinkle with ½ teaspoon of salt and almost immediately the squash will begin to water. Squeeze the mass two or three times to remove excess liquid.

Melt butter and sauté the squash for 1 minute. Off heat, add pepper, lemon juice, dill and sour cream.

Bake the large squash shells in a 350° oven for 15 minutes, then spoon in the grated filling. Dot with butter and bake for an additional 15 minutes. Sprinkle with parsley. Each squash will cut easily into 3 or 4 serving sections. Good company for a roast chicken.

Zucchini and Basil Gratin

SERVES 4 TO 6

6 medium zucchini
Olive oil
1 large tomato, seeded and sliced
Salt and pepper
½ cup freshly grated Parmesan cheese
1½ cups whipping cream
20 basil leaves

FOR GARNISH
Additional Parmesan

Wash, trim and cut the zucchini lengthwise in ½-inch thick slices. Salt and leave to drain for ½ hour. Pat slices dry, then fry in olive oil until crisply browned. Drain zucchini on paper towels to absorb extra oil.

Lightly oil a gratin dish. Spread a layer of zucchini on the bottom, then a layer of tomato slices. Season with salt and pepper.

Stir cheese and cream together. Pour half over the tomatoes and press basil into the cream. Add another layer of zucchini and cover with remaining cream. Grate more parmesan on top and put to bake in a 350° oven until nicely browned (about 30 minutes).

Squash and Lemon Salad

SERVES 8 TO 10

3 or 4 medium zucchini
3 or 4 medium yellow summer squash
3 firm tomatoes
1 small tomato half
2 lemons
1 ⅓ cups dry white wine
⅔ cup olive oil
Juice of 1 lemon
2 cloves garlic, minced fine
1 teaspoon thyme or *lemon thyme*
Salt and pepper

Slice zucchini and summer squash into ¼-inch rounds. Cut tomatoes into wedges and arrange first zucchini, then summer squash, then tomatoes in concentric circles in a round gratin or quiche dish. The pattern should be first an outer rim of green, then yellow, red, green and yellow circles. Place a small tomato half cut with zigzag edges in the center. Pare the skin from 2 lemons and cut into wedges; remove seeds and scatter lemon sections over squash. Add wine, olive oil, lemon juice, garlic, thyme and generous seasoning. Bake for about 25 minutes at 350°. The lemon and wine acidulation ensures that the watery yellow squash and zucchini will retain shape and body during cooking. Taste a slice of squash toward the end of baking time. It should retain some firmness and a bit of crunch. Serve this dish cool but not chilled, on the day it is made. Fresh bread should accompany the salad to absorb its savory juices.

Grilled Zucchini Salad with Herb Flowers

SERVES 4 TO 6

4 medium zucchini
Salt
Olive oil
2 or 3 tablespoons vinegar
Juice of 1½ lemons
Pepper
Thyme or *oregano flowers* or *just fresh leaves*

Wash, trim and cut the zucchini into slices lengthwise. Salt slices and leave them to drain for a half hour. Wipe dry. Coat with oil and grill under a broiler or over the coals of a dying fire when the meat is finished. Baste often with more oil. When the slices are golden brown on both sides, layer them into a serving dish. Over each layer, sprinkle vinegar, lemon juice and seasoning. Over the whole, pour a thin coat of olive oil. Scatter herb flowers, crumbled into small leaves and petals, on top. Cover with aluminum foil and leave to marinate overnight in the refrigerator. Remove from the cold before serving so the oil will liquify.

Rough and Wild Greens with Grilled Chapons and Walnut Sauce

SERVES 6 TO 8

There is a time, in early May, when tender sprouts appear. First, from the garden, I gather small leaves of roquette (arugula) from a late fall planting, a few tiny sorrel leaves, some tarragon which has doubled its garden area since last summer, lemon thyme, hyssop, and chives. From the yard and along the road come the smallest dandelion plants and the yellow flowers and tender upper leaves of wild winter

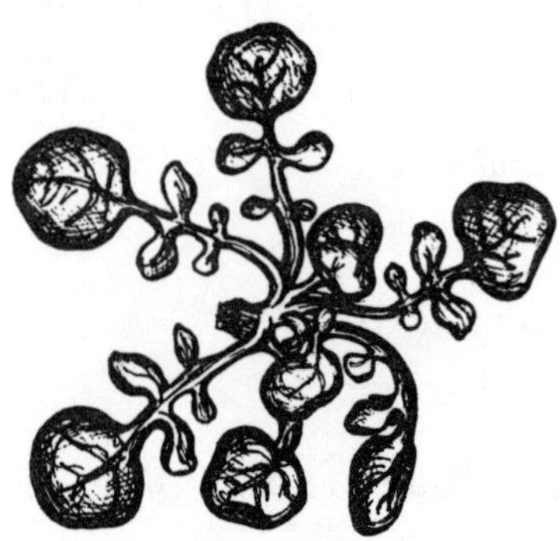

cress. Roughly torn romaine extends quantity while allowing the salad to remain '*sauvage*' in character.

The greens are carefully washed in at least two waters, then toweled and patted dry. The sauce is composed in a garlic-rubbed salad bowl, the romaine placed on the bottom, then rough leaves scattered on top. The look wanted is that of a newly mown meadow, with whole chives and dandelion leaves supplying a cut-grass effect and the bowl crowded to overflowing.

As the season and garden plantings progress, small nasturtium and chard leaves, basil, salad burnet–anything that will provide amusing piquancy–is added. The salad can complement a flavorful grill or peasant dish, or stand on its own. The chapons (large, crusty croûtons) are best grilled over coals, but under a broiler is also fine.

FOR THE CHAPONS

4 or 5 slices of homemade bread, cut a generous ½-inch thick
1 large garlic clove
Red wine vinegar
Salt
Olive oil

The bread should be slightly stale or dried enough in the oven so that the surface is rough and firm. Cut crust off the bread and rub slices on both sides with a peeled garlic clove which will wear itself away in flavoring. Sprinkle the slices lightly with vinegar and salt, then moisten with olive oil until the bread is damp but not soggy. Grill slices until brown on both sides. Cut into 1-inch squares and use to garnish salad.

FOR THE WALNUT SAUCE

1 tablespoon English walnuts
1 tablespoon blanched almonds
1 garlic clove
½ slice bread, crumbled
Salt and pepper
1 tablespoon white wine vinegar
Juice of ½ lemon
2 tablespoons whipping cream
Olive oil

In the salad bowl or a mortar, pound walnuts, almonds, garlic, bread and seasoning to a fine paste. Stir in vinegar and lemon juice. Add cream, then enough olive oil to make a sauce of medium consistency. Taste for seasoning and make sure the dressing leans to salt and acid.

Flower Blossom Salad with Herbed Vinaigrette

SERVES 6 TO 8

3 perfect heads of Boston lettuce

FLOWERS

Nasturtiums, marigold petals, chive blossoms separated into flowerets
Thyme or *oregano blossoms*
Violets, mustard flowers
Tiger lily buds, rose petals
Hyssop flowers, etc.

FOR THE VINAIGRETTE

¼ teaspoon coarse salt
Pepper
1 tablespoon fresh parsley, chives, tarragon, mixed
2 tablespoons red wine vinegar
1 tablespoon lemon juice
Olive oil to taste

Twist the core from each lettuce. Hold the head together and rinse under cold water. Shake as much water off as possible then gently wrap lettuce in two or three layers of paper towels and place upright in a bowl to drain. Refrigerate until needed. Place the lettuces in a shallow bowl. Arrange so they look like entire, loose heads. Tuck whole blossoms between the leaves and scatter petals over the top. Serve vinaigrette on the side.

Place salt and fresh-ground pepper in a heavy bowl or mortar. Add herbs and work with a pestle until the rough salt is pulverized and the herbs are a green paste. Add vinegar and lemon juice, continue stirring, and slowly add olive oil. Taste for seasoning.

Green Bean and Shrimp Salad

This salad must be made with the tenderest of garden fresh beans. They should be about three inches long—older, tougher beans simply will not do.

SERVES 6

1 pound unshelled shrimp

FOR THE MIREPOIX

1 medium onion, chopped
1 clove garlic, minced

2 small carrots, chopped
2 tablespoons chopped parsley
Half a bay leaf
Pinch thyme
4 tablespoons olive oil

½ cup dry white wine
1 pound green beans
Boston lettuce
6 firm white mushrooms, sliced thin
6 lemon wedges
2 tablespoons fine-chopped parsley and chives, mixed
Salt and pepper
Juice of 1 lemon
Approximately ½ cup cream

Rinse and dry the shrimp.

Make a *mirepoix* by placing onion, garlic, carrots, herbs and olive oil in a frying pan. Cook for 25 minutes over gentle heat, stirring frequently and making sure the vegetables don't brown.

Turn up the heat, add wine and shrimp, and cook shrimp until fully pink. Set aside and when cool, shell and devein the shrimp. Place the *mirepoix* and shrimp peelings in a sieve and press to extract juices. These will form the base of the dressing. Measure, and if the amount exceeds 4 tablespoons, reduce over high heat to that amount.

String the beans. Plunge them into rapidly boiling, well-salted water. Cover and return to a boil as soon as possible. Taste beans until they are cooked to the still crisp *al dente* stage. Drain and refresh immediately under cold water.

Arrange the salad on individual plates. Place a leaf or two of lettuce as a base. Arrange green beans, aligned in the same direction, on top. Put shrimp in the center and garnish with thin raw mushroom slices. Add a lemon wedge on the side.

For the dressing, mix reduced cooking juices, parsley and chives, seasoning and the lemon juice. Add approximately ½ cup of cream, tasting as you go until a well seasoned but delicate dressing is formed. Pour over salads.

For convenience: cook, peel and shell shrimp the day before. Reduce juices. The salad should be served lukewarm or cool but not cold.

Molded Spring Vegetables in Herbed Jelly

A particularly pleasing display of orange, white and green vegetables suspended in a translucently aromatic gel.

SERVES 8 TO 10

FOR THE JELLY

6 cups well-seasoned, homemade chicken stock, clear of all fat
1 bay leaf
Several sprigs of parsley, thyme and savory
1 stalk lovage or *celery, sliced*
Several green scallion tops

2 pounds asparagus
1 pound small, tender carrots
2 cups sliced whites of scallions
2 egg whites and egg shells
2 envelopes plain gelatin

FOR GARNISH

Leaves of Italian parsley or *salad burnet*
Herbed mayonnaise

Place stock, herbs and scallions in a saucepan and reduce to four cups. Cool to room temperature.

Break asparagus off at its tender point and cut into ¼-inch slices. Wash, scrape, and slice the carrots thin.

Boil carrots in well-salted water until perfectly tender but not overcooked. Strain out with a wire skimmer. Boil scallions in the same water. When cooked, strain out into a second bowl. Add the asparagus last and cook at a rolling boil until tender but still bright green. Put all vegetables, in separate containers, to cool.

Whisk the egg whites and crumbled shells together until light. Soften gelatin in ¼ cup cold water. Combine eggs, gelatin and stock in a saucepan and heat gently. Whisk continuously until the mixture comes to a boil and forms the thick matting of albumen and herb stalks which will draw off all impurities. Stop stirring and let the broth maintain a slow boil for 15 minutes. Cover, remove from heat, and let sit for 10 minutes.

Rinse a clean dish towel with cold water, wring out, and use to line a large sieve. Place sieve over a deep bowl and carefully pour in broth. Allow the broth to drip of its own accord. If jelly is not perfectly clear, let it filter through the frothy debris again. (The sieve bottom must not touch and defile the clear liquid beneath.)

Pour a ¼-inch thick layer of jelly into an 8- or 9-cup soufflé dish. Place decorative leaves of parsley or burnet on top and refrigerate until set. Cool the remaining jelly. When the mold bottom is firm, add carrots in a smooth layer, then onions, then asparagus. Pour the cooled jelly over all and return to the refrigerator until completely set. Unmold and serve with herbed mayonnaise.

For convenience: make a day or two before serving.

A Macédoine of Grated Vegetables

Vegetable amounts will depend on numbers to be served and size of container. This is most effectively presented as a party dish.

Beets
Romaine lettuce
Turnips
Tomatoes
Radishes
Carrots
Cucumbers
Spinach
Salt and pepper
Fresh herbs of choice
Vinaigrette sauce with garlic
Croutons

A glass serving bowl

Cook, peel, and grate the beets.

Cut romaine into thin shred (*chiffonnade*).

Cut a thick peel from the turnips and grate. Let sit for ½ hour, then squeeze dry.

Core and cut the tomatoes in half, crosswise. Press out all seeds and juice and slice into thin strips.

Grate radishes.

Grate carrots, let sit ½ hour, and squeeze dry.

Peel cucumbers, grate, salt lightly and let rest for 45 minutes. Press out moisture.

Wash and rib spinach. Cut leaves into thin shred (*chiffonnade*).

Season each ingredient. Layer vegetables into serving bowl in the listed order with beets on the bottom. Add herbs to lettuce and spinach layers. Moisten each layer (except for lettuce and spinach) with a goodly amount of vinaigrette dressing. Leave to marinate for 4 to 5 hours. Before serving, sprinkle top with freshly made croutons.

An Oriental Salad Plate

A pretty salad based on oriental ingredients available in most large grocery stores. It appears a copious amount when heaped upon the plate but in fact is of little substance and almost calorie free.

SERVES 4

1 small, firm cucumber
1 medium tomato, peeled and seeded
6 dried oriental mushrooms
4 ounces snow peas
1 head bok choy, washed and sliced thin
4 gingko nuts
6 white icicle radishes
8 ounces alfalfa sprouts
2 cups cooked, shredded breast of chicken
or
½ pound small, cooked, peeled shrimp
2 hard-boiled eggs
1 quart peanut oil (for frying)
3 ounces maifun (rice threads or sticks)

FOR THE DRESSING

1 garlic clove, minced
Pinch sugar
3 tablespoons soy sauce
2 tablespoons white wine vinegar
1 teaspoon sesame oil
Peanut or *salad oil to taste*

Wipe cucumber clean of any wax. Cut into three sections and core out the seeds. Squeeze tomato flesh in a dish towel until only the driest pulp remains. Stuff pulp compactly into cucumbers and chill.

Soak mushrooms in cold water for 20 minutes. Cut off the tough stems and parboil in salted water 1 minute. Strain and cut into strips.

String the snow peas. Boil peas and bok choy briefly until just tender. Cool and pull peas into halves.

Crack four gingko nuts and parboil until the skin can be slipped off.

Cut radishes into thin rounds and chill in ice water.

Arrange 4 salad plates. Mix alfalfa sprouts, bok choy and radishes and heap on each plate. Place mushrooms and chicken (or shrimp) on top. Arrange 5 or 6 snow peas as a fan at the right. Remove yolk from the egg half, place a gingko nut in the white, and crumble the yolk over. Slice the stuffed cucumber thin and arrange 3 slices on the left. (The plates can be covered with plastic wrap and refrigerated at this point.) Mix dressing ingredients to taste.

Heat the oil 15 minutes before salads are to be served. Break rice threads into 2-inch pieces and deep fry until puffed and golden. Place around rim of salad. Serve sauce on the side.

Jack Heerick's Dutch Potato Salad

A meaty twist on a classic salad and an opportunity to garnish a substantial buffet dish creatively.

SERVES 10 TO 12

3 pounds new or all-purpose potatoes, peeled and cooked
1 pound beets, cooked
3 apples, peeled and cored
1 pound cold, cooked beef
3 dill pickles, chopped

1 small jar cocktail onions
Salt and pepper
4 cups Homemade Mayonnaise (*see page 145*)

FOR GARNISH
Pickles, 4 hard-boiled eggs, parsley, Bibb lettuce

Dice the potatoes, beets, apples and beef into uniform cubes no larger than ½-inch square. Mix all ingredients but garnish, turning gently until everything is coated with mayonnaise. (If the mixture is at all dry, a small amount of olive oil can be added.) Pack and mound the salad on a lettuce-covered round or oval platter.

Chill for 3 to 6 hours before eating. Garnish with pickle fans, thin slices of hard-boiled eggs and chopped parsley.

Warm Potato Salad in Basil Cream

SERVES 4 TO 6

2½ pounds small new potatoes
⅓ cup olive oil
10 large basil leaves
1 clove garlic, minced
1 tablespoon white wine vinegar
1 cup whipping cream
Salt and pepper
1 teaspoon capers

FOR GARNISH
Small basil leaves

Peel the potatoes and cook in salted water. When tender but still slightly firm, drain and cut in half.

Put olive oil, basil and garlic in a medium-sized sauté pan, and as the oil heats, mash the basil with a spoon to release its volatile essence. When the leaves look wilted, turn off heat and steep for 10 minutes.

Remove basil, reheat oil and add vinegar, cream and seasoning. Mix well, add potatoes and stir and shake the pan while the cream simmers. As soon as the sauce thickens, taste for seasoning (it may need more vinegar or salt), and pour the creamed potatoes into a rustic serving dish. Sprinkle with capers and a quantity of small basil leaves. (The delicate leaves of dwarf Greek basil are particularly well suited to this dish.)

Wild Rice Salad

SERVES 4 TO 6

⅔ cup wild rice
½ pound mushrooms, chopped
1 tablespoon oil
1 cup ham, cut in small dice
⅓ cup mixed, fine-chopped parsley and chives
Vinaigrette Dressing without herbs *(see page 92)*
Lemon juice
Salt and pepper

Rinse and wash rice carefully. Bring 4 cups of well-salted water to a boil and add rice. Regulate to a gentle simmer and cook until just tender. Cool.

Sauté the mushrooms in 1 tablespoon of oil. As soon as they give off their liquid, take the pan from the heat; these flavorful juices will be part of the dressing.

Mix rice, ham, mushrooms and their liquid, herbs, and dressing. Taste for seasoning. The rice absorbs quantities of dressing and heavy saltings seem to disappear. Add lemon juice, more vinaigrette and seasoning if the salad seems bland after chilling.

For convenience: the salad is better if made at least a day ahead.

Tabbouleh Rolled in Bibb Lettuce

SERVES 6

2/3 cup burghul (a crushed wheat available at food specialty shops)
1 cup fine-chopped parsley
1/2 cup chopped chives
1/2 cup mint leaves (preferably spearmint), torn fine
4 medium tomatoes, peeled, seeded and chopped
Juice of 1 large lemon
2 or more teaspoons salt
Pepper
Olive oil
2 Bibb lettuces, separated into leaves and washed

Place burghul in a large bowl and cover with cold water. Let the wheat sit until it becomes bite tender. Strain and place burghul on a clean kitchen towel. Wrap and twist the wheat, wringing out all moisture and leaving a fluffy, dry grain. Mix in herbs, tomatoes, lemon juice, salt, pepper and enough olive oil to lightly moisten the salad. Heap into a pretty bowl and serve a platter of lettuce leaves on the side. Each person spoons tabbouleh onto a leaf, rolls the leaf up, and eats it in the manner of an egg roll.

Rolled, Stuffed Nasturtium Leaves

SERVES 4 TO 6

1 cup cooked rice
1 cup cooked fish or *chicken*
Zest of ½ lemon, grated fine
1 tablespoon minced parsley and chives, mixed
Salt
Olive oil
Lemon juice

36 large nasturtium leaves
Pepper
A few nasturtium flowers

Place rice, fish or chicken, lemon zest, herbs and salt in blender or food processor. Purée, adding just enough olive oil to bind ingredients into a thick paste. Chill.

Bring a pot of salted water to a boil. Turn off heat, add nasturtium leaves and cover. Remove leaves after 30 seconds and drain on paper toweling. Place a spoonful of rice in each leaf and roll up. Arrange in a rustic serving dish and sprinkle with olive oil, lemon juice, salt and fresh-ground pepper. Let chill and marinate for up to 8 hours before eating. Garnish each serving with a fresh nasturtium blossom.

Baked Artichokes in Mint and Garlic

Put this dish to bake along with a chicken and both will be ready to eat at the same time. Artichokes prepared in this manner are particularly rich and meaty and can easily stand on their own as a separate course.

SERVES 4 TO 6

8 large artichokes
¾ cup olive oil
¼ cup dry white wine
1 tablespoon lemon juice
Salt and pepper
20 large garlic cloves, peeled
25 mint leaves
2 egg yolks at room temperature

Turn the artichokes to produce hearts: break off the stems and snap back leaves until the tender, pale center is apparent. Using a stainless knife, cut off the top, leaving only an inch of base with the furry thistle exposed. Slant the knife at a 45° angle and cut out the spiky core. Aim for the point just under the thistle and try not to remove any of the heart proper. Rub exposed surfaces with a cut lemon. Trim the exterior of the tough green outer leaf ends, and place the smooth, hollow heart in a small bowl containing ¾ cup olive oil.

When all artichokes are turned, place them, cupped side up and single layered, in a gratin dish. Add the oil, white wine, lemon juice, and seasoning. (There should be oil swimming in every heart.) Place a garlic clove in the center of each artichoke and scatter the rest on the bottom. Tear mint leaves over the whole and cover the dish with aluminum foil. (The mint will heighten flavor but will not be overpowering in the finished dish.) Bake, along with a chicken, at 375°. Baste a few times during the cooking, and in 40 to 45 minutes, the hearts should be easily pierced with a knife tip.

Remove the artichokes, strain juices through a sieve and reserve. Press the garlic through a sieve with a pestle and place in separate small bowl.

Cool oil to room temperature. In blender or food processor, beat the egg yolks until light and thickened. Slowly dribble in the olive oil. When mayonnaise-like sauce has formed, stir in the garlic purée and taste for seasoning. Place artichokes in a rustic dish, coat with sauce, and leave to cool for 1 hour before eating.

Onion Flowers with Pine Nuts

To accompany cold roast veal or pork:

1 large, sweet Spanish onion per serving
Salt
Red wine vinegar
Olive oil
Pine nuts
Pepper
Lemon
Chopped parsley

Peel the onions, leaving the stem trimmed but intact. Cut in thin, ¼-inch slices but do not cut through the stem. Turn the onion at right angles and slice again into a chrysanthemum flower design. (There will be a few loose onion sections in the middle—just leave them as they are.) Salt the onions and place in a lightly oiled baking dish. Sprinkle 1 teaspoon of red wine vinegar over each onion. Dribble olive oil until the onions are oiled and there is some extra in the pan for basting.

Cover lightly with aluminum foil and bake in a preheated 250° oven for 2 hours, basting several times. Add a few pine nuts to the center of each onion and continue baking for 1 more hour.

Remove from oven, add pepper and squeeze lemon juice over the onions. Add a small amount of olive oil if need be to ensure 3 or 4 tablespoons sauce per serving. Sprinkle with parsley and refrigerate. Serve cool or at room temperature.

For convenience: bake the day before so the 3-hour oven time won't overheat the kitchen before a meal. The onions are attractive when baked and served in either brown earthenware or white porcelain. Because of the sweet nature of this dish, it is rather difficult to place within a menu. Follow it with an acid salad and either fruit or cheese, but certainly no dessert which could vie in sweetness with the onions.

Pickled Cucumber Salad

A salad meant *only* to accompany a cold plate of corned beef or sliced sausage.

SERVES 6 TO 8

2 long, firm burpless cucumbers
Salt
1 cup white wine vinegar
1 teaspoon coriander seeds
A few peppercorns
1 bay leaf
A pinch each of thyme and tarragon
Olive oil
Small black Niçoise olives
8 slices thick bacon
Ground pepper, perhaps salt

Wash, dry and trim the cucumbers. They can be cut simply into inch-thick slices or, for a more decorative look, turn them into fat, crinkle-cut pickles. Slant a small, sharp knife through the cucumber at a 45° angle, then keep cutting zig-zag angles until the crinkled top is free. Move down 1½ inches and repeat the slanted cuts until the section separates. Keep cutting in this manner.

Generously salt the slices, leave them to disgorge their water for 45 minutes, then rinse well.

Put the vinegar, spices and herbs into a pan along with 6 cups of water. Bring the broth to a slow boil and cook for 5 minutes. Add the drained cucumbers and cook for about 5 minutes. Keep testing a large slice, for you want only the faintest of pickling effects. Strain as soon as the peel is tender. (The interior should still be crunchy.)

Cool slightly, pour off any accumulated vinegar water, and coat the cucumbers with a thin film of olive oil. Add a handful of Niçoise olives and refrigerate.

Cut the bacon into 1-inch squares. Parboil briefly in a small pan of water to rid it of excess salt and smoky flavoring. Dry the bacon, then fry until crisp. Blot bacon on paper towels and mix it gently into the cucumbers. Add pepper and taste for seasoning. Serve within an hour of the bacon addition.

For convenience: the cucumbers can be made and combined with the olives a day or two in advance. The bacon must be added shortly before serving.

Grilled Pepper Salad

To accompany cold roast beef

SERVES 4 TO 6

6 large, perfect, red or green peppers
12 basil leaves
1 carrot, sliced thin
1 small onion cut into thin rings
1 pimento cut into thin strips
1 garlic clove
Salt and pepper
1 tablespoon red wine vinegar
Olive oil

Grill or broil the peppers in order to remove their skins. Place them first on their sides until they blister and char, then turn them stem ends up. Roll and move carefully with fingers and spoon. (A fork would puncture the skin and cause the loss of valuable juices.) When all peppers are blistered, dark and withered (a process that will take some time), remove them to a dish to cool.

Place a large sieve over a bowl and peel the peppers over it. Cut peppers in two lengthwise, remove the stem with its seed attachment, and keep all peels, seeds and stems in the sieve.

Place a basil leaf on each pepper half and fold the pepper over. Arrange in a rustic dish. Scatter the carrot, onion and pimento on top.

Squeeze and press the residue in the sieve to extract juices. Grind the garlic clove to a pulp in a mortar; add salt, pepper and vinegar. Stir in the pepper juices, then, tasting as you go, add olive oil and seasoning until a pleasant, slightly acid dressing emerges. Pour it over the peppers and marinate for 24 hours in the refrigerator.

Crusted Eggplant

To accompany cold lamb

SERVES 4

2 firm, 1-pound eggplants
Salt
Olive oil
1½ cups thick, homemade Tomato Sauce *(see page 39)*
1 clove garlic, minced
1 tablespoon fine-chopped parsley
1 tablespoon chopped oregano, thyme, basil, mixed
Pepper
½ cup freshly grated Parmesan cheese

Wipe clean, trim off the stem ends and cut the eggplants in two, lengthwise. Make several deep slits in the flesh and salt the cut sides well. Leave to drain cut side down on a platter for 1 hour. Squeeze the eggplants to rid them of additional moisture and pat dry.

Fry, cut side down, in olive oil over medium heat. When the flesh is very tender, remove the halves from the pan and drain on paper towels. Scrape flesh from the outer shells, mash it well, and add tomato sauce, garlic, parsley, herbs, seasoning to taste, and half the cheese. Spoon back into the shells and top with the remaining Parmesan. Place in a lightly oiled pan and bake at 350° for 30 minutes. Cool. Sprinkle lightly with olive oil.

For convenience: make a day or two ahead and refrigerate. Serve as a first course or as a side dish with lamb.

Leftover Chicken Salad

Approximately 2 cups cooked chicken
1 carrot, sliced thin
3 tablespoons white wine vinegar
½ teaspoon salt
2 cloves
Pinch mace
White wine
Tender spinach leaves
Olive oil
Pepper

Skin the chicken and pull into bite-sized pieces. Put chicken and carrot in a small bowl, add vinegar, salt, cloves, mace and enough wine to form a marinade. Refrigerate overnight. Drain off any extra marinade, remove cloves, and arrange chicken on spinach leaves. Dress lightly with olive oil and grindings of fresh pepper.

Leftover Beef Salad

Beef
Thinly sliced shallots
Lemon juice
Olive oil
Salt and pepper
Romaine lettuce
Tomatoes
Fresh parsley, thyme, savory

Slice beef paper-thin. Place it and the shallots in a bowl, add strained lemon juice, oil and seasoning to make a marinade. Refrigerate overnight. Make individual servings on romaine, garnish with tomatoes and herbs, and add more oil if necessary.

Leftover Lamb Salad

Lamb
A well-garlicked vinaigrette dressing
Small, fresh green beans
Roquette (arugula)
Thyme or lemon thyme

Cut lamb into thin slices. Put it to marinate in the vinaigrette. Cook green beans until crisp and *al dente*. When they are just warm, mix lamb, beans, roquette and herbs and serve on individual salad plates.

Main Courses

(PASTAS, FISH, POULTRY, MEATS)

Italian arborio rice is a risotto-making necessity. Easily found in food specialty shops, this fat, starchy grain is the only one which can slowly absorb and expand into the creamy mass that is risotto. In Venice, this *alla primavera* (springtime) dish is served *all'onda* (in the manner of waves); i.e. it moves and runs slowly on a tipped soup plate. It is delicious in that authentic state but makes for a grander presentation when firm enough to mold. Decide either consistency by the amount of liquid added.

Molded Risotto alla Primavera

SERVES 6 TO 8

2 medium carrots in large-pea dice
1½ cups green peas
½ cup sliced celery

⅔ *cup peeled, seeded, dry tomato pulp*
1 *cup sliced small mushrooms*
10 *tablespoons butter*
1 *packed cup fresh spinach shredded extra thin*
2½ *cups chicken stock mixed with 2½ cups water*
3 *bunches scallions, the tender parts sliced thin*
2 *cups Italian arborio rice*
½ *cup dry white wine*
½ *cup Parmesan cheese, freshly grated*
Salt and pepper

FOR GARNISH
Minced parsley
1 *small, firm tomato*

It is most expedient to prepare the vegetables and garnish ahead, for once the rice is started, it demands constant attention. The carrots, peas and celery must be cooked *al dente*. Throw the carrots into boiling, salted water. When almost tender, add the celery and peas, then everything can be strained out together when just cooked.

Give the dry tomatoes a good, coarse chop. Sauté the mushrooms in a tablespoon of butter. Place carrots, peas, celery, tomatoes, mushrooms and spinach in a bowl and set aside.

Bring stock and water to a simmer in a pan.

Melt 4 tablespoons butter in a heavy sauté pan large enough ultimately to hold all ingredients, and cook the scallions over medium heat until limp. Add the rice and stir until it gains a pale translucence. Pour in the wine and continue stirring. It will quickly disappear into the rice.

Add a large ladle of simmering stock and lower the heat. There should be no evident boil. As each addition of broth is slowly absorbed, add another ladle of liquid. Stir regularly and thoroughly (a wooden fork is the correct utensil) so rice does not stick. The rice will cook approximately 24 to 28 minutes in all.

After 20 minutes, start tasting the rice from time to time, particularly if you are new to the risotto process. Feel and taste as the grains expand from firm to chewable to that perfect moment when there remains still a slight "bite" to the kernel, when each particle remains distinctive unto itself, yet there has formed a unified whole cohesively bound by creamy, exuded starch. At that point, throw in all vegetables and the grated cheese.

Blend the mass carefully so as not to break the delicate grains. Grind on pepper, taste for salt, and add 4 tablespoons of butter cut in chunks. Remove from heat, cover, and let rest for 3 minutes during which time the cheese will melt and the spinach turn a vivid green.

Butter well an 8-cup charlotte or soufflé mold. Press the risotto into the dish, let set 2 minutes, then invert over a warm serving platter. Give a good shake and turn out. Rim the risotto top with minced parsley. Cut a thick skin-peel from the tomato as you would a long, coiled orange peel, and curl it into the semblance of a flower in the middle.

Rigatoni with Eggplant and Basil

SERVES 5 TO 6

1 large firm eggplant
Olive oil
15 ounces ricotta cheese
1 cup thick, homemade Tomato Sauce (see page 39)
1 cup whipping cream
½ cup freshly grated Parmesan cheese
2 tablespoons fine-chopped parsley
Salt and pepper
1 pound quality rigatoni, preferably Italian made, like DeCecco
6 tablespoons unsalted butter
½ cup fresh basil leaves

Wash and trim the eggplant. Slice it in two lengthwise and cut into unpeeled, half-moon slices about ½-inch thick. Salt slices and let them rest 30 minutes. Wipe away the moisture with paper towels and sauté slices in olive oil until crisp and brown on both sides. Keep warm.

Mix the ricotta, tomato sauce, whipping cream, cheese, parsley and seasoning together.

Cook rigatoni in plentiful boiling, salted water to which two or three tablespoons of oil are added. (This helps keep pasta strands separate.) Do not overcook. Drain and mix in the sauce. Put it all over gentle heat, stirring and warming to melt the cheese. Add butter in chunks and when melted, add the basil leaves torn, at the last moment, into small pieces. Turn pasta immediately into a heated earthenware serving dish and overlap the eggplant slices in an edging border. A sprig or two of basil can garnish this pretty dish.

Green Green Pasta

SERVES 6 TO 8

This green pasta is most efficiently composed in a large pan that can hold all ingredients and also be placed directly on table for service. A 10- or 11-inch *sauteuse*, made from copper or aluminum, will repay its initial expense many times over in usefulness for this and other dishes. Of course the elements can also be combined at the end in a large, hot serving dish.

FOR THE PASTA

5 ounces spinach
3 whole eggs and 4 egg yolks
½ teaspoon salt
Approximately 2⅓ cups quick-blending flour

FOR THE SAUCE

4 *medium zucchini*
Salt
1 *bunch scallions*
4 *ounces unsalted butter*
2 *cloves garlic, minced fine*
¾ *cup small green peas*
1½ *cups whipping cream*
¾ *cup Parmesan cheese, freshly grated*
½ *cup fine-chopped herbs (parsley and chives predominating, oregano, marjoram, tarragon, thyme in moderation)*
Pepper, ground fresh
Additional unsalted butter

Wash and rib spinach. Cook in a large pot of boiling, salted water until tender but still bright green. Drain, refresh under cold water, and squeeze out excess moisture. (The spinach must be very dry or it will complicate rolling out the pasta.) Chop or purée the mass well and press spinach through a sieve with a heavy spoon or pestle. The fine greening that results will color the pasta.

Break eggs in a large bowl. Add salt and spinach green and, blending with fingers, stir in flour until a firm mass is formed. Turn out of bowl onto a floured surface and work in flour until the dough no longer feels sticky.

If you are rolling pasta by hand: knead the dough vigorously until smooth and elastic. (The pasta should have a leathery sheen and a smooth ancient-girdle feel.) More flour may have to be worked in during kneading if spinach moistens the dough. Cover with plastic wrap and refrigerate for 30 minutes. Divide dough in two and roll out each half as thin as possible on a floured surface. Let the sheet of dough dry briefly over an outstretched broom handle. When edges feel slightly firm and dry, roll up dough and cut into thin spaghetti strips. Toss noodles lightly in a bit of flour, shake off excess and place on a platter. Cover with a dish towel.

If you are using a machine: knead dough briefly, then cover with plastic wrap and refrigerate for 30 minutes. Divide into four parts. Knead each portion through the wide opening until smooth. If the dough is sticky, keep rolling in flour between kneads. When perfectly smooth and elastic, thin the strip down through each succeedingly narrow roller. Stop at next to the last notch. Hang strips of pasta over a broomstick until they firm and crisp slightly at the edges. Run strips through wider cutting blade. Toss lightly in flour, shake off excess and place on a platter. Cover with a dish towel.

To make the sauce, grate the zucchini and sprinkle lightly with salt. Let sit in a bowl for 30 minutes then squeeze firmly to extract water.

Trim and slice fine the white parts and 1 inch of the scallion greens.

Melt butter, add scallions and garlic and simmer until the onion is soft. Stir in the grated zucchini and sauté briefly. Place in a bowl. Cook green peas in boiling, salted water and add to scallions. Keep everything as green as possible.

Whip cream until thickened but not firm.

Cook pasta in a large pot of boiling, salted, oiled water. Taste pasta and strain into a colander when perfectly *al dente.*

Over low heat, rapidly mix pasta, greens, cheese, cream and herbs. Carefully lift and turn the mass with two wooden forks or spoons until everything blends and melts in a sensuous sauce and the herbs release their fragrance. Add good grindings of pepper, some pats of butter, more salt if needed, and serve at once.

For convenience: have all ingredients at the ready for the final assemblage. Students always ask if they can make pasta ahead and dry or freeze it. This can be done, but the whole point and pleasure of *fresh* pasta is lost. One might as well use the boughten article.

Pasta with Scallops à la Provençal

SERVES 6 TO 8

Fresh pasta
3 cloves garlic
⅓ cup chopped parsley
Flour
1½ pounds scallops, patted very dry
⅓ cup olive oil
¼ cup firm breadcrumbs
Juice of 1 lemon
Salt and pepper

Make pasta according to preceding recipe (page 113) but omit the spinach greening. Cook in boiling, salted, oiled water and drain, when *al dente*, into a sieve. Place the sieve over a pot and fill with hot (not boiling) water. The pasta will keep warm for the time necessary to cook the scallops.

Flour the dry scallops. Sauté in olive oil in a large pan so they will not overcrowd and stick together. When crusted and golden on all sides, throw in the garlic-parsley mixture, then the breadcrumbs. Shake the pan briefly until scallops are coated with green and the crumbs have absorbed oil. Squeeze on lemon juice and season. Drain pasta and add enough olive oil to form a thin, redolent coating. Top with scallops.

An Elegant Shrimp "Pizza"

This is an amusing dish to present for lunch or as the first course of an elegant dinner party. It will look rather like a plain pizza but the relationship goes no further. Have your fishmonger peel the shrimp and reserve shells. He will also provide extra fish bones.

SERVES 8

FOR THE FUMET

Head and bones from 1 large fish
Shells from 1 ½ pounds shrimp
1 carrot, sliced
1 celery stalk, sliced
1 onion, quartered
1 bay leaf
Parsley and thyme sprigs
3 lemon slices
½ teaspoon salt
⅔ cup dry white wine
4 cups water

4 ounces unsalted butter

FOR THE SAUCE

2 tablespoons unsalted butter
2 tablespoons flour
1 ½ cups fish fumet
4 large tomatoes, peeled, seeded, chopped or *one 28-ounce can tomatoes, well drained*
The shrimp butter
Juice of ½ lemon
1 egg plus 1 egg yolk
Salt and pepper
Cayenne

FOR THE "PIZZA"

Rough Puff Pastry for pizza shell *(see page 199)*
1 ½ pounds peeled shrimp
4 ounces mushrooms, cleaned and sliced
1 large ripe tomato
Salt and pepper
The sauce
½ cup Parmesan cheese, grated fresh

FOR GARNISH

Chopped parsley

Cover all stock ingredients with 4 cups water. Bring to a boil and immediately reduce heat to an easy simmer. Cook 30 minutes. Strain, gently pressing bones and vegetables to release their juices. Remove shrimp shells from the debris and reserve. Measure the stock to see how much you have, then reduce to about 1 ½ cups over brisk heat.

Make a shrimp butter by grinding the shrimp shells with 4 ounces unsalted butter in a mortar or food processor. Press the shrimp-flavored butter through a sieve and reserve.

To make the sauce, melt the tablespoon unsalted butter, stir in the flour and let the resulting *roux* cook gently for 2 minutes. Stir continuously, making sure the mixture does not brown. Whisk in the fish fumet and continue stirring over low heat for another 5 minutes. Cool slightly, then add tomato pulp (be sure it is as dry as possible), shrimp butter, lemon juice, eggs, salt, pepper, and 3 good shakes of cayenne.

Cover a 15-inch pizza pan with rough puff pastry rolled fairly thin. Cut a long, inch-wide strip of pastry to use as a rim. Moisten the outer edge of the rolled dough and, with minimal water, "glue" the rim on and notch a decorative edge.

Arrange shrimp and mushrooms over the top. Cut the tomato in two through the middle and squeeze out seeds and juice. Cut flesh into thin strips and scatter them over the shrimp. Season. Dab the sauce around, sprinkle with cheese and bake for 50 minutes at 350° or until pie is golden and bubbling.

For convenience: the entire sauce can be made the day ahead. Have cheese grated and pastry shell rolled out and chilling.

Shrimp on a Bed of Spinach

SERVES 4 TO 5

2½ pounds fresh spinach
12 scallions
4 slices firm, crustless bread
1 cup olive oil
2 medium cloves garlic, minced fine
Salt and pepper
1½ lemons
1 pound peeled, deveined shrimp
1 tablespoon capers

Wash and rib the spinach. Trim the scallions and slice the tender green and white parts thin. Bring a large pot of well-salted water to a boil. Throw in the spinach and scallions and cook, uncovered, until the spinach is just tender and still green. Drain and refresh under cold water. Squeeze all liquid from spinach and chop roughly. Cut bread slices in two, diagonally.

Use ⅓ cup of olive oil to fry the bread croûtons until golden brown on both sides. When all are uniformly crisp, roll up the croûtons in 3 thicknesses of paper towels and set aside.

To the same pan, add another ⅓ cup of oil and half the garlic. When hot, throw in the spinach and scallions, season well and stir rapidly over high heat for 1 minute until the oil is absorbed. Squeeze juice of half a lemon onto the spinach and turn it out on the bottom of a small gratin dish.

Add the final ⅓ cup of oil and the remaining garlic to the same pan. When sizzling, sauté the shrimp. Squeeze the juice of another half lemon over them and season well. Scatter shrimp over spinach. Sprinkle with capers, add 5 or 6 decorative lemon rounds cut very thin, and place the croûtons around the edge. To be eaten lukewarm.

Simple Summer Sauces

There are several reduction-based sauces used throughout this book, for their unctuous richness can turn even the roughest grill into an elegant meal and their rapid though last-minute preparation means a minimum of summer stove work. Here are four adaptably basic suggestions for summer sauces:

1. The easiest "sauce" is based on a simple reduction of cream. Over medium heat, reduce 2 cups of whipping cream to 1 cup, stirring frequently so a skin does not form. The result will be the consistency of a medium white sauce (Béchamel) and should serve four. Season with salt and pepper. For variations:

– Add a handful of fine-shredded sorrel to the reducing cream.

– Color and flavor reduced cream with 1 tablespoon of *fines herbes* and/or spinach purée.

– Stir in ½ cup chopped, sautéed, pressed dry mushrooms or duxelles.

– Add Dijon-type mustard as in recipe for Grilled Lamb, page (172).

2. Take a quantity of tomato sauce and reduce it until well thickened (or keep a supply in the freezer). Purée the sauce and thin with whipping cream to desired consistency. Or reduce sauce and an amount of cream at the same time, pass through a sieve and whisk in 2 or 3 tablespoons unsalted butter for gloss and flavor.

3. Make a sauce based on reduced stock or pan glazings. Reduce 2 cups of defatted chicken, veal or strong fish stock and ¼ cup white wine down to 3 or 4 tablespoons of shiny, syrupy glaze. Let cool briefly, then start whisking in chunks of chilled, unsalted butter. Move pan back over heat from time to time. The butter will emulsify and build into a thick sauce. The butter's chill helps to regulate the heat but at no time should the sauce become so hot that you cannot rest a finger in it. If it becomes too hot the butter will melt and swim rather than build and emulsify.

A simple sauce can also be produced from the crusted proteins that stick to the pan bottom when meat is fried. Do not waste this delicious flavor. Instead, pour off any fat (blot surface lightly with paper towels if necessary) and add ½ cup of wine. Scrape pan until the coagulated brownings are mingled with the wine, then reduce to a thickened glaze and, using heat precautions described above, whisk in butter. Taste for seasoning. One note of caution regarding this procedure. In cooking down stock or pan glazes, there comes a point in reduction after which the syrup will caramelize, i.e. the natural sugars and proteins will take on the taste of caramel. This flavor is so permeating that all suggestion of fish, chicken or meat will be lost to its pervasive and undesirable presence. If this overdone glaze is left to cool somewhat, it will thicken and spin strands when touched by a spoon. Aim for a syrup that still moves in the pan, not as a sludge, but as a slightly thin honey that is still able to coat a spoon.

4. The most famous reductive sauce is *beurre blanc* (white butter) in which a quantity of wine (sometimes vinegar), salt and shallots are slowly cooked down until juices disappear, leaving only a coating of stained purple shallots on the pan's bottom. The reduction is then mounted with butter. Likewise, a vegetable essence with little acid properties of its own (such as the mushroom base for the sauce on page 77) can be reduced along with wine and in so doing, incorporate its characteristic flavors usefully. This principle gives rise to many variations, and any highly acidified reduction will support this treatment as in the buttery sauce built on lemon juice in the following recipe.

Shrimp Brochettes with Lemon and Dill Sauce

SERVES 6

FOR THE BROCHETTES

1 pound large, firm mushrooms
1 ½ pounds shelled jumbo shrimp
6 tablespoons unsalted butter
Juice of 1 lemon
½ cup fine dry breadcrumbs
Salt
Pepper

FOR GARNISH

Watercress

Lightly oil 6 skewers. Wipe the mushrooms clean and remove stems. Thread skewers alternately with shrimp and mushrooms. Melt butter and lemon juice together and brush over the brochettes. Sprinkle with breadcrumbs and salt. Broil under a flame or over a grill until done, turning frequently and brushing on the remaining lemon butter half way through the grilling. Pepper.

FOR THE SAUCE

¼ cup strained lemon juice
2 tablespoons minced shallots
Large pinch salt
1 ½ sticks chilled unsalted butter, cut in chunks
½ cup cream, firmly whipped
1 tablespoon fine-chopped dill
Pepper

Put lemon juice, shallots and salt in a small, heavy saucepan. Reduce slowly until the shallots appear dry on the bottom of the pan. Remove from heat. Start whisking 2 or 3 lumps of butter at a time into the reduced shallots. Keep adding butter and whisking continuously. Put the pan back on a very low flame from time to time, but do not let the butter melt. Instead, it should mount into a thick, pale, creamy sauce, held in suspension by the acidity of the lemon. When all butter is incorporated, stir in the whipped cream. Add dill and pepper to taste.

Place brochettes on watercressed plates. Sauce and serve immediately.

For convenience: the brochettes may be composed several hours in advance of grilling, and kept, foil-wrapped, in the refrigerator. The lemon juice and shallots can be reduced ahead of time but the rest of the sauce is basically last minute. Warm shallots gently before continuing the butter additions.

Shrimp and Zucchini Fritters

Although one does not want to pass too much summer time over a deep fryer, the season never seems complete without at least one session turning out crisp fritters. A particularly auspicious time for such an undertaking is on those days when squash plants are prolific with blossoms crying out to be batter dipped. It is easy to execute a mixed fry for two or three by oneself, but because of the last minute preparation involved, extra participants and a production line speed the process when more people are to be fed. Let one person coat ingredients with batter and drop them in the oil. Another does fry duty, and a third dries, salts and covers each fritter.

SERVES 6

FOR THE BATTER

- 1 *cup sifted flour*
- ¼ *teaspoon salt*
- 2 *tablespoons melted unsalted butter*
- 1 *tablespoon cognac*
- 1 *cup lukewarm water*
- 3 *egg whites at room temperature*

Combine the flour and salt and make a well in the middle. Add butter, cognac and water, gradually whisking in more and more of the flour until the mixture seems smooth. Let rest, covered with a towel, for 1 hour. Beat egg whites to firm peaks and fold into the batter. Use at once.

FOR THE FRITTERS

1½ pounds large shrimp
2 cloves garlic
Lemon juice
5 medium zucchini
Pepper
Squash or zucchini blossoms (optional)
Olive or peanut oil for frying
Salt
1 small bunch parsley, preferably Italian flat leaf

FOR GARNISH

Lemon wedges

FOR THE DIPPING SAUCE

1½ cups Homemade Mayonnaise (see page 145)
3 tablespoons dry tomato pulp

Peel the shrimp, leaving tails on if possible. Devein shrimp and butterfly them in the process by slitting deeply, spreading shrimp open, and pressing down to flatten. Season. Press 1 garlic clove and squeeze some lemon juice over shrimp and leave to marinate.

Wash and stem zucchini. Cut into ⅓-inch thick rounds. Press 1 clove of garlic over the vegetable, moisten with lemon juice and add pepper.

Expell any ants from the squash blossoms.

Heat the oil and test for correct frying temperature by dropping in a small piece of batter. It should immediately sizzle and remain on the surface.

Fry zucchini first. Dip slices in batter, tap off any excess and cook until brown on both sides. Do not overcrowd. Remove finished fritters with a slotted spoon and place first on 3 thicknesses of paper toweling to drain, then on a heated serving platter. Salt and cover with a large napkin.

Dip and fry blossoms next and shrimp last. At the end, throw in the parsley bunch (both stems and leaves). It will hiss loudly. Remove in less than 30 seconds, when the leaves have turned a dark, bright green.

Scatter parsley over fritters, garnish with lemon wedges, and serve with a dipping sauce of homemade mayonnaise colored with sieved tomato pulp.

Crab and Onions in a Crumb Crust

A crumb crust is a simple, different base on which to build a variety of quiche-like tarts. An excess of bread, even stale bread, can be used economically, and the amount of butter is much less than in a pastry crust. The egg and cream will seep through the solid crab filling, soaking the crumbs and causing them to expand and bind into a solid, sliceable shell.

SERVES 4 TO 6

4 slices firm bread
Approximately 5 tablespoons unsalted butter
½ pound uncooked claw crabmeat
2 eggs
½ cup whipping cream
Salt and pepper
The white parts only of 3 scallions, minced fine
1 teaspoon fine-chopped chives

FOR GARNISH
Lemon wedges

In a blender or food processor, crumble bread into small (but not fine), even crumbs. Melt butter in a frying pan and stir in crumbs, tossing them until they are uniformly buttery. Stir over medium heat until they turn a shade or two darker and start to look a toasty brown. There should be no melted butter remaining in the bottom of the pan.

Add only enough to flavor and fry crumbs without leaving them soggy.

Spread the crumbs in a 9-inch pie dish, smoothing them over the bottom and up the sides in approximation of a crust.

Place crabmeat in the pie shell. Beat the eggs, cream and seasoning together. Add the fine-chopped white parts of the scallions and the chives. Pour mixture over the crab. The scallions will remain on the surface, which is as it should be. Place 6 small shavings of butter over the top.

Bake pie in a 350° oven for 35 minutes. Run a knife around the edge and turn out on a plate, upside down. Invert a serving platter over the tart and turn it right side up. Serve in slices, garnished with lemon.

Lobster à l'Américaine

One of the easiest dishes from the classic French repertoire, Lobster *à l'américaine*, served with an attendant rice pilaf, provides a splendid, short-order meal. If the lobster is set aside after cooking, and the remaining juices are drawn off and sieved, the result is Sauce Américaine which plays an elegant role in the Shrimp Mousse recipe following after.

SERVES 2 TO 4

4 shallots, chopped fine
6 large, ripe tomatoes, peeled, seeded, chopped
1 clove garlic, minced
1 tablespoon fine-chopped parsley
3 leaves tarragon, chopped (optional)
Salt, pepper, cayenne
An inch of dried orange peel
½ cup dry white wine
½ cup cognac
½ cup chicken stock

1 hen lobster, approximately 2 pounds
6 tablespoons olive oil
Rice pilaf
1 stick unsalted butter, cut in chunks
Juice of ½ lemon

FOR GARNISH
Chopped parsley

Have all ingredients measured and prepared ahead. Place shallots, tomatoes, garlic, herbs and orange peel in a bowl. Measure wine and cognac into 1 cup, stock into another. Arrange all ingredients in easy proximity around the stove.

Twist the lobster in two where the tail meets the carapace (the smooth upper back). If unsure of strength and nerve, place a cleaver

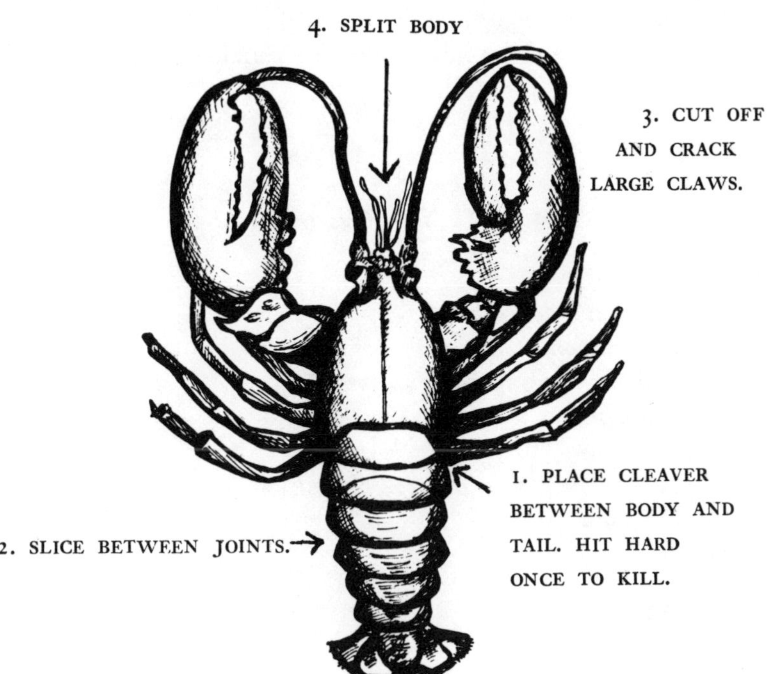
4. SPLIT BODY
3. CUT OFF AND CRACK LARGE CLAWS.
1. PLACE CLEAVER BETWEEN BODY AND TAIL. HIT HARD ONCE TO KILL.
2. SLICE BETWEEN JOINTS.

on the spot and strike down on it with a small, heavy frying pan. Cut the tail in two or three sections. Twist off the claws and small legs. Cut the body in two lengthwise.

Remove the tomalley (the pale green liver), and any coral (eggs) and set aside. Remove and discard the small gritty sac at the head. Scoop the water (blood) from the lobster into a small bowl.

Heat olive oil in a large sauté pan. Add lobster sections and stir over a good heat until they are scarlet. Add wine and brandy. Touch with a lighted match and shake the pan until the flames are gone. Immediately add the tomatoes and stock and season, using enough cayenne to sharpen but not overwhelm the lobster flavor. Cover and cook briskly for 18 minutes. Shake pan frequently during this time.

To serve, heap a bed of rice in a serving dish. Remove the lobster pieces and place on rice but keep the sauce simmering. Add tomalley, coral and blood and cook another minute. Off heat, whisk in the butter and lemon juice. Spoon the rough sauce over the lobster and serve, sprinkled with chopped parsley.

As this is a participation dish, each diner should be provided with a finger bowl after the meal.

Shrimp Mousseline with Sauce Américaine

SERVES 8 TO 10

Lobster meat, chopped and
Sauce Américaine (page 126)
1 pound peeled, deveined shrimp
2 egg whites
Unsalted butter
1½ cups whipping cream, well chilled
½ teaspoon salt
Pepper

FOR GARNISH
Chopped parsley

Make Lobster *à l'américaine* up to the final addition of butter. Pick out the lobster meat and sieve the sauce. Set aside.

Make a forcemeat of shrimp. Pound shrimp and egg whites in a mortar or purée in a food processor. Pass the resulting paste through a sieve, preferably a drum sieve (*tamis*) to ensure a uniformly smooth texture. Pack shrimp into a small bowl and cover tightly with plastic wrap. Chill for at least 1½ hours in the refrigerator.

Generously butter a 2-quart soufflé mold. Cut a round of brown paper to fit the bottom. Place in dish and butter its top side.

To assemble mousse, take shrimp from refrigerator and place in a large bowl. Stir in ½ cup of the chilled cream to lighten the mixture. Add seasoning. Whip the other cup of cream until thickened but not firm. Fold it and the reserved lobster meat into the shrimp. Spoon the mousse into the soufflé dish.

Poach in a *bain marie* on top of the stove: place a cake rack in the bottom of a large pan, fill the pan ⅓ full of steaming water, and lower the soufflé dish onto the rack. The water should come ⅔ of the way up the mold. Funnel a bit more in if necessary. Cover the pan and cook over low heat. At no point should the water boil. Poach for 1 hour.

To serve, heat the reserved Sauce Américaine and whisk in lemon juice and the final butter enrichment. Remove mousse from *bain marie*. Blot off any water from the top with paper towels and unmold onto a serving dish. Peel off paper. Encircle with sauce and garnish with parsley.

For convenience: make sauce (except for late butter and lemon additions) and pick and chop lobster meat the day before. Purée and sieve the forcemeat and leave to chill. Add cream only before poaching.

This mousse does not mind sitting covered, but with the heat turned off, for 20 minutes or so before unmolding.

Scallop Mousseline with Watercress Sauce

Another mousse of ethereal and particular refinement, this dish provides an elegant first course for a splendid dinner party or a good luncheon selection when something pretty, light but hot is desired. The recipe can easily be halved, in which case, poach the mousse in individual soufflé dishes.

SERVES 10

1 pound scallops, preferably fresh, but frozen will do
2 eggs, separated
10 ounces mushrooms, cleaned
1 tablespoon unsalted butter
10 ounces fresh spinach
Salt
1½ cups whipping cream, well-chilled
Pepper
Nutmeg

Pat the scallops dry with paper towels. Purée scallops and egg whites until perfectly smooth. This can be done bit by bit in a blender or, more easily, in a food processor. There is no need to sieve. Pack the purée into a small metal bowl. Press plastic wrap over the surface so no air can enter to dry and crust the mixture, and place in the refrigerator for at least 1½ hours.

Chop the mushrooms fine and sauté them in 1 tablespoon of butter over fairly high heat. The mushrooms will render their juices. Continue cooking until the liquid is gone and the pan bottom appears dry. (The mushrooms often squeak at this point when stirred.) Let cool.

Wash and rib the spinach. Cook uncovered in the water that clings to its leaves and a dash of salt. When just cooked, drain in a strainer, refresh under cold water, and gently squeeze the mass to remove all moisture. Purée spinach with the 2 egg yolks.

Cut a circle of kitchen parchment or brown paper to fit the bottom of a 2-quart soufflé dish or charlotte mold. Butter paper on both sides and also the dish. Fit paper into the bottom of the mold.

Take the scallop purée from the refrigerator. Stir in ½ cup chilled cream to lighten the mixture. Whip the remaining cup of cream until thick but not firm. Fold the beaten cream into the purée, then the mushrooms, 1 teaspoon of salt, pepper and a scraping of nutmeg. Spoon and smooth half the mixture into the mold.

Add the spinach in a thin, level layer. Use fingers to flatten and spread it as evenly as possible.

Spoon in the other half of the mousse, smooth the top and tap the whole dish gently but firmly on a towel-covered table to settle the contents.

Select a large pot with a cover to act as a *bain marie*. Place an object (such as a small cake rack or cookie cutter) on the bottom to keep the mold from resting directly on the pot. Fill the pot with enough water to come ⅔ of the way up the mold. Bring water to a boil then regulate heat to the barest simmer. Set the mold in the water and cover the pot. The water should steam but have no hint of a boil about it. There should be no noise from the pot, no bubbles breaking under the mold to move it about. Stay in the general vicinity of the stove for the first few minutes. Poach mousse for about 60 minutes, at which point the surface should feel quite firm to the touch. (With heat off, the mousse can rest in the water and wait for 20 minutes if necessary.)

Remove mold from water. Let it sit 5 minutes. Run a knife around the edge and gently invert onto a warm serving platter.

To serve, cut two slices off one side, then cut the remaining mousse in half-slices. A lemon wedge and a small scoop of pilaf should be the only accompaniments. Ribbon the pale green sauce over mousse and rice.

Watercress Sauce

2 bunches watercress
2 cups whipping cream
1 cup dry white wine
2 tablespoons lemon juice
½ teaspoon salt
2 sticks unsalted butter, chilled and cut in chunks
Pepper

Wash and strip the watercress leaves. Blanch in a small pot of boiling, salted water. As soon as cress is bright green, drain and refresh under cold water. Dry thoroughly and purée.

Reduce cream, white wine, lemon juice and salt in a small, heavy pan until there remains only 1 cup of thick sauce base. Let cool a moment, then whisk in the butter bit by bit. The butter must not melt but should build into an emulsive sauce. Add watercress and pepper and give a few hard whisks. Taste and add more lemon juice or salt if needed. Serve immediately.

For convenience: purée scallops and cook mushrooms and spinach the day before. The next day, add cream to forcemeat and proceed to assemble dish. The cream and wine reduction for the sauce can be finished early, covered with plastic wrap and refrigerated so no crust can form. Reheat gently and add butter before serving. Make half a recipe of this delicious sauce to serve with baked or poached fish for four.

Scallop and Herb Pie

A great comfort of a cool, damp summer's evening.

SERVES 4 TO 5

1½ pounds scallops
3 tablespoons flour
8 ounces firm mushrooms
1 teaspoon each chopped parsley and chives
1 small onion, chopped
1 cup white wine
3 tablespoons melted unsalted butter
Salt and pepper
Rough Puff pastry (*see page 199*)
Egg yolk for glaze
½ cup whipping cream
1 egg
1 tablespoon fines herbes (*parsely, chives, tarragon, chervil*)

Pat scallops dry and roll in flour. Shake off excess.

Wipe mushrooms with a damp cloth, cut off any dry stem ends, and slice.

Mix scallops, mushrooms, parsley, chives, onion, wine, butter and seasoning. Place in a casserole or soufflé dish that will hold ingredients and leave 1 inch to spare at the top.

Roll out the pastry. Cut a 1-inch wide strip and place it flat against the upper inside rim of the dish. Cover top with pastry and crimp the two edges together. Cut a circle 1½-inches in diameter in the center of the pie but leave dough in place. Decorate with scraps.

Beat the egg yolk with 1 teaspoon of the cream and brush glaze over the pie. Bake in a 350° oven. After 40 minutes, remove from oven and lift out the center circle of dough. Beat together the remaining glaze, the remaining cream, 1 egg and the herbs and pour into the hole. Poke the cream into the recesses with a spoon handle if need be. Return to oven for another 10 minutes.

A calm summer's night off the Carolina coast: the stars, the very faintest thumbnail moon above, and below, under the small flat-bottomed skiff, the dark, full, flood-tide sea.

Far in the distance there is another fisher's boat, but we have left the common grounds behind, pressing past Harker's Island and Atlantic to Drum Inlet and unlighted shores. We cannot see them now, but all around are the fish—squat flounder up from the deep, edging their way in to land. In winter we would use a different boat, a different harvest method, for then the fish, leaving the coastward bays and inlets, seek deep muddy bottoms for their wintering, and the fisherman, hunting with trawler, stirs the bottom first with tickler chain to startle the fish, then sweeps his conical net across the swirling flat to gather in his catch. But in summer, when the moon is right, the flounder come to shore to feed on plankton and there they are for the taking—the simple thrust of a steel-pronged, fifteen-foot-long gig.

We cut motor and turn in toward the bank, letting current drift us up. The fisherman at the fore eases his gig into the sea, and for the last distance it trails the water. I, along for ballast and company, sit at the stern. There is no sound to frighten the fish, to give evidence of the fact that we wait there, poised like malevolent Neptune with spearing gig in hand.

At shore, the fisherman slowly swings his gig around to the front. He will not, cannot spear down, for the fish would dart at the very sound of breaking water. Instead, he will reach out, and with a quick, noiseless jab, fix his prey. We float quietly for a moment, then turn a powerful shine light on, and all around and to the sides the bottom sand lights up. Then we see one, a dark ellipse unmoving on the sand, with its nose almost on the bank. And then there is another and another, some obvious to our view and others not so open but visible only as faint sand-covered outlines.

We and they wait, motionless. (The blind white side is vulnerable but you'd think the brown side, with its strange flat eyes peering always upward, would register some boding sense of danger. Has a great skate never sailed above? A hovering shark never circled overhead and cast its fearful shadow?)

Suddenly the fisherman thrusts his gig forward and then begins a slow swing of flounder-laden spear through the water and around the boat. A quick flip and the fish is over the side and into the fish box. Back swings the gig in slow arc around the boat, but having stirred the waters we must wait until silt settles, wait until other fish come trustingly to feed.

After three silent hours in the night, we turn back up the shore with forty pounds of flounder.

Kathleen Taylor's Stewed Flounder

A down-home method, reminiscent of French *cotriades* and *chaudrées*, for preparing steak-cut slices of any firm, white fish. Both bluefish and flounder are cooked in this manner on the outer banks of North and South Carolina. Butter can replace the salt pork for a more delicate dish.

SERVES 4

Salt and pepper
Flour
One 1½-pound flounder cut across in inch-wide steak pieces
Salt pork
1 large onion, chopped
2 large potatoes, diced
Lemon juice
Chopped parsley

Salt, pepper and flour the fish steaks. Shake off excess.

Render approximately 3 tablespoons of melted salt pork in a pan large enough to hold all ingredients. Brown the fish lightly on both sides in the fat, then remove from pan.

Add chopped onion and potatoes, stirring briefly. Pour over 1 cup water into the pan and replace fish slices on the vegetable bed. Cover pan and stew very slowly until the potatoes and onions are tender. Season, add lemon juice and a strew of parsley and serve.

Mackerel Brochettes with Saffron Sauce

SERVES 6

10 inch-thick slices of king mackerel
2 medium onions
2 medium tomatoes
1 zucchini
½ cup dry white wine
Olive oil
1 clove garlic, crushed
1 teaspoon mixed dried herbs
Salt and pepper

FOR THE STOCK

Fish trimmings
1 carrot
1 onion
1 celery stalk
1 bay leaf
Parsley and thyme sprigs
3 lemon slices
Salt and pepper

FOR THE SAUCE

3 tablespoons unsalted butter
3 tablespoons flour
1½ cups strained stock
A generous ¼ teaspoon saffron
½ cup whipping cream

Lemon juice to taste
Salt and pepper

Lemon wedges
A rice pilaf

The fish slices are divided into 4 quarters by thin membranes. Punch out the fat, scallop-like nuts of flesh in each of the 4 sections. Use trimmings for stock.

Cut onions into quarters, leaving each piece well attached at the root end. Parboil gently for 3 minutes. Cut the tomatoes into 6 wedges. Rid them of juice and seeds. Slice zucchini.

Place fish and vegetables in a bowl and moisten with white wine and a small amount of olive oil. Add garlic, herbs and seasoning and marinate for at least 1 hour. Thread skewers with alternating fish and vegetables. Reserve marinade.

Place the fish trimmings and other stock ingredients in a small pan. Add 2½ cups water and bring to a boil. Immediately regulate heat to low, and simmer for 30 minutes. Strain.

Make a *velouté* sauce: melt the butter in a small, heavy saucepan. Add flour and whisk over low heat for 3 minutes. Do not let flour brown. Whisk in 1½ cups strained stock, add the saffron and cook gently (the sauce should emit slow, heavy bubbles) for 20 minutes. Skim off any skin from time to time and drag a wooden spoon over the bottom to make sure nothing is sticking.

Thin the sauce with the cream. Whisk in lemon juice to taste and adjust seasoning.

Broil or grill the brochettes, basting occasionally with marinade. Serve with lemon wedges and a pilaf, the last necessary to absorb the abundant, saffron-yellow sauce. Serve sauce separately.

For convenience: the fish and vegetables can rest in the marinade all day. The stock and sauce may be made the day before up to the point of adding cream. When the *velouté* has cooled, pour a thin film of melted butter over the surface to prevent a skin forming. Reheat gently when needed, and whisk in cream and surface butter.

Cold Paupiettes of Salmon and Flounder

If fresh salmon is unavailable for the forcemeat, substitute trout or flounder. The delicate juxtaposition of peach, white and green will be lost in the paupiette itself, but this deficiency can be overcome by lightly tinting the accompanying mayonnaise with reduced tomato sauce.

The given amounts will produce four large main course servings. By using smaller ramekins and quarter-pound filets, these same ingredients could also serve to provide eight small, first course portions.

SERVES 4

4 half-pound filets of flounder, skin on
½ pound skinless fresh salmon
1 egg
1 tablespoon fine-chopped chives and parsley
Salt, pepper, nutmeg
1 cup whipping cream, chilled
Fine-minced parsley for garnish
Homemade Mayonnaise *(see page 145)*
Cream

Butter 4 small soufflé dishes or ramekins, about 4 inches in diameter. Pat the flounder filets dry and coil them in the dishes, skin side against the edge. Cut off any fish that protrudes above the rim. Refrigerate the ramekins.

Purée the skinless salmon with the egg, herbs and seasoning, in a food processor or, bit by bit, in a blender. Pack into a small bowl, cover with plastic wrap, and place in refrigerator for at least 1 hour to firm.

To assemble, mix ½ cup of the cream into the firm purée. Whip remaining ½ cup until thickened but not firm. Fold into purée. Spoon mixture into the centers of the ramekins, tapping each dish firmly to settle its contents. Place ramekins in a large pot with enough hot water to reach ⅔ of the way up the small dishes. Cover and poach on top of the stove for 25 minutes. The water should be steaming and near a simmer but never break into a roiling bubble. No noise should come from the pot.

Remove ramekins from water and let them sit and compose themselves for 5 minutes. Place each dish upside down on a cake rack to drain off any juices. Unmold and carefully remove outer skin with a knife point. Roll the edge of each paupiette in fine-minced parsley, cover with plastic wrap, and refrigerate until serving time. The accompanying mayonnaise should be diluted with a touch of cream until it pours thickly. It can also be flavored with an addition of chopped herbs or tomato purée.

For convenience: make everything the night before. Keep paupiettes covered and in ramekins until needed.

Whole Fish "Soufflé"

A combination of forcemeat and soufflé procedures produces the firm yet melting consistency of the following dish. The "soufflé" will neither rise nor fall much, and it can be held 5 to 10 minutes in a warming oven before serving with no great damage. Red snapper provides the prettiest presentation, but trout or bluefish yields a more refined and pronounced flavor.

SERVES 6

FOR THE SOUFFLÉ

One 3½ pound gray or speckled trout, bluefish or snapper
4 whole eggs and 4 egg whites
3 tablespoons butter
1 cup whipping cream, chilled and lightly whipped
Salt and pepper
Nutmeg
¼ cup Gruyère or Parmesan cheese, grated fine

FOR THE SAUCE

1½ cups thick, dry tomato sauce (see page 39), sieved
1 cup whipping cream
4 tablespoons unsalted butter

FOR GARNISH

Chopped parsley
Lemon wedges

Have a fishmonger scale, gut and trim the fish. The tail should be left intact.

With a large knife or cleaver, cut off the tail a good 2½ inches above the actual finny end. Cut off the head behind the gills. Rinse and set both pieces aside.

Filet the fish. Run a sharp knife down along the backbone, shaving as close to the bone as possible and lifting off the filet as you go. Remove filet from other side. Skin filets by making a small incision at the tail end between meat and skin. Holding the skin down firmly, slip the knife along its surface and separate off the flesh. (A fishmonger will do all of the preceding steps if you so instruct, but as there is no need for impeccable filets, now is a good time to practice technique.)

Cut half of one filet into thin strips and set aside. Purée the remaining flesh, along with 2 whole eggs and 2 egg yolks, in a food processor or blender. Pass purée through a sieve to strain out membranous filaments, pack into a small bowl and cover with plastic wrap. Refrigerate for at least 1 hour. Place 6 egg whites in a dish so they will be at room temperature when needed.

To assemble, preheat oven to 350°. Heat 3 tablespoons butter in a large, oval gratin dish.

Stir 1 cup cream into the fish forcemeat; season and add 3 scrapings of nutmeg. Beat the egg whites by hand until they form firm peaks. Stir ⅓ into the fish to lighten the mixture, then fold in the rest.

Place the reserved strips of fish in the hot gratin dish. When they start to sizzle, heap on the soufflé and sprinkle with cheese. Place the fish tail at one end, the head at the other and hurry dish into the oven. Bake for 30 minutes.

Heat tomato sauce and cream together, then whisk in butter. Ladle sauce around soufflé and sprinkle lightly with parsley. Rim with cut lemons.

Grilled, Smoked Fish with Braised Celery

SERVES 6 HANDSOMELY

6 small celery hearts, 5 to 6 inches long
4 tablespoons unsalted butter
2 tablespoons anise-flavored liqueur
Salt and pepper
Fresh herb fennel
One 3½- to 4-pound fish (bass, trout, rock fish, bluefish or other good griller), gutted, scaled and trimmed
Olive oil

FOR GARNISH

3 lemons, halved

Prepare a bed of coals, indoors or out. You will need a 20-inch fish grill.

Trim the celery ends, pare the outer stalks to remove strings, and wash hearts under running water. Blanch them for 10 minutes in boiling, salted water. Cut hearts in two lengthwise, and place them, cut side down, in a large pan containing 4 tablespoons melted butter. *Start the celery braising 10 minutes before the fish is put to grill* and the two should finish together. To braise, add ⅓ cup water, 1 tablespoon of liqueur and seasoning. Cover and cook over low heat. From time to time, shake the pan and check to see that liquid remains. Add more water if necessary. At the end of the braise, turn the hearts over. They should be lightly browned, the excess water should have evaporated and only a lovely, condensed vegetable essence will be left as a coating. Season, sprinkle with chopped fennel leaves and place around fish on serving platter.

Stuff the fish with many feathery fennel leaves and stalks. Rub well with olive oil, salt, pepper and a sprinkling of liqueur. Oil the grill and place fish in it. Grill about 6 minutes per side or until the fish appears to be browning and crisping nicely. Then set two bricks upright or make an andiron arrangement that will allow the fish to be raised 8- to 10-inches above the fire. Wet some fennel greenery and throw it on the coals to smoke and perfume.

Let the fish sit above the fire for another 25 minutes, turning it over once and misting the coals occasionally to cause continued smoking.

Open the grill out flat, flip the fish firmly over onto a serving platter, and garnish with the braised celery and lemon halves. A small pitcher of olive oil should be placed on table as sauce.

For convenience: trim and blanch the celery in the morning. Let the fish marinate in oil, chopped fennel and Pernod all day. In early spring and fall, substitute bulb fennel for celery.

A summer's scene, the mid-season Grand Aïoli in a small, Provençal town. Old stone tables in the village park, more tables overflowing the street, dappling light filtered down through plain trees, a broad bordering stream washing over countless bottles of wine acool in the moss green depths . . .

Business is closed for the day. Everyone is spirited and happy. Whole families of three, sometimes four, generations group and kiss, touch and laugh as they wait for the feast to begin. Because I am alone and no one should be on such an occasion, I am invited to sit at a large table with a mother and father, two sets of their married children, some assorted grandchildren and a small, aged aunt. The old lady, in widow-black dress and knitted grey stockings, is propped in a folding chair brought especially for her. She has the brightest eyes I have ever seen, and she cocks her head and regards me, bird-sharp. Everyone is curious.

Where do I come from in the States?
North Carolina draws a blank.
Is it near Chicago? Have I ever been to Chicago? Is it dangerous there with all *les gangsters?*

The feast is a progress of salt cod, snails, eggs and vegetables. Artichokes, beans, potatoes, beets are heaped upon our plates, and a prodigious amount of powerfully garlicked mayonnaise is centered on table. We dip our bites communally into the aïoli, that pungent, heavy sauce that seems to hold within itself the very soul of the meridional people. And we don't dip lightly; we immerse. The old lady has a knife which she uses to spread on a double thickness. I keep up with them, bite for bite, but still they ask . . .

Is the aïoli too strong?
Perhaps I am not used to so much garlic?
Ah but it is good for the system the aïoli–good for the heart, excellent for the digestion and it allows one to drink more by oiling the liver so the wine slips through . . .

When the eating ends, the wine continues, and the toasts, and the songs–three hundred people laughing and swaying at the old stone tables under the ancient trees with the stream endlessly flowing and the long light slanting through a summer's afternoon.

Do we, they ask, have such feasts in the United States?
Alas, no.

Le Grand Aïoli

A Grand Aïoli can involve a variety of ingredients: chickpeas, cauliflower, beets, carrots, green beans, artichokes, salsify, potatoes, Jerusalem artichokes, hard-boiled eggs, snails, octopus, salt cod and even lamb or beef left over from a daube.

A "Petit Aïoli" need include only two or three items, but the following ingredients marry best with garlic mayonnaise, to my taste. Fresh flounder filets will be easier to come by than salt cod for most people and are less time consuming to prepare. A large summer party might be simplified if many guests contribute, one bringing beans, another artichokes, yet a third the eggs, and so on. The host would then be left to provide aïoli sauce, bread, a salad and an icy dessert. A vulgar but non-sweet rosé, well chilled and with added ice cubes, traditionally accompanies the feast.

SERVES 1

1 artichoke
1 hard-boiled egg
2 or 3 small new potatoes
A handful of green beans
A cauliflower or broccoli portion
A filet of flounder (reserve the bones for a fumet) (see page 117)
or
10 large shrimp, cooked but unpeeled
or
A slice of cold, roasted lamb

Sauce Aïoli (see page 146) using 1 egg yolk per person plus an additional batch or two

Trim the artichokes by breaking off the stems to pull away any rough strings. Using a stainless steel knife, even the bottom so the artichoke can sit upright. Slice off the upper two inches of useless leaf and cut all sharp leaf points off with scissors. Rub a cut lemon over the surface to prevent discoloration. Cook in a large quantity of boiling, salted water to which is added the juice of ½ lemon. The artichokes are cooked when a knife point easily pierces the stem. Drain upside down.

Boil the potatoes, green beans, and cauliflower, each in a separate pot of salted water.

Poach the filets in fish *fumet.* Or boil the shrimp. Or slice the lamb.

To serve, arrange all elements on individual plates. For a large group, have everyone serve himself from heaped platters. Place a bowl of aïoli on table and a generous dish into which people can deposit shells and peelings.

On Aïoli and Homemade Mayonnaise

Aïoli is made by the same classic methods as plain mayonnaise, the only difference being that a goodly quantity of puréed garlic is added to egg yolks and seasoning before the incorporation of olive oil.

It is possible to make a sort of mayonnaise wondrously fast in various machines. Slip in the eggs, pour in the oil, whiz it all up and out comes mayonnaise to be sure. But one has only to compare this to a hand-made batch to see the difference. The machine product is lighter in both color and texture for the simple reason that it has suffered a certain amount of aeration in its high-speed spin. It will lack the sleek gloss and richly oiled density that evolves from slow hand turning, and the maker will lose the opportunity to control and learn from the rhythmic build of emulsifying ingredients. If a truly large batch is needed, use the machine for some but not all of the sauce.

Sauce Aïoli and Homemade Mayonnaise

10 large garlic cloves, peeled (omit for plain mayonnaise)
¼ teaspoon salt
Fresh-ground pepper
A lemon half
4 egg yolks at room temperature
Quality olive oil such as James Plagniol or *Bertolli*
1 teaspoon boiling water

Have all ingredients at room temperature. Pound the garlic to a purée with mortar and pestle; add salt, several grindings of pepper, and a squeeze of lemon juice. Add egg yolks and stir with pestle until they thicken and appear a shade or two lighter in color.

Have olive oil ready in a small, easy-to-handle pitcher. From now on, stir always in the same direction and at the same relaxed speed. Start dribbling in oil, slowly at first, until a thin mayonnaise has formed and is apparent. Now continue pouring oil in a small but steady stream. Once or twice add a squeeze of lemon juice. At no time should the oil be added so quickly that it remains on the surface. Look and listen for the following as the sauce builds: toward the end of the process, the mayonnaise will "sound", i.e. it will make small, sticky "clicks" as the pestle revolves in the thick mass, a sign that the oil will soon reach its limit. More important is the visual appearance. The oil starts hitting in a different way. Instead of almost immediate absorption, it cracks the mass lightly, leaving oily traces in the pestle's wake. A little of this can be tolerated, but if the aïoli is as thick as it should be (it should hold the pestle upright) one might as well stop. Add 1 teaspoon of boiling water to stabilize the sauce. Taste for lemon and salt and add more if need be. Store tightly covered with plastic wrap so no skin can form.

If you go beyond the limits of what the yolks can absorb and excessive oil breaks the sauce, stir up another egg yolk in a clean bowl and work the sauce (like the initial oil) into the egg—a rescue that will never prove necessary if ingredients are at room temperature and one observes what is happening. Though a first mayonnaise moves slowly, it is surprising how rapidly subsequent batches will churn themselves out, and how much more oil will be used when one has the assurance to build with a free hand. A large egg yolk will probably absorb a scant ½ cup for a beginner, but more like ⅔ cup for a more experienced cook. If the taste of pure olive oil is found offensive in plain mayonnaise, try ½ olive oil and ½ vegetable oil of choice for a milder version. An aïoli demands to be made entirely of olive oil, however.

Bourride

Once a winter I have a great hunger for bourride and fix it, but this divine soup never feels right unless prepared and consumed on an intense summer's day. Though not so widely known as bouillabaisse, bourride should be made in preference to that more famous soup to which we, lacking the correct fish, cannot do justice. Bourride provides an authentic Provençal taste and, if savored near a beach in lazy hot mid day, an authentic Provençal sensation of blissfully garlicked, soporific sate which can only lead to siesta.

Although the following recipe is devised for ten, the per-person formula is readily evident and easy to act upon. (For every person you need one cup of stock; one filet, one potato, one egg yolk to thicken the stock, and aïoli made from one egg yolk.) The more people served, the more complex become those few moments before the soup is ladled. Let guests help disperse croûtons and side plate elements as you will need to remain at the stove to watch the thickening broth.

SERVES 10

FOR THE STOCK

8 cups water
2 cups dry white wine
2 carrots, sliced
1 large onion, chopped
1 clove garlic, crushed
2 tomatoes, peeled, seeded, chopped
1 bay leaf
Whole sprigs of parsley, thyme, fennel
A 3-inch length of orange peel
4 slices of lemon
Heads and bones from fileted fish
Salt

Put all stock ingredients in a covered pot, bring to a boil, then simmer for 30 minutes. Strain, pressing just enough to extract all juices, and reserve.

FOR THE SIDE PLATE

1 loaf of firm French or *Italian bread*
Olive oil
1 clove of garlic
10 medium potatoes, peeled and halved
1 medium-sized fish filet per person (choose a variety: trout, flounder, bluefish, bass, etc.)
1½ pounds unpeeled shrimp (or *if expense is no problem, 10 lobster tails*)
Optional: 1 slice of eel, 2 or 3 mussels per person
*Aïoli made from 10 egg yolks** (*see page 146*)
10 egg yolks to thicken broth
1 cup whipping cream
Salt and pepper
Chopped parsley

* *Note:* it will be easier to make this quantity of aïoli in 2 or 3 batches.

FOR GARNISH

5 large lemons, halved
Parsley sprigs

Cut the bread into ½-inch slices and fry in olive oil. The large croûtons should be golden brown on both sides and thoroughly crisp. Blot with paper towels and rub one side with a cut clove of garlic. Hold in a warming oven.

Boil the potatoes in salted water. Hold in a warming oven.

Poach the filets, shrimp and any other seafood in the just simmering fish stock. The easiest method is to place the stock in a fish kettle (*poissonière*) and lower all fish on the rack which can then be lifted out intact and the seafood carefully slid onto a hot serving platter. Failing that, place stock and fish in the largest pan available and gently lift filets out with a spatula. Put platter in the warming oven.

Stir half the aïoli, the 10 yolks for thickening, and the cream together in a large bowl. Slowly ladle in hot stock, whisking all the time, then return broth to pan and stir over gentle heat until it thickens. *Beware of curdling the eggs*. The final consistency will be that of a light cream soup. Stir with a flat wooden spoon so that you feel contact with the pull and drag of currents. Add pepper, and taste for a pleasing saltiness.

To serve: place croûton in a heated soup plate. Center a blob of aïoli and a sprinkling of parsley on it.

On a serving plate to the left, put a filet of fish, a potato, seafood, a lemon half and a sprig of parsley. The guests should be seated.

At the last moment, ladle soup over the croûtons. Place the remaining aïoli on table. The participants must immediately mash potato, filet, and croûton into the broth and start eating. Each guest peels his own shrimp and there should be a bowl on table to receive litter.

Keep extra portions of bread or fish warm. Place remaining soup in a hot tureen, and ladle out, along with more aïoli, when needed. It would be a pity to rush this meal.

For convenience: make aïoli the day before; simmer and strain broth in the morning. Have bread sliced, potatoes peeled, eggs separated, parsley and lemon garnishes prepared. Though this may all sound like a production, it is one of the easier full meals to prepare. Finish with a simple, inclining-to-acid salad, and an icy dessert.

Chicken Legs with Aïoli

SERVES 4

FOR THE MARINADE

1 cup white wine
2 tablespoons white wine vinegar
2 tablespoons chopped parsley
1 bay leaf
1 teaspoon oregano and thyme, mixed
1 medium carrot, sliced
1 small onion, sliced
1 large clove garlic, minced
Salt and pepper

4 chicken legs
4 tablespoons olive oil
Aïoli made from 1 large clove garlic and 2 egg yolks (see page 146)
Salt and pepper

FOR GARNISH

Chopped parsley

Place all the marinade ingredients over the chicken legs and let them marinate at least 1 hour. (Overnight is also fine.) Remove chicken, pat dry and fry in olive oil until lightly browned. Drain legs on absorbent toweling and pour off the pan oils. Immediately deglaze the pan by adding the marinade and scraping the bottom with a wooden spoon. The acid wine will soften the encrusted juices and allow them to be incorporated usefully in the continued cooking.

Place chicken back in the pan. Add 2 cups water, cover, and simmer slowly for about 30 minutes or until the chicken is fork tender.

Make aïoli.

Place the chicken legs on individual dinner plates. Strain the cooking juices, then reduce them over high heat until only 3 or 4 tablespoons of thick glaze remain. Cool and whisk into the aïoli. Taste for seasoning. If the reduced glaze has not provided enough salt, add more. Pour sauce over the chicken, grind on fresh pepper and sprinkle with parsley. Eat warm, luke or cool.

Stuffed Chicken "Cutlets"

SERVES 4

4 whole chicken legs
⅔ cup Spanish olives
1 clove garlic, peeled
¼ cup chopped parsley and chives, mixed
3 tablespoons softened unsalted butter
Pepper
2 cups chicken stock
Flour
1 egg, beaten
⅔ cup fine, dry breadcrumbs
Olive oil for frying

Bone the chicken legs. With a small, sharp knife, cut the flesh around the top of the thighbone and scrape down the length of the bone to the drumstick joint. Cut against and around the knob until it is free of all flesh and tendons, then continue scraping down the drumstick.

Cut the bone off with a firm cleaver stroke, leaving 1½ inches of bone in the base of the leg. Reserve bones.

Pit the olives by spiraling off their flesh from the pit exactly as one would peel the skin from an orange. Put the olives into a small saucepan, cover with water, and bring to a boil. Drain and repeat the boiling step to ensure that olives are not unduly salty. Chop olives, garlic, herbs, butter and pepper together in blender or food processor until they form a fine paste. Stuff legs with the mixture then sew up the opening to neatly enclose the stuffing.

Simmer chicken, sewn side up, for 35 minutes in chicken stock with enough water added to just cover the legs. Add the bones to enrich the stock.

When cooked, drain and cool. Place compactly together on a platter and cover with another plate on which is placed 3 pounds of weight (canned goods will do).

Refrigerate, weighted, overnight. This will press the legs into "cutlets."

Remove strings from legs. Dust with flour, dip in beaten egg, and roll in fine crumbs. Chill at least 20 minutes, then fry in oil until the coating is crisp and brown. Dress the leg bone with a cutlet frill if desired. Serve hot or cold. A good picnic dish.

For convenience: cook legs a day ahead. Coat in crumbs in the morning and refrigerate between two layers of waxed paper until needed. Fry an hour before serving.

Chicken and Cucumbers

SERVES 4

4 medium cucumbers
4 chicken breasts
6 tablespoons unsalted butter

¼ cup dry white wine
6 ounces sour cream
1 tablespoon chopped fresh dill

Peel cucumbers, slice in half lengthwise and scoop out the seeds. (An apple corer does the job most efficiently.) Cut the cucumbers in ¼-inch slices and salt them. Leave in a bowl to drain for 30 minutes. Gently squeeze cucumbers twice to remove as much water as possible.

Remove skin and bone from the breasts and cut meat into thin, 1½-inch-long strips. (Slice with the grain.)

Place two sauté pans on the stove; melt 3 tablespoons of butter in each and cook chicken in one, cucumbers in the other. Think Chinese, stirring and frying rapidly, until the chicken shows no sign of pink and the cucumbers are tender but still crisp. Combine chicken and cucumbers in one pan, pour off most of the juice, and add the white wine. Shake the pan over high heat for 1 minute to dissipate the alcohol. Turn heat low, add sour cream and dill, and when everything is warm, serve out over rice or herbed, buttery noodles.

Chicken in Sorrel Cream

SERVES 4

One 3-pound chicken
Flour
3 tablespoons unsalted butter
Approximately 2 packed cups sorrel
1½ cups whipping cream
Salt and pepper

Cut chicken into serving pieces. Dry the pieces and coat lightly with flour. Brown chicken in the butter, allowing the breasts to color on only one side. Drain on paper towels, blotting off as much fat as possible.

Wash, rib and dry the sorrel. Gather it into large handfuls and shred it thin into *chiffonnade* strips. Place half the sorrel on the bottom of a gratin dish. Arrange the chicken pieces, browned side up, on top and season. Mix the remaining sorrel with cream and pour over chicken. Season. Bake in a 350° oven for 35 to 40 minutes, basting once or twice in this time. Before bringing to the table, spoon off any small amounts of fat that might show on the cream's surface.

A summer's day, skimming the waves on a sleek hydrofoil with gray Leningrad receding in the distance and only the deep blue Bay of Finland stretching ahead. We (four Russian student friends and I) are bound for a day at Peterhof, the summer retreat of the Czars, though the students can ill afford it.

Twenty-five miles along, we glide to a smooth stop and there, rising up from the sea and leading to the palace, is a wide expanse of stairs and ornate gardens. Through the grounds we go, and though my friends have seen them many times, still they point and wonder at the splendors all about: the hidden fountains set to trip and spray unwary strollers; the gilded palace rooms; the curious paneled dining room, each panel painted with a royal portrait so that Grand Dukes and Duchesses and Czars of noble blood stare down in perpetuity on any hapless diners. But what they most want me to see is back behind the palace, down twisting, overgrown paths, past fragrant hedges and disguising rose bowers. There, nestled in a grove and far from prying palace eyes, is a gazebo, built, they tell me, by Catherine the Great and used by her until old age for countless trysts and rendezvous. It is here we are to eat a picnic lunch.

Our old basket, with its faded napkin covering, is opened, the napkin centered on the wooden floor, and three packages removed. First are two long halves of chicken—boned, pressed, redolent of lemon, oil and garlic; then a thick rough-grained loaf of bread. The chicken is cut in six pieces, the bread twisted into chunks; the oil from the chicken used to anoint the coarse crumb and our hands. We share around the napkin. The chicken is delicious and one portion remains. There suddenly begins a noisy Russian counting game (a sort of Slavic "One potato, two potato" according to my English-speaking friend), to choose who is to receive the portion. Everyone gets tapped on the head and eliminated until suddenly I am presented the remaining chicken leg. I protest that one of the men should have it but, they say, the winning means the eating so I comply.

Left in the basket are six green containers of intricately woven grape leaves each holding a handful of large blackberries. We eat them with the remaining bread, and again there is a portion left and again the boisterous counting game begins, only this time it lasts twice as long and is more complex and people are getting tapped very hard on the head and everyone is laughing uproariously and I win . . . again.

On the trip back to Leningrad, I accuse my friend of rigging the game. He answers, "We would not have you come so far to us only to lose."

In my week's stay, I never saw in all of Leningrad a single blackberry. But what few chickens I saw for sale cost eight dollars each.

Pressed Lemon Chicken

SERVES 4 TO 6

One 3-pound chicken
1 garlic clove
1 ½ lemons
½ teaspoon celery seed
Salt and pepper
¼ cup olive oil

Use poultry scissors or a knife to cut the chicken in two down one side of the backbone. Cut off backbone and tail. Remove wishbone at the immediate opening of the chest cavity by running a small knife along the slender bone, scraping back the flesh, and snapping the bone out. With chicken opened skin-side down, note the spoon-shaped breastbone with its gristle handle. Remove this bone by slipping a knife along both sides of the gristle and up along the bone. Bend and twist gristle (which may break off) and bone out of chicken. Cut bird down the middle of the breast so there are two lengthwise halves. Make small slits through the breast into which the wing tips can be slipped and held compactly. This preparation allows optimum skin browning when the chicken is fried.

Squeeze garlic clove through a press and rub over chicken, both inside and out. Season with juice of ½ lemon, the celery seed, salt and pepper and leave to marinate 1 hour.

Heat oil in a heavy pan that can hold the entire chicken. Place halves, skin-side down, and brown lightly. Place a lid or small pan directly on the chicken and weight with 2 or 3 heavy cans. Let chicken turn a deep, golden brown, then remove weight and turn chicken skin-side up. Slice a lemon half thin and place rounds on the browned skin. Baste with olive oil and replace weighted lid. Cook another 25 minutes over moderately low heat.

Baste a final time and squeeze the remaining lemon half over the chicken. Divide into serving portions. If a vegetable garnish is desired, small browned potato balls are a good complement or, curiously, a rough chop of collard or turnip greens doused with lemon juice holds its own against the savory bird.

Boned, Roasted Chicken with Country Pâté

SERVES 8 TO 10

One 3½-pound chicken

FOR THE PÂTÉ

½ pound chicken livers
¼ cup finely chopped salt pork
2 slices bread
1 small onion, minced
2 cloves garlic, minced
⅓ cup finely chopped parsley
1 teaspoon mixed herbs (thyme, oregano, savory)
1 egg
Salt and pepper

1 bay leaf
Olive oil
Thyme, oregano and savory (fresh or dried)

The chicken will be boned without cutting the skin at any point and, in effect, will be turned inside out and the carcass removed more or less whole. Lay the chicken on its back with the chest cavity open toward you. Keep the skeletal diagram (below) for reference. Use a

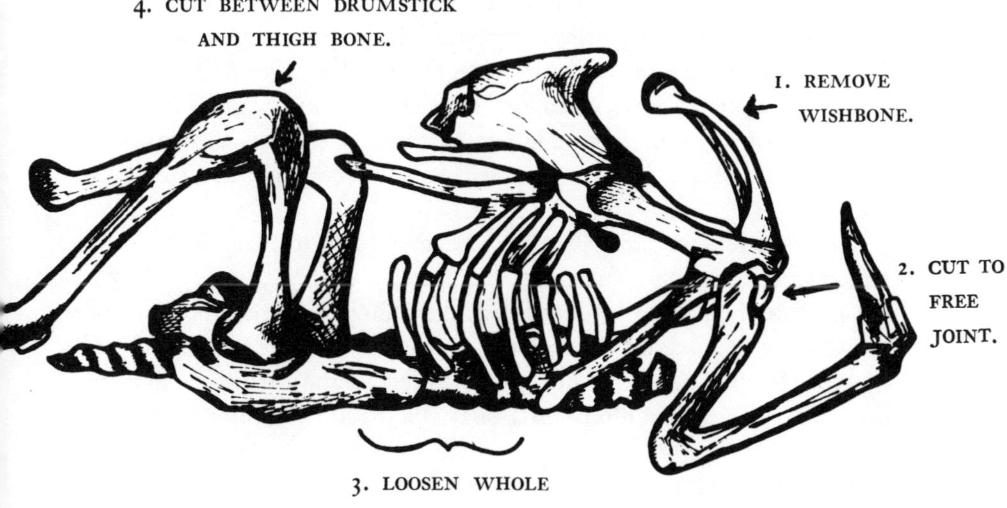
4. CUT BETWEEN DRUMSTICK AND THIGH BONE.
1. REMOVE WISHBONE.
2. CUT TO FREE JOINT.
3. LOOSEN WHOLE CARCASS.

small, very sharp knife and your fingers for the boning, and remember to cut on the bone and away from yourself.

1. Remove wishbone. At the immediate cavity opening, the arching wishbone appears faintly through the flesh. Locate it, run a knife along the outline between bone and flesh, and press flesh away from bone with your fingers. Snap it out.

2. The wing bone will be left in. Wiggle the wing to locate the socket then sever all ligaments at this joint. The "collapsing-L" shaped bone that you have just freed consists of a long, unattached shoulder blade and a stubby bone joined to the large breastbone by soft gristle. Outline the stubby bone with a knife, pushing back the flesh until you get a clear view of the bone-blade configuration. Hook a finger through and firmly, carefully, pull out the "L." Repeat at the other wing.

3. Start running a finger around the carcass, close to the bone structure. Break any filaments away and turn flesh and skin back as you go until the whole midsection is free.

4. Push the drumstick up to reveal a smooth fleshly "knee" where drumstick joins thighbone. Cut between the two bones. *Leave the drumstick in* (it is easy to pull out the wrong bone first time around) and remove the thighbone. Scrape the flesh down toward the hip socket and twist the thigh out. Repeat with other leg.

5. The rest is easy. Continue scraping with a finger down the pelvic bone. Holding the bone structure with one hand and the flesh with the other, pull skeleton down and away. Leave the tail on or cut it off as you please. Turn the mass right side out by pushing the legs through first and then the breast. The chicken will look like an empty suit of long johns.

Collect any loose and fallen flesh. Dice and add to pâté. Sew up the tail opening.

To make the pâté, pick over livers, discarding any green portions or fat. Chop well, rocking a knife back and forth over the mass until it is a pulp. Dice the salt pork fine. (The easiest method is to cut it right on the rind, then slice thinly off.) Soak the bread in water and squeeze dry.

Put all pâté ingredients in a large bowl and work well with the hands until uniformly mixed. Prop up the chicken in a bowl and fill with pâté. Slip a bay leaf (a fresh one will show up best) under the skin at breast center. Sew up the top.

Oil a roasting pan and place the chicken in it, breast up. Tie the drumsticks together at the ankles, and do a rough tie of the wings (run and tie the attaching string under the bird). Rub olive oil and herbs into the chicken and roast at 350° for 1 hour. Baste during this time. Leave chicken to cool, then place a flat lid or plate on the bird and weight with a 2-pound can. Chill and press for at least 5 hours. To serve, remove wings and drumsticks and cut bird into cross-slice. Serve with thin toast, unsalted butter and cornichons.

Vinegared Chicken with Tomatoes and Croûtons

SERVES 4

4 slices firm, crustless bread
1½ sticks butter
1 clove garlic, cut, and 1 large clove garlic, minced
4 large tomatoes, peeled, seeded, cut in strips
One 3-pound chicken, cut in serving pieces
Salt
¼ cup red wine vinegar
¼ cup dry white wine
½ cup water
½ cup whipping cream
Pepper, freshly ground

FOR GARNISH
Chopped parsley

Cut the bread slices in two diagonally. Fry the large croûtons in 4 tablespoons of the butter until nicely crisp and brown. Drain on paper towels and rub with 1 cut clove of garlic. Keep warm.

Peel tomatoes by placing them briefly in boiling water. Slice in two through the middle and squeeze out seeds and juice. Cut into strips.

Dry chicken pieces with paper towels. Salt and sauté chicken in 4 tablespoons butter until golden on all sides. Remove chicken, pour off excess fat, and deglaze pan with vinegar and white wine. Scrape congealed juices with a wooden spoon and allow the liquid to simmer briefly before returning chicken to pan. Pour ½ cup water over chicken, add minced garlic, cover pan and cook for 30 minutes.

Remove chicken to a heated platter and spoon off any fat noticeable on the remaining sauce. Add tomato strips and cream; simmer briefly. Off heat, whisk in 4 tablespoons butter. Pour the creamed tomatoes over the chicken, grind on pepper, garnish with parsley, and place the croûtons around the platter's edge.

Herbed and Jellied Chicken

MAKES 8 TO 10 GENEROUS SLICES

One 4 to 4½ pound stewing hen
1 small onion, quartered
1 carrot, sliced
1 bay leaf
Several parsley sprigs
½ teaspoon salt
Pepper
¼ cup fines herbes (*parsley, chives, tarragon, chervil, minced together*)

Pull out as much fat from the bird as possible. Cut chicken into serving pieces and place pieces in a large pan. Add onion, carrot, bay leaf, parsley sprigs, salt and water to just cover all ingredients. Slowly bring to a boil and immediately skim off the scum that floats to the surface. Lower heat until the broth maintains a slow simmer. Cover and leave to cook for 1½ hour.

Strain out the chicken and vegetables. Let the stock sit until the fat surfaces, then carefully spoon it off. Reduce the remaining stock to 2 cups.

When the chicken has cooled, remove all skin, bones and gristle and pull large sections of flesh into bite-sized pieces. Pepper chicken generously and mix in half of the herbs.

Scatter remaining herbs on the bottom of a terrine or loaf pan and place chicken on top. Check the reduced stock for seasoning (it should be slightly salty), and when it is room temperature, pour it over the fowl. Give the mold a hard tap to settle contents. Fold 3 layers of heavy aluminum foil to fit directly over the chicken. Place 3 pounds of weight along the foil (canned goods will do) and put to chill from 5 hours to overnight.

To serve, run a knife around the edge of the terrine, dip the bottom briefly in hot water and unmold. Serve with a flavored mayonnaise (curry; tomato and paprika; a *gribiche* with hard-boiled eggs, mustard, and capers; or just more herbs would all do nicely), and garnish with toast and cornichons.

Rolled, Stuffed Omelets with Chicken Livers and Basil

SERVES 6

FOR THE FILLING

½ pound chicken livers
2 large zucchini
3 cooked chicken breasts
or
2½ cups leftover chicken
Olive oil
½ cup ricotta cheese
¼ cup freshly grated Parmesan cheese
3 tablespoons whipping cream
1 teaspoon thyme and oregano, mixed
Salt and pepper

FOR THE OMELETS

6 large eggs
1 teaspoon water
Salt and pepper
Olive oil

2 cups Tomato Sauce (see page 39)
3 tablespoons freshly grated Parmesan cheese
12 fresh basil leaves, shredded

Look over the chicken livers, discard any green portions or fat, and cut livers in half. Rinse, trim, and cut zucchini into medium dice. The chicken should be skinned, boned and shredded.

Sauté zucchini in a small amount of oil. When cooked, remove zucchini and place livers in the same pan. Add more oil if necessary and sauté briefly. The livers should retain a certain pinkness at the core. Press them lightly with the back of a spoon and pour off juices. Mix all of the filling ingredients together.

To make the omelets, beat six eggs, with 1 teaspoon of water and seasoning until well blended. Heat 1 tablespoon of olive oil in a 9-inch skillet and when quite hot, pour in a very thin coating of egg, tipping the pan to cover the surface. Fry on one side only. When the underside is speckled with brown, remove omelet, add more oil and fry another. Make six omelets.

Divide the filling among the omelets and roll each one up. Place in a lightly oiled gratin or baking dish that can also be used for service. Spread tomato sauce over omelets, sprinkle with grated cheese, and dribble 2 or 3 tablespoons of oil over the cheese.

Bake in a 350° oven for 30 minutes, then transfer briefly to a heated broiler to crust and brown the top. Scatter on shredded basil.

Vitello Tonnato Loaf

SERVES 10

FOR THE LOAF

7 ounces water-packed tuna, drained
4 anchovy filets, patted dry
2½ pounds ground veal
2 eggs
Zest of 1 lemon
Juice of 1 lemon
1 slice bread, crumbled
1 clove garlic, minced
¼ cup diced pimento
¼ cup chopped parsley
¼ cup chopped black olives
1 teaspoon salt
Pepper, freshly ground

FOR GARNISH

6 anchovy filets
Pimento
Parsley
Homemade Mayonnaise (see page 146)
Capers

Grind the tuna and anchovy in a blender or food processor.

Place all loaf ingredients in a large bowl and work together by hand until thoroughly mixed.

Butter a loaf tin (9½ x 5¼ x 2¾ inches) or terrine. Crisscross the six garnishing filets of anchovy in three X's at the bottom. Pack in the loaf mixture and bake at 375° for 50 minutes. When cool, unmold, wrap, and refrigerate overnight.

To serve, center small rounds of pimento in the middle of each crossed anchovy and place the loaf on a parslied platter. Accompany with fresh bread and a lemony, homemade mayonnaise laden with capers.

Veal Chops with Herb Sauce

SERVES 4

1 packed cup greens, washed and dried (spinach, parsley or *watercress predominating; chives, thyme, sorrel flavoring)*
½ cup whipping cream
1 egg yolk
Salt and pepper
4 large veal chops
Oil and unsalted butter for frying
½ cup dry white wine
4 tablespoons unsalted butter cut in chunks

Purée the greens in blender or food processor. Mix with cream, egg yolk and seasoning and set aside.

Trim the chops, dry them with paper towels, and salt. Fry veal in a minimum of mixed butter and oil. Remove meat to a warming oven platter, drain off excess fat from pan, and deglaze with white wine. Scrape pan bottom with a wooden spoon and cook wine and juices down until there remains only 1 tablespoon of thickened glaze.

Over low heat, whisk the herbed cream into the pan glaze. Stir constantly until the sauce thickens (a matter of moments). Remove from heat, whisk in 4 tablespoons of butter and taste for seasoning. Pour the sauce over chops and dish out individual portions.

Braised Shank of Veal with Spring Vegetables and Turnip Purée

SERVES 6

6 large slices shank of veal or enough for 6 servings
Salt
Flour

Oil and unsalted butter for frying
1 cup dry white wine
2 cups hot, homemade veal or chicken stock
1 medium onion, chopped
1 pound turnips
8 large garlic cloves, peeled and crushed
6 large carrots
1 stick unsalted butter
8 ounces pearl onions, peeled
Small pinch sugar
2 cups fresh green peas
Salt and pepper
6 thick, crustless rounds of buttered toast rubbed with a garlic clove
Chopped parsley

Trim and salt the shanks. Roll them lightly in flour and brown in a mixture of oil and butter. Remove shanks, spoon off cooking fat, and deglaze pan with 1 cup of wine, stirring and scraping congealed juices with a wooden spatula. Replace veal and pour on stock. Add enough water to just submerge the shanks. Cover and cook at the barest simmer for 45 minutes.

Pare turnips and cut into large dice. Scatter turnips, chopped onion and garlic cloves over the shanks, replace cover, and simmer another 45 minutes.

Scrape carrots and trim them into large rounded olive shapes. A half hour before the veal is done, place 4 tablespoons butter in a heavy frying pan, add pearl onions and carrots, a pinch of sugar, and a small ladle of the meat juices. Cover and set to braise over very low heat. Shake the pan from time to time and make sure the contents are moist by adding more stock if necessary. Twenty minutes later, add the peas and in 10 minutes, everything should be cooked and glazed with a light, buttery syrup.

When the meat is cooked, remove it to a heated platter. Strain out the vegetables and purée in blender or food processor. Reduce the cooking juices down to 3 or 4 tablespoons and add them to the turnips. Whisk in 4 tablespoons of butter and taste for seasoning.

Serve individual portions. Place a shank on a toast round, sauce generously with loose floating purée, sprinkle with parsley and add a spoon of glazed vegetables.

For convenience: braise veal 3 hours ahead. Let it sit in the purée and gently reheat when needed. Have vegetables peeled and trimmed in advance.

Crisp Sage and Liver

A Venetian specialty.

SERVES 4

1⅓ pounds pale calves liver
8 tablespoons unsalted butter
Salt and pepper
Lemon juice
30 fresh sage leaves, brushed clean

Cut the liver into thin, ¼-inch wide strips, trimming out any membranous filaments in the process. Melt 4 tablespoons butter in a sauté pan large enough to hold the liver without overcrowding. When butter sizzles, add liver and do a rapid sauté over high heat for a very brief time. Shake the pan, tossing the contents, and guard against overcooking. The whole process should take no longer than 1 minute. Add salt, pepper, a squeeze of lemon and place liver in a heated serving dish. Quickly melt the remaining 4 tablespoons of butter, throw in the sage and swirl the pan until the butter turns nut brown. At this point, the leaves will be totally crisp and the butter nicely flavored with sage. Pour butter and leaves over the liver and serve at once.

Cold Neapolitan Potato Cake with Sausage

SERVES 8

2 pounds boiled, all-purpose potatoes
2 eggs
6 ounces ham, diced
8 ounces salami, chopped
⅔ cup diced mozzarella cheese
⅓ cup freshly grated Parmesan cheese
¼ cup chopped parsley
2 cloves garlic, minced
1 teaspoon salt
Pepper
Olive oil
3 cups firm breadcrumbs

Rice the potatoes by pushing them firmly through a sieve with a pestle or large spoon. Mix potatoes, eggs, ham, salami, cheeses, parsley, garlic and seasoning together.

Pour ⅓ cup olive oil into a 9- x 13-inch cake pan. Pack in half the breadcrumbs. Moisten hands with water and pat the potato filling over the crumbs. Scatter remaining bread on top and dampen with driblets of oil. Bake in a 350° oven for 40 to 45 minutes. Cool to room temperature, then cover and refrigerate until chilled.

Cut in squares and serve with a green salad for a light lunch. Keeps well two or three days.

Stuffed Pizza

Doubling pizza into a large turnover provides extra capacity for fillings and an opportunity to create sophisticated variations on a common theme. The interior could hold a quantity of grated vegetables bound with egg, cheese and herbs, or a thick ragôut of seafood. Though this recipe contains traditional elements (which children will like), the effective tomato topping should be used with any choice of filling.

SERVES 6

FOR THE DOUGH

1 scant teaspoon dry yeast
⅓ cup lukewarm water
1 teaspoon olive oil
½ teaspoon salt
Approximately 1 cup flour

FOR THE STUFFING

1 large onion, sliced thin
2 tablespoons olive oil
1 pound lean hamburger
½ pound Polish sausage (kielbasa)
¼ pound mushrooms, sliced
Salt and pepper
1 teaspoon fine-chopped oregano
1 tablespoon chopped parsley
10 ounces ricotta cheese
8 ounces mozzarella cheese
Olive oil
½ cup thick Tomato Sauce *(see page 39)*

To make the dough, dissolve yeast in water. Add oil, salt and ⅔ cup flour. Stir and turn dough out on a floured counter. Continue adding flour and kneading until dough is no longer sticky but still somewhat soft. When smooth and elastic, let rest in a towel-covered bowl for 1 hour.

Cook the onion in oil until soft. Add hamburger and sauté. Strip casing from the sausage, chop or crumble it and add to hamburger. Let the sausage briefly render some of its fat over heat. Place meat mixture in a strainer and press off excess moisture. Sauté the mushrooms. Mix meat, mushrooms, seasoning, herbs and ricotta until smooth. Cut mozzarella into thin, ½-inch strips.

On a floured surface, roll and pat the dough into a thin, large circle. Place it on a lightly oiled baking sheet. Spread filling on half the dough, leaving a 1½-inch border clear. Place half the mozzarella slices on top of the filling, fold the dough over, and crimp the edges together. Brush the top crust lightly with olive oil. Brush on tomato sauce and sprinkle with salt. Lattice the remaining mozzarella strips on top. Bake at 350° for 45 minutes, protecting the top with aluminum foil if it threatens too much brown. Serve 1 hour out of the oven. Good picnic fare.

A Rapid Roast of Beef with Sauce Rémoulade

SERVES 10 TO 12

One 4-pound prime eye of round roast
Salt and pepper
2 cloves garlic
¼ cup chopped parsley
Olive oil
12 firm white mushrooms about 1½-inches in diameter
6 barding slices of salt pork

FOR THE SAUCE

Homemade Mayonnaise (see page 146)
1 teaspoon Dijon mustard or more, to taste
1 teaspoon anchovies, minced to purée
2 tablespoons chopped gherkins
1 tablespoon capers
2 tablespoons fine-chopped parsley and chervil, mixed

Trim the roast of any outer fat. The flattest side of the beef will show a long, smooth grain. Make three or four ½-inch cuts on this side to keep the meat from arching while in the oven. Turn roast over, round side-up, and cut into 12 slices, leaving them attached at the bottom. Cut straight down to within an inch of the base. Cut in at the sides so that the slices become round leaves held only by a central stem. Salt and pepper between slices.

Mince the garlic and parsley together. Moisten with 3 tablespoons of oil and rub some of the mixture between each slice. Place a mushroom cap sideways between each of the slices. Cover roast with the barding fat and tie slices in place with several loops of string.

Put meat in an oiled roasting pan. Place in a preheated 450° oven for 18 minutes, then turn the heat off. Remove the barding fat and baste. Leave sitting in the oven for 15 more minutes (basting occasionally) at which time the beef should be perfectly brown outside and a tender pink at the center. Place on a serving platter to cool.

Mix all the sauce ingredients together. Taste for seasoning.

Serve beef warm or cold, surrounded by watercress, with the sauce in a boat on the side.

Grilled Steak and Vegetables à l'Orientale

SERVES 4

One 1½-pound steak (T-bone or *sirloin)*
Soy sauce
5 tablespoons olive or *peanut oil*
4 garlic cloves, sliced paper thin
4 sweet red peppers
Salt
2 large onions
3 medium zucchini
6 egg roll wrappers

FOR THE SAUCE

½ cup soy sauce
½ teaspoon lemon juice
1 clove garlic, minced
Small pinch powdered ginger

Trim steak. Marinate the meat for 2 hours in 1 tablespoon of soy sauce, 2 tablespoons olive oil, and the thin-sliced garlic.

Rinse the peppers and quarter them, removing stem and seeds. Slice onions into ½-inch thick rings and parboil in salted water for 5 minutes. Drain and place on a sheet of aluminum foil. Sprinkle with salt and 1 teaspoon soy sauce and wrap into a thin packet. Parboil the peppers for 5 minutes. Cut zucchini into 1-inch-thick diagonal slices. Sprinkle both peppers and zucchini with soy sauce.

Cut the egg roll wrappers in two. Rub the remaining 3 tablespoons of oil over the wrappers, salt them, and fold the halves over into squares.

Mix the sauce ingredients together.

Grill steak, peppers, zucchini and the onion packet. Remove to a platter and grill the egg roll wrappers briefly until they are lightly browned and bubbled on both sides. Cut steak in thin slices and arrange meat and vegetables on a platter. Surround with crisp pastry. Strain the sauce and serve on the side.

Grilled Breast of Lamb Riblets with Artichokes and Mustard Cream

SERVES 6

2 lamb breasts
2 cups chicken or *veal stock*
Salt and pepper
Mustard
Olive oil
½ cup fine dry breadcrumbs
6 large artichokes
Lemon
3 firm medium tomatoes
12 small new potatoes
A handful black Niçoise olives
Chopped parsley
Fresh thyme, stripped from its branch

FOR THE SAUCE

3 cups whipping cream
2 teaspoons Dijon mustard
Salt and pepper

Trim the breasts and poach, at a bare simmer, in the stock with enough added water to cover. Test with a fork and when perfectly tender (about 50 minutes), drain and cut into riblets. When cool, season and brush lightly with mustard. Dip in olive oil and roll in fine breadcrumbs. Wrap and refrigerate until needed.

Turn the artichoke hearts. Break off the stems and pull off outer leaves until the pale green center is evident. Slice off ⅔ of the top with a stainless steel knife and rub the artichoke with a cut lemon half. Boil in salted water to which is added 1 tablespoon of lemon juice. When the bottom is easily pierced with a knife tip, drain and cool. Trim artichokes down to hearts by digging out the thistle-like cores and cutting off any tough, dark green exterior. Coat with olive oil.

Cut tomatoes in two crosswise and gently squeeze out most seeds and juice. Season and oil lightly.

Scrub the potatoes; salt and oil them.

Put the potatoes to grill first, then artichokes, lamb and tomatoes. Heap everything in an earthenware dish and sprinkle with olives, fresh herbs and seasoning. Serve sauce on the side.

To make the sauce, reduce cream, at a gentle boil, down to 1½ cups. Stir in mustard and seasoning.

For convenience: prepare lamb riblets and artichokes the night before.

Leg of Lamb in a Crust

Have your butcher leave the shank end of the leg of lamb long and uncut. The American practice of chopping through the bone robs one of the succulent few bites of gelatinous meat at the knuckle which the French lovingly call the *souris* (mouse). Cutting off the bone also complicates carving in that there is nothing left to grasp hold of and slice against.

Though a roasted leg seems best to me in its virginal state, this crust harmonizes with and does not soggily detract from the purity of lamb as does a pastry covering.

SERVES 8 TO 10

1 cup cooked rice
3 slices firm bread
4 anchovy fillets
2 large garlic cloves
⅓ cup fine-chopped parsley
1 tablespoon mixed rosemary, oregano, thyme (fresh or *dried)*
Salt and pepper
Olive oil
One 4 to 5 pound leg of lamb, trimmed of fat

Blend together the rice, bread, anchovies, garlic, herbs and seasoning. Add olive oil until the whole forms a thick, pliably moist paste.

Salt the lamb and spread paste over the top meaty side of the leg, patting and packing the mixture down smoothly with the fingers.

Place leg on a small rack in a baking dish and roast in a preheated 475° oven. After a few minutes, the lamb will start to sizzle and spit. Let it carry on for a good, noisy 5 minutes, then turn heat down to 250°. The leg will remain in the oven 1 hour from start to finish. Halfway through the cooking, baste with olive oil and pan juices. The crust should end a crisp, golden brown. Check it 40 minutes along, and if it appears to be turning too dark, cover lightly with aluminum foil.

Desserts

PEACH cake is a large edition of the miniature *pêches* found in French pastry shops. Those individual *petits fours*, composed of two rum-moistened hemispheres of *savarin* hinged together with whipped cream, provide the inspiration for this pretty, useful version composed from *génoise* batter. The cake must be made a day or two ahead so it can firm and dry. Another necessity is a metal bowl (or preferably two) of precise size for molding and baking. I use two 1½-quart stainless steel mixing bowls 8-inches in diameter, the kind available at all restaurant supply houses. If you have only one bowl this size, divide the following recipe in two and make a second batch after the first half is finished, as *génoise* batter must not wait before baking. Always treat a *génoise* with soufflé reverence.

Peach Cake

SERVES 12 TO 15

FOR THE CAKE

8 eggs plus 2 egg yolks
1 cup sugar
1 teaspoon vanilla
1 teaspoon fine-grated lemon zest
1 1/3 cups all-purpose flour, sifted after measure
3 tablespoons melted unsalted butter
Grand Marnier liqueur
3 cups whipping cream
or
1 quart softened ice cream plus 1 cup whipping cream
Confectioner's sugar

FOR THE PEACH FUZZ

½ cup sugar
Red and yellow food coloring
Fresh green leaves for garnish

Generously butter and flour the baking molds. Shake out excess flour. Have all ingredients measured and ready. Preheat oven to 350°. It will be easiest to make the cakes in a heavy mixer or with an electric beater.

Break the eggs and extra yolks into a large mixing bowl. Add sugar, vanilla, and lemon zest. Gently warm the bowl over low heat, all the while whisking the ingredients until they are just warm. Beat the mixture by machine for exactly 9 minutes. Take bowl off the mixer and start adding flour in a slow stream. Using your right hand with fingers stiffly spread, fold in the flour. Plunge deep into the batter, gently reaching to the bottom of the bowl and lifting and folding the comforting mass while the left hand turns the bowl and continues to add flour. Don't overwork or the cake will be dense and coarse textured. You are through as soon as there are no feelable or visible slicks of flour. Sprinkle on the butter and fold again briefly. The whole process will take less than 1 minute. Immediately fill the molds. Put them on a cookie sheet and place in the oven. Bake for 35 minutes. Remove and cool briefly before turning out on a lightly oiled cake rack.

When cool, trim and round off crisp edges from the top rim with scissors. Put a sieve over the cakes and let them sit out a day to firm.

To fill, cut a coned circle from the flat top of each cake. Dig out crumb until a 1¼-inch thick shell remains. Sprinkle the center with liqueur and fill the two halves. Because the cake is bland, it can be flavored and filled in any way imaginable. Crumble the cut-out core into crumbs and add them to 2 cups of stiffly whipped cream flavored with confectioner's sugar and vanilla. Or fold crumbs into softened ice cream with perhaps some diced fruit or nuts. Spoon the filling into the hollows and over the top edge. Sandwich the halves together and cut off a thin slice from the bottom edge so the "peach" can stand upright. Place in freezer until firm. Prop if necessary.

To make peach fuzz, add 3 drops each of red and yellow food coloring to ½ cup of sugar and stir until it is a uniform color. Put a doily or some large green leaves on a platter. Set the cake on the platter. Brush cake lightly with water and rub generously with the colored sugar. It will turn a deeper shade of peach and the brown portions of cake will blush under their sugary coating.

Whip the remaining cup of cream very stiff. Add some confectioner's sugar to sweeten and fill in any crevices between the peach halves. Pipe a neat row of rosettes to cover the center joint. The cake can reenter the freezer for 1 hour at this point, if desired. Place a sprig with 2 small leaves as a stem on top before service.

For convenience: bake the cakes ahead and freeze in airtight containers. Defrost and heat gently to freshen when needed. A handy, help-yourself dessert to serve, along with bowls of peach slices, raspberry purée and ice cream, to a large crowd.

Crusted Blueberry and Cream Cake

SERVES 10 TO 12

FOR THE CAKE

1 quart blueberries
1 1/3 cups all-purpose flour
1 teaspoon dry yeast
Pinch salt
4 eggs
3/4 cup sugar
1 teaspoon vanilla

FOR THE SYRUP

1 cup sugar
1/4 cup water
2 tablespoons light rum or Grand Marnier
1/3 cup boiling water
1/3 cup sugar

Butter a 10-inch spring-form pan and cut a round of parchment paper to fit the bottom. Butter the paper, also.

Rinse and pick over the blueberries. Set aside.

Sift together the flour, yeast and salt. (If need be, pulverize the yeast in a mortar before sifting.)

Place the eggs, sugar and vanilla in a large mixer bowl. Over very gentle heat, whisk eggs and sugar until quite warm, but don't allow the eggs to set around the edges. Continue beating by machine until the mixture mounts to a thick, almost white foam that forms a ribbon and has at least tripled in volume.

Pour a slow stream of flour into the mixture and fold in quickly but gently. Cut a spatula deep into the mass, lifting and turning to amalgamate flour and eggs. Don't overwork as it is most important to keep egg volume.

Place a dense but single layer of blueberries into the mold. Pour on half the batter, sprinkle on remaining berries and cover with the rest of the batter. Bake in a preheated 350° oven for about 40 minutes.

Prepare a caramel syrup. Place 1 cup sugar and ¼ cup water in a small, heavy pan over medium heat. Stir just until the sugar is dissolved, then leave alone. Let the sugar gently bubble until it starts to turn first to straw, then to deeper shades of yellow and gold and finally to amber. Remove from heat and cool slightly. Add liqueur and ⅓ cup boiling water to make a pourable syrup.

Test cake for doneness by inserting a knife in the center. It should come out clean. Unmold onto a serving platter and pour warm caramel syrup over the blueberried top. Sprinkle a layer of granulated sugar (about ⅓ cup) evenly over the cake and place briefly under a broiler until the sugar crystalizes into a crisp topping. Serve with whipped cream.

Lemon "Terrine"

An amusing dessert served in its terrine container, this variation on the *génoise* theme is dense, moist and studded with nuts. It is best eaten two days after making.

SERVES 10

½ *cup skinned pistachio nuts*
½ *cup slivered almonds*
1½ *cups pound cake or* génoise *crumbs*
Zest of 4 lemons, grated fine
5 *eggs*
⅔ *cup sugar*
Juice of 4 lemons, strained

Skin the pistachio nuts by dropping them in a small amount of boiling water. Remove from heat, let sit for 3 minutes, drain, then rub the nuts in an old dish towel. The skins should easily come loose. Freshen almonds in the oven until lightly browned. Chop the nuts roughly, mix with cake crumbs and lemon zest in a large bowl, and set aside.

Butter a 9- or 10-cup terrine or loaf pan. Sugar it generously (the sugar will provide a slight crust for the terrine) and set aside.

Place eggs, sugar and lemon juice in a mixer bowl. Place the bowl directly over a very low burner and whisk until quite warm. Remove from heat and continue beating by machine. Place the bowl over heat again halfway through the beating. Whip until the mixture turns thick and forms a ribbon, i.e., when the beater is lifted, there should fall from it a thick strand that remains visible on the surface.

Fold the dry ingredients into the warm eggs gently and rapidly. Don't overwork. The volume will decrease due to its heavy load of nuts and crumbs.

Pour into the sugared terrine and bake for 30 to 35 minutes at 350°.

Remove from oven, place a piece of plastic wrap over the top, and cool to room temperature. Refrigerate at least overnight. The terrine will be moist, cold, slightly chewy, and more a loaf than a full blown cake. Keeps well for two or three days. Good picnic fare.

Raspberry "Pâté"

This dessert, with its overtones of English summer pudding, must be made a day (or even two) before serving. Under refrigeration, it turns into a solidly encrusted "pâté," the moist magenta interior held firm by surrounding crumbs.

SERVES 8 TO 10

1½ pounds good quality Scotch shortbread
Approximately 3 tablespoons whipping cream
Sugar
3 cups raspberries
A pinch of cinnamon

FOR GARNISH
Whipped cream

Crush the shortbread to a fine crumb in a blender or food processor. Put aside 1 cup. Bind the rest of the crumbs lightly with cream until the mixture is just moist enough to pack.

Sprinkle the bottom of a small terrine or loaf pan (about 4½ by 7 inches) with 2 tablespoons of granulated sugar. Pat a thin layer of "dough" onto the bottom and up the sides to the height of 1½ inches.

Mix raspberries with cinnamon, the reserved cup of crumbs, and enough sugar so they taste distinctly sweet. Spoon berries into the crust and cover with remaining moist crumbs. Put a layer of aluminum foil on top of the pâté and weight it with small cans or jars. Refrigerate at least overnight.

To serve, run a knife around the edge and dip the mold bottom briefly into hot water. Reverse the mold sharply down onto a towel-covered counter. Slide the pâté onto a serving dish and slice off one crusted end.

Cut pâté into ¾-inch slices, dipping the knife in hot water between cuts. Garnish each slice with a small rosette of sweetened whipped cream.

Chilled Chocolate Framboise Cakes

My version of a cake glimpsed through the window of Fauchon in Paris.

SERVES 15 TO 18

FOR THE PRALINE

3 ounces unpeeled almonds
¾ cup sugar
¼ cup water

FOR THE CAKE

8 ounces semi-sweet chocolate
2 sticks unsalted butter
5 large eggs
1 cup superfine sugar
The praline
¼ teaspoon salt
1 ¾ cups sifted flour

FOR THE BUTTER CREAM

3 large eggs at room temperature
6 tablespoons superfine sugar
2 teaspoons vanilla
3 sticks unsalted butter

Framboise (*or Grand Marnier*)
1 cup raspberry jam
6 ounces confectioner's chocolate (*couverture*) (*see addresses, page 250*) or *chocolate chips*
Cocoa

Praline, like vanilla, is a flavoring agent, therefore it is necessary to make it as intensely pungent as possible. To this end, toast the almonds until dark but just short of burned. Stir the sugar and water together in a small, heavy saucepan, then let the sugar cook over medium heat. *Do not stir* once the mixture starts simmering. The sugar will turn to caramel, passing from a light, straw color through deeper shades of gold to a rich, dark amber. At this point, add the almonds, swirling the pan to coat the nuts, then pour out on a greased marble slab or the back of a cookie sheet. When completely cool, grind to powder in a blender or food processor. There should be about 1⅓ cups. Reserve.

To make the cake, melt the chocolate and butter together over low heat. Off heat, break and stir in the eggs one at a time. Add the sugar, praline powder, salt and sifted flour slowly, continually stirring so the batter does not turn lumpy. When very smooth, pour into a buttered, 9- x 13-inch rectangular cake pan. Bake at 350° for 45 to 50 minutes. The cake should be firm on top but still slightly soft in the middle. Let cool completely before turning out of the pan. Trim off any crisp edges.

While the cake bakes, make the butter cream. Whisk eggs, sugar and vanilla together (a mixer does the job rapidly) until they form a thick, white sponge. Remove eggs from bowl and, without washing the bowl, add butter and beat until creamed. Slowly beat in the egg mixture. This is a no-fail butter cream. If it looks curdled, simply continue beating and it will pull itself together.

To assemble, cut the cake in two, lengthwise. Carefully slice each half into 3 long layers (a serrated tomato knife works well here) and sprinkle each layer with Framboise. Heat the jam and sieve out any seeds. Spread a generous coat of raspberry on each layer. Spread butter cream on one side of 4 different layers, then form back into 2 long cakes. (There will be 3 layers of cake and 2 of butter cream in each.) Brush jam on the sides and tops of the cakes.

Melt the confectioner's chocolate. With a flat spatula, spread thin layers on kitchen parchment or waxed paper. Refrigerate and when firm, peel the paper off the thin bark. Affix chocolate to the sides and tops of the cakes, breaking pieces where necessary. A rough but covered look is desired. Cut 5, 1-inch-wide strips of paper. Lay them an inch apart on top of the cakes and sieve cocoa over the surface so that it coats the interstices in a pleasing design. Carefully lift off the papers and chill cake until needed.

Remove from refrigerator 10 minutes or so before serving so the chocolate will cut without breaking.

For convenience: the cakes can sit, covered with aluminum foil, overnight. Wait to sieve on the cocoa until shortly before serving. If desired, one cake can be composed and eaten, while the other half, minus jam and butter cream, is frozen for later use.

Choux Cake with Almond Cream and Strawberries

SERVES 8 TO 10

FOR THE CAKE

1 cup water
6 tablespoons unsalted butter
Pinch salt
1 tablespoon sugar
Zest of 1 lemon, grated
1 cup unbleached flour
5 large eggs

3 or 4 tablespoons sugar

FOR THE ALMOND CREAM

1 cup milk, scalded
1½ tablespoons cornstarch
½ cup light brown sugar
1 egg plus 1 egg yolk, lightly beaten together
1 teaspoon vanilla
3 ounces whole almonds, toasted and ground
1 cup whipping cream
1 tablespoon almond liqueur (optional)

Sliced strawberries

To make the cake, combine water, butter, salt, sugar and grated zest in a heavy saucepan. Bring to a rolling boil over medium heat and pour in all the flour at once. Keeping the pan over heat, stir vigorously with a large wooden spoon until the ingredients merge into a smooth pasty ball. Keep spreading and stirring the glutinous mass so that it firms and dries. A covering film of paste on the bottom of the pan is a good indication that the dough is dry enough. (The successful expansion of choux paste depends on the fact that egg whites puff and rise best if unhampered by excess moisture.)

Remove from heat, let cool a moment, then stir in the 5 eggs, one at a time. Each egg addition will cause the mass to break apart but firm stirring will return it to cohesion.

Oil or butter a 9- or 10-inch soufflé dish, charlotte mold or other metal pan with straight sides. Spoon in the paste and bake in a preheated 400° over for 50 minutes. Remove from oven, carefully slice off top and dig out all soft, undercooked dough from both top and base. Place the cut-out lid on a cookie sheet and return both sections of cake to the oven for another 10 minutes. Brush the lid lightly with water and sprinkle 3 or 4 tablespoons of sugar over it. Place lid under a broiler briefly to crystallize. Let cake cool to room temperature before filling.

To make the cream, pour scalded milk over the combined cornstarch and brown sugar. Whisk milk into the eggs, then return custard to gentle heat and continue whisking until thick. Add vanilla and ground almonds. Chill. When cool, whip the cream and fold it into the custard along with the optional liqueur. Fill the bottom of the cake with cream, heap on sliced berries and replace lid.

On Custards

A brief word on custards, for they appear in abundance from this point on as bases for bavarians, tarts, and ice creams. In each recipe, due warning is given that the egg and milk mixture should not approach a boil—a moment's excessive heating and the whole will turn into a mass of curdled eggs swimming in milk. To prevent this disaster, one should remain in close and observant contact with the custard itself. Some general rules:

1. As the milk comes to a scald, stir it with a flat wooden spatula, both to prevent a skin forming and to feel the pan bottom for symptoms of scorch.

2. Stir the eggs lightly. Dribble in the hot milk, all the while stirring smoothly with the wooden spatula. (Whisking or excessive stirring only churns a froth of bubbles atop the liquid, which in turn obscures the view when the custard is put to thicken over heat.)

3. Place custard over medium heat and continue stirring with the flat spatula. It is only with and against such a surface that one can feel the mounting, flowing pressure as the custard thickens. Stir smoothly over the bottom, using a figure-eight motion that scrapes against all corners and hits the center (where scorch is most likely) twice. (It is not necessary to stand by for a lengthy time while the custard slowly heats over a low flame. A good medium heat will move things faster. It *is* best not to raise the heat in the middle of cooking, however.)

4. Watch as well as feel. As the boil approaches, tiny bubbles will form at the outer edges; there will be a certain amount of steam from the surface, and you can feel the heat as you bend over the pan. If in doubt, it is always better to stop short. Bavarians will solidify because of their gelatin, custard tarts will set in baking, and ice cream bases will freeze firmly, anyway. It is only custard sauces that must be brought to denser consistency.

5. A well-made custard will "coat a spoon." Lift out the spatula and run a finger down its center. If, in a sort of Red Sea effect, the waters stay neatly to either side of the dry, middle path, then even a light custard is thick enough.

Eggs in an Orange Nest

This old-fashioned dish consists of two separate bavarian mixtures. The vanilla custard is spooned into empty egg shells and left to harden while the orange bavarian sets in a round bowl. The vanilla "eggs" are then peeled and placed on top, and glacéed strips of orange zest are added to form a straw nest border. Empty egg shells in advance and at your leisure. Prick a small hole on one side of the shell and shake out the contents. Clean the empty eggs under running water and replace in an egg box until enough have accumulated.

SERVES 10 TO 12

FOR 1 BATCH BASIC BAVARIAN

4 egg yolks
½ cup sugar
1¼ cups milk, scalded
1 teaspoon vanilla
1 package (tablespoon) unflavored gelatin softened in ¼ cup water
1 cup whipping cream

16 large, empty egg shells
3 navel oranges
1 cup sugar
¾ cup water

Make a vanilla bavarian to fill the egg shells. Beat the egg yolks and sugar together until thick and pale. Add the hot milk little by little, whisking all the time, then place custard on heat. Stir until the mixture thickens and coats a spoon. Do not allow to boil. Immediately add vanilla and softened gelatin. Stir until gelatin dissolves, strain, then cool custard in the refrigerator. Just before the custard threatens to set, add 1 cup cream, whipped thick but not firm. Rinse the empty egg shells with cold water, shake out the excess, and fill at once using either a funnel or a small, lipped ladle. Allow to set in the refrigerator for at least 5 hours.

To make the orange nesting material, cut thin strips of peel. If you have a vegetable stripper, use it to cut 1½- to 2-inch ribs from the 3 oranges. Grate off the remaining zest (only the outer orange skin, not the bitter white underneath) to use as flavoring. If you have no stripper, cut a thin skin from 2 of the oranges with a small knife. Cut the lengths into narrow strips and grate the zest from the third orange. Make a sugar syrup by simmering 1 cup of sugar with ¾ cup water for 5 minutes. Add the orange strips and let them cook gently until the sugar starts to color a light gold. Swirl the pan carefully from time to time. Strain out the strips and scatter them on a lightly greased baking tin. Pour the remaining sugar out separately and reserve.

For the orange bavarian, squeeze and strain the juice from the 3 oranges. Make another batch of basic bavarian but add the grated zest and juice instead of the vanilla. (This mixture will be slightly thinner than the vanilla bavarian.) Cool and add whipped cream. Pour the orange custard into a round shallow bowl. Let it chill completely.

To assemble, dip vanilla eggs in a bowl of hot water for a brief instant, holding a thumb over the hole so they don't become waterlogged. Crack the eggs carefully and peel. Arrange eggs on top of the orange bavarian. Place the sugared shreds of orange around the edge. Crush the caramelized orange sugar and sprinkle on top.

For convenience: both bavarians can be done a day ahead. The orange can be glacéed, but keep it in an airtight container and scatter it on before serving.

Chocolate and Vanilla Pudding with Poached Pears

This pretty, two-toned pudding, with its delicate layer of poached pear, needs to sit from ten to twelve hours before serving. The easiest mold to shape it in is a 10-inch spring-form pan, but a large soufflé dish or charlotte mold, while making a thicker dessert, would also serve.

SERVES 10 TO 12

FOR THE PEARS

1½ cups sugar
1½ cups water
1 teaspoon vanilla
1 large or 2 small firm pears

FOR THE PUDDINGS

½ cup milk, scalded
4 eggs, separated
1¼ cups sugar
Large pinch salt
2 envelopes unflavored gelatin
1 tablespoon lemon juice
1 pound cream cheese
8 ounces ricotta cheese
4 ounces semi-sweet chocolate
2 or 3 tablespoons water
1 teaspoon vanilla
1 cup whipping cream

FOR THE CHOCOLATE SAUCE

8 ounces semi-sweet chocolate
1½ cups water
½ cup sugar
1 teaspoon cognac

To poach the pears, simmer the sugar and water together for 5 minutes. Add vanilla. Peel the pears, cut them in half and remove core. Poach the pear halves immediately to avoid discoloration. The pears should cook until they are tender enough to be pierced by a fork but retain some firmness. Remove from syrup. Pat dry and cut in very thin slices. Cool and reserve.

Prepare the puddings. Scald the milk. Beat the egg yolks, sugar and salt until thick and pale lemon in color. Whisk the milk slowly into the eggs and place custard on a gentle heat to thicken. Stir constantly and do not allow to boil.

Soften gelatin in ⅓ cup water and stir into the custard just as it is removed from heat. Keep stirring until the gelatin is totally dissolved. Add lemon juice and strain custard through a sieve to insure a perfectly smooth texture. Cool but do not allow to gel.

Mash cream cheese and ricotta together with a fork or electric mixer until smooth and soft. Melt the chocolate with 2 or 3 tablespoons of water.

When custard is slightly cool, stir it into the cheeses thoroughly.

Move rapidly now. Divide custard equally into 2 bowls. Add the melted chocolate to one half, the vanilla to the other.

Whip the cream until thick but not stiff. Add ½ of the cream to each mixture.

Beat the 4 egg whites to firm peaks. Fold ½ into each mixture.

Run cold water into a mold and shake out the excess. Add vanilla custard first, smoothing the top. Layer the pear slices next, then pour on the chocolate custard. Give the filled mold a gentle tap on a hard surface to settle the contents. Cover with plastic wrap and put to chill and develop essence.

For the sauce, melt chocolate in the water. Add sugar and stir over low heat until dissolved. Whisk two or three minutes as the sauce simmers. Add cognac. Strain through a fine sieve and cool. This is meant to be a covering chocolate, not a heavy fudge sauce.

To serve, run a knife around the pudding edge, then turn mold upside down on serving platter. If pudding doesn't shake out immediately, place a hot towel on top and the custard will unmold in its own time. Pour chocolate sauce over the pudding in a light, covering coat. Put extra sauce on table in a sauce boat.

Café Brûlot and Cream

SERVES 6

2 envelopes unflavored gelatin
1 cup water
3½ cups strong breakfast coffee

1 tablespoon cognac
1 cinnamon stick
3 cloves
A 3-inch piece of orange zest
1 cup whipping cream

FOR GARNISH
Whipped cream, sugar and cinnamon sticks

Soften gelatin in ½ cup of the water.

Heat (but don't let boil) the coffee, cognac, cinnamon stick, cloves, orange zest and remaining ½ cup water. Add gelatin, stirring until dissolved, then leave coffee to infuse for 5 minutes. Strain and cool.

Whip the cream until firm but not stiff. Stir cream into coffee. The brew can then be poured into a 6-cup mold or individual coffee cups. (Glass containers will allow the two-toned coffee, with its frothy cream on top, to show to advantage.) Chill at least 3 hours.

To serve, give mold a quick dip in hot water. Gently pry a small edge of the gelled mixture away from the side with a knife, blow hard in the crevice to insure a broken vacuum, and unmold. (If serving in cups, simply place them on saucers.)

Garnish with large rosettes of whipped cream flavored with vanilla, and center a cinnamon stick in each rosette. Place a container of sugar on table. The crunch of sugar on top of the creamy coffee is an amusing touch to my taste, but if you don't like the idea of sugar in the mouth, sweeten the coffee before gelling with ½ cup of superfine sugar.

A summer scene, July, 1969, the night of the first moon landing and the most memorable summer meal I never ate. A congenial group seated around the second-best table at La Tour d'Argent, surrounded by the accoutrements of grand, three-star luxe: gold and silver, cream and crystal, pristine linen, solicitous service.

At the best table, the front corner with its spectacular view across the Seine to the lighted buttresses of Notre Dame, sits a very pretty young American girl and a rouged and elderly French *roué*. He, most obviously Somebody, is entertaining her for the first time. But who is she? A never-met niece on her first trip abroad? The granddaughter of an old friend? Oh surely not . . . but perhaps?

At any rate, she is bored. She sulks and fidgets at the table. Nothing pleases her. She refuses wine.

We are each unimaginatively eating a different variety of duck when Claude Terrail, the owner, wends his way through the tables murmuring, "The Americans have landed on the moon."

There is a polite smattering of applause in the restaurant, and across the river, a famous American novelist's house lights up in a modest display of fireworks. The young lady is not moved.

Finally the *roué* summons the *maitre d'* and there is a whispered consultation. Both gentlemen seem pleased with themselves. In a few moments, a waiter appears pushing a service cart. On it, a green salad, a huge cold lobster, a bottle of vintage Krug on ice, and a tall crystal pitcher filled to the brim with raspberries. The waiter gently mashes down on the berries and fills the pitcher with champagne. He stirs, then pours the rosy liquid out, filtering it through a finely meshed sieve into frosted tulip glasses holding yet more raspberries. (Oh the frivolity of that ephemeral fruit . . . the merging lush and lust . . . the small red kisses inherent in the very form . . .) The young lady perks up.

We finish the last bites of our sauced duck and move into cheese.

The *roué* expertly tosses the salad himself. Why is he showing off? (Why do *we* all seem to be eating a hot soufflé for dessert?)

As we take our sated leave, I catch one last glimpse. He is feeding her bites of lobster; she, shoes off, is spooning out raspberries, and the champagne is all gone.

Oh surely not . . . but probably.

Champagne Jelly with Raspberries

SERVES 4

1 envelope unflavored gelatin
1 ¾ cups water
¾ cup sugar
Juice of 1 lemon
Zest of 1 lemon, cut in wide strips
1 egg white and 1 egg shell
½ cup dry white wine
¾ cup quality champagne
Raspberries

Soften gelatin in ¼ cup of the water. Heat 1 ½ cups water, add gelatin, and stir until dissolved. Add sugar, lemon juice and zest (the outer yellow skin with no white attached). Heat just to the point where liquid is about to break into a boil. Remove from heat, cover, and let steep 20 minutes.

Whisk egg white, the crushed egg shell and white wine together until lightly foamy. Whisk in the gelatin syrup and replace pan over medium-low heat. Continue a lazy whisking action. As liquid heats, the egg white albumen will gradually rise to the top, bringing with it specks of dross that might otherwise cloud the jelly. As soon as a frothy scum forms and the liquid breaks into a simmer, stop stirring and cook slowly for 10 minutes. Cover, remove from heat, and let stand 5 minutes.

Rinse a clean dish towel with cool water. Wring out and use to line a sieve. Place sieve over a large bowl, making sure there is a goodly space under the sieve. Carefully pour in the syrup and let it drip through of its own accord. Do not allow the clear jelly to touch the sieve or it could recloud.

Cool jelly. Watch, and as soon as it turns cold and just before it sets, stir in the champagne. Pour into 4 champagne or balloon wine glasses. Leave to set until thoroughly cold. Serve with raspberries, sugar, and more champagne.

Lemon Omelet Soufflé

A last minute but spectacularly light dessert.

SERVES 8

Sugar
1 quart lemon ice cream or *sherbert*
Zest of 1 lemon, grated fine
1 teaspoon vanilla
6 eggs plus 2 egg whites at room temperature

Butter a metal platter or quiche dish (either round or oval) and sugar it well. Refrigerate. Preheat oven to 425°.

Rapidly shape the lemon ice cream with hand and spoon, into a mounded half circle (or oval, depending on the shape of the serving dish). Return to freezer immediately.

Add lemon zest and vanilla to ⅓ cup of sugar and work briefly with the fingers to flavor the sugar.

Separate eggs. Place yolks and flavored sugar together in a mixer bowl and let them beat away by machine while the whites are beaten separately. (If you have no mixer, let another person whisk the sugared yolks; if you have no other person, beat yolks first, then whites, then yolks again briefly, but this is not so satisfactory.)

Beat the whites, preferably by hand in an immaculate copper bowl. (An easy way to clean the bowl interior is to throw in a handful of salt and scour away with a used lemon half, the juice of which provides an acid cleanser, the lemon itself a handy scouring pad.) When the whites have risen to firm peaks, quickly fold in the yolks which should, by this time, be thick and pale. Never mind if the two mixtures are not completely amalgamated.

Spread ⅓ of the eggs 1 inch thick on the baking dish. Place the ice cream block in the middle (eggs should extend 2 inches beyond the block). Swirl the rest of the egg over the ice cream. If you desire, some of the egg can be piped in a decorative design on the soufflé top and sides. Sprinkle with a large handful of sugar and place immediately in the preheated oven.

Keep an eye on the dish, for in a matter of a minute or two, the top will brown and the moist soufflé be ready to eat.

Cold Caramel Soufflé

SERVES 4 TO 6

Sugar
3 *tablespoons water*
2 *ounces whole almonds, lightly toasted*
2 *or 3 tablespoons hot water*
½ *cup whipping cream*
5 *egg whites at room temperature*

Butter and sugar a 2-quart soufflé dish. Lightly grease a baking sheet and set aside.

Place ½ cup sugar and 3 tablespoons water in a small, heavy saucepan. Bring to a gentle boil and let cook until the sugar caramelizes. Do not stir during this process. Just as the caramel reaches a medium amber shade, remove it from heat. Pour about ⅓ of the caramel into a small metal bowl. Add the almonds to the remaining syrup, swirling the pan to coat them, and pour out onto the baking sheet to cool and harden.

The caramel in the small bowl will be used to make a light sauce. Let cool somewhat, but add 2 or 3 tablespoons of hot water before it can harden. (Add just enough water to allow the caramel to remain a flowing syrup.) When the caramel has further cooled, stir in the cream. Chill.

When the caramelized almonds (praline) have cooled, grind them to a fine powder in blender or food processor.

Beat the egg whites to firm peaks, preferably by hand in a clean copper bowl. Stir ⅓ of them into the praline and fold in the remaining whites. Pour into the soufflé dish.

Place in a *bain marie* (a larger pan containing water halfway up the mold), and bake at 350° for 30 minutes.

Let soufflé rest briefly, then run a knife around the edge and invert onto a rimmed platter or quiche dish. Scatter 3 tablespoons of sugar over the top and place under a hot broiler briefly to crystalize. Cool to room temperature, then refrigerate for up to 5 hours.

Before serving, pour the creamy caramel syrup around the soufflé.

Bittersweet Chocolate Tart

SERVES 8

FOR THE FILLING

Zest from 2 large oranges
½ cup sugar
1 cup milk
1 cup whipping cream
6 ounces French or Swiss bittersweet chocolate
3 eggs, lightly beaten
Large pinch salt
1 teaspoon vanilla

FOR THE SYRUP

½ cup sugar
½ cup water

1 half-baked 10-inch pie shell (*see page 200*)
1 cup whipping cream
⅓ cup confectioner's sugar
Vanilla, to taste

FOR GARNISH

1 orange slice
Sugar

Strip zest (the outer orange skin with no white attached) from oranges with a vegetable peeler. Put the zest into the ½ cup of sugar and work it gently for 2 minutes with your fingers so that an orange essence is imparted to the sugar. Remove zest from sugar and reserve both.

Make the sugar syrup with *another* ½ cup of sugar and ½ cup of water. Gently boil for 5 minutes, then place the reserved zest into the syrup and simmer for about 20 minutes until zest becomes transparent. Remove the zest from syrup, let it cool and harden, then chop well or grind in a blender.

Place the milk, cream, chocolate and orange-flavored sugar in a saucepan and stir until the chocolate is melted and the mixture almost comes to a scald. Pour the mixture slowly onto the eggs, whisking constantly.

Add chopped orange zest, salt and 1 teaspoon vanilla and return mixture to the saucepan. Place over gentle heat, and stir with a wooden spoon until slightly thickened. Do not let custard approach boil.

Pour the filling into the half-baked pie shell and bake in a preheated 350° oven for 35 minutes.

Serve chilled and covered with masses of stiffly whipped cream sweetened with confectioner's sugar and flavored with vanilla to taste. Swirl the cream on with a spatula or pipe rosettes through a pastry star tube. Garnish the center with a slice of orange, slit ⅔ through, twisted, and rolled in sugar.

For convenience: tart can be made the day before and kept refrigerated. The whipped cream garnish should be added shortly before serving. Keeping a jar of homemade glacéed peel on hand allows one to skip the sugar syrup step.

Flemish Tart

SERVES 10

Another tart with a baked custard base, this one an attempt to render an old Dutch masterpiece into culinary terms. Crowd the "canvas" with as many fruit flowers as possible. I usually make this dessert in July when mint and lemon verbena are in blossom.

FOR THE CUSTARD

3 cups milk
4 eggs
½ cup sugar
Pinch salt
½ teaspoon cinnamon
Nutmeg

1 round 11- or 12-inch half-baked pie shell (see page 200)

FOR THE GARNISH

Black currant preserves
A variety of fresh fruits: peaches, strawberries, blueberries, a banana, green and purple grapes, apples
Mint sprigs
Lemon verbena or mint blossoms, if possible

Whipped cream

Scald the milk. Beat eggs and sugar together until thick and light. Whisk in the milk slowly. Add salt, cinnamon and a scraping of nutmeg and place over medium heat. Stir constantly until the mixture thickens. Do not allow to boil.

Pour custard into the half-baked pie shell and place in a 350° oven for about 45 minutes or until custard is set and gently browned at the edges. Let cool completely.

Melt a cup of preserves and strain. Brush a thin coating onto the custard. Arrange a compact design of flowers made from fruit slices—tulips from peaches, giant peonies of thin-sliced strawberries, lilies of the valley from green grapes, etc. Make stems and leaves from mint sprigs. Arrange any herb blossoms like sprays of baby's breath. Gently glaze the fruit with the remaining preserves to provide an antique patina. Serve with sweetened and lightly cinnamoned whipped cream.

For convenience: the custard can be baked in the morning and allowed to sit, covered and refrigerated through the day. Decorate and glaze 1 hour before serving.

On Rough Puff Pastry

From preference, most pastry crusts I make are based on the following formula: equal weight measures of unsalted butter and unbleached flour, appropriate salt, and enough ice water to bind into a dough. It is the laziest of formulas, and one usually reserved for full puff pastry, but it makes, in whatever form, a crisp, meltingly flavorful crust. When a plain pie dough is wanted, it is a simple matter to work the fat into flour to an oatmeal flake. For rough puff pastry, the butter is left in larger chunks and the formed dough is given several turns. (I always give plain dough a turn or two if I've time, for even that small effort results in a layered effect and therefore more flakiness.)

Rough Puff Pastry

2 heaped to overflowing cups of unbleached flour
¼ teaspoon salt
2 sticks chilled, unsalted butter, cut in ½ tablespoon chunks
Approximately ¾ cup ice water

Mix flour and salt in a heavy bowl. Add butter and work into flour until butter is thoroughly mixed throughout but still remains in rough, almond-sized slicks. The most effective method is to rub the mixture between the thumbs and stiffly held fingers of both hands. Work rapidly and stop too short rather than overworking.

Make an open space (well) in the middle, pour in some ice water, and lightly mix until the dough can be packed together in a holding ball. (You will probably use between ⅔ to ¾ cup water, but instinct should guide rather than a set amount. It is better to err on the side of slightly too much water as it is easier to work flour into a damp pastry than water into a tightly bound dough.) Give the dough two or three kneading motions, then wrap in foil and put to chill at least ½ hour.

On a floured surface, roll pastry into a neat rectangle no larger than necessary for the dough to be easily folded into thirds. (Over-rolling simply stretches and toughens.) Fold dough into thirds or, in pastry parlance, give the dough a turn. Roll out again into a rectangle and give another turn. Wrap and refrigerate. Wait at least ½ hour, then give two more turns. Wrap and refrigerate ½ hour, then roll into shape. (A finished crust should also sit for a time before baking so it does not oven-shrink. The rest periods between turns insure that the tensile gluten relaxes enough that the final crust won't toughen.)

This is an easier, quicker way to gain lift in pastry than making full puff pastry, and far less troublesome in hot weather. Rough puff can, as puff pastry always must, be given six turns if time permits. The rest periods can last anywhere from ½ hour minimum to overnight.

The listed ingredient amounts yield enough pastry for 2 medium tarts, but it is impossible to make a smaller batch and still have enough volume to make the turns. It is perhaps easiest simply to double the recipe and keep 2 or 3 formed tart bases at the ready in the freezer.

TO PREBAKE A PIE SHELL (OR BAKE A PIE SHELL BLIND)

Shape a square of heavy aluminum foil to the interior of a pie tin. Leave three inches of foil extending over the edge. Remove and reserve.

Roll pie crust, place it in the tin and trim edges. Fit the foil into the pie crust and fill with small raw beans or lentils. (It is not necessary for the beans to sit thickly in the pie's center. Rather they should weight the edges and sides to hold them in place while baking.)

Bake the crust in a preheated 350° oven for about 12 minutes, or until nicely set. Carefully lift off the bean-laden foil. If the crust is to receive a liquid filling (as for a quiche), brush the bottom lightly with egg white which will act as a sealer and allow the finished tart to retain a crisp crust. Continue baking the shell to the right degree of brown.

Crisp Orange and Almond Pastry

SERVES 12

6 ounces sliced or slivered almonds
Rough Puff Pastry (see page 199)
1 ½ sticks unsalted butter
½ cup sugar
Zest of two oranges, grated
4 tablespoons whipping cream

Lightly brown the almonds under a broiler or in the oven. Set aside.

Roll pastry out thin and cut a 12- or 13-inch circle. Transfer dough to a baking sheet or pizza pan. Prick the surface with a fork and pinch a decorative border around the edge. Bake in a 350° oven for 15 minutes, or until the pastry has risen, begun to set and turned pale gold.

Melt the butter, add sugar and bring to a boil. Immediately stir in almonds, orange zest and cream. Spoon the mixture over the half-baked crust, cover the surface evenly with nuts, and make sure the syrup glazes the entire crust except for a ½-inch border at the edge.

Return tart to oven, lower temperature to 350° and bake another 15 or 20 minutes. The light syrup will melt, spread, crystallize and eventually caramelize. The tart is finished when it appears a dark gold. Keep a watch for this.

Remove pastry from the baking dish and cool on a cake rack. Slice in pie wedges.

Bing Cherry Flan

SERVES 8

2 pounds Bing cherries
Well chilled Rough Puff Pastry (see page 199)
1 cup sugar plus 2 tablespoons
¼ teaspoon cinnamon
Kirsch or crème de cassis

Pit the cherries, using either a cherry stoner or your fingers. Reserve 1 cup.

Roll pastry into a rectangle 14 inches long and 10 inches wide. Transfer to a baking sheet. Cut the edges into a scallop pattern with a knife. Using the end of a cannoli tube or a pastry nozzle, cut small circles from the center of each scallop.

Strew cherries down the center of the tart and fold all edges over on top to make a lacy border. Sprinkle cherries with 1 or 2 tablespoons of sugar and place in a 350° oven until the crust is golden brown (about 40 to 45 minutes).

Chop the reserved cup of cherries fine and place them, the cup of sugar and the cinnamon in a small, heavy saucepan. Let simmer while the tart bakes. Skim off the pale purple foam that forms, and give a gentle stir from time to time. When tart is finished, strain the cherries through a sieve. Flavor the resulting glaze with a dash of kirsch or cassis and pour over the tart. Serve with whipped cream or ice cream. (This basic recipe can easily be adapted to other fruits.)

Quick Jam Tart

SERVES 6

Rough Puff Pastry (see page 199)
Raspberry or strawberry jam
Blueberry or blackberry jam
Peach or apricot jam
Whipped cream

Roll out a 9- or 10-inch circle of pastry. Place on baking sheet, pinch up a decorative edge, and prick bottom with a fork. Cut six ½-inch-wide strips of dough about 10 inches long. Divide the tart into six portions by making V-shaped divisions, like pie wedges, with the dough strips. The two points will rest at the rim, the sharp angles will all meet at the center. Trim the edge and bake the crust in a 375° oven until crisp and golden.

When cool, spread the six divisions with alternating flavors of jam. Make a small rosette of thick whipped cream in the center and another rosette in each of the jam sections at mid-rim. An easy dessert to satisfy children, an excellent way to use up leftover pastry scraps.

Berry Turnover

This dessert can function as a large container for a variety of fruits. It appreciates being served on a doily-covered silver tray.

SERVES 10

Rough Puff Pastry (see page 199)
1 ½ quarts strawberries, raspberries or *blueberries*
½ to 1 cup sugar
Juice of ½ lemon
1 egg yolk
1 cup whipping cream

Roll out a 15-inch square of pastry ¼-inch thick. Transfer it to a baking sheet and chill.

Pick over and stem the berries. Rinse and dry if necessary. Heap them on one triangular half of the dough, leaving a good 1-inch border clear. Mound the berries in the center, sprinkle with sugar according to the sweetness of the fruit and squeeze the lemon juice over them.

Fold the free half of the dough over the top and seal the edges together with a bit of thin flour-water paste to make a triangle. Crimp the two long edges, then cut a hole, 1 ½ inches in diameter, directly in top center. Use any scraps of leftover dough for ornamental designs if desired.

Beat the egg yolk with a small amount of water and brush over the pastry to glaze. Place turnover in a 350° oven for 45 to 50 minutes. If necessary, cover the top with aluminum foil to prevent burning during the last minutes.

Remove from oven and cool to room temperature. Whip the cream until lightly thickened and pour or pipe it down through the hole on top.

Blackberry Pudding with Latticed Suet Crust

A dish which can be adapted to many kinds of fruit; try raspberries, blueberries or cherries in the summer, pears or apples in colder weather. I make this in a traditional English deep pie dish, a white porcelain oval 13 inches long and 3 inches deep. The depth is necessary, but bowls of other shapes and materials will be found accommodating. The single thick suet top crust is delicious and holds its shape nicely when soaked with pudding juices.

SERVES 8

FOR THE CRUST

3 ounces suet
3 ounces unsalted butter, cut into chunks
¼ teaspoon salt
3 cups all-purpose flour
Approximately ¾ cup ice water

FOR THE FILLING

3 to 4 quarts berries, or enough fruit to heap packed and high, in the dish
1½ to 2 cups sugar, depending on fruit's sweetness
¼ teaspoon cinnamon
1 beaten egg, for glaze

To make the crust, crumble suet into a bowl. Remove any thin membranes or small red veinings running through the fat and continue crumbling to a small grain. Add butter and mix the two fats together until relatively smooth.

Add salt to flour and rapidly work in the combined fat. Work the dough by rubbing masses of it between the thumb and four fingers held stiffly together. When the dough resembles oatmeal, add enough ice water to bind into a ball. Wrap and refrigerate for ½ hour. (This will be sufficient dough for two pies, but it is senseless to make in smaller batches. Freeze half for later use.)

Place a small, inverted oven-proof dish or cup on the bottom of the pie dish to help prop the center crust. Place fruit in the dish, heaping it in the middle and remembering that the contents will shrink a good deal during baking. Sprinkle with sugar and cinnamon.

Roll out dough ¼-inch thick. Cut a long, 1½-inch-wide band and attach it around the rim of the dish with a slight moistening of water. Cover fruit with lattice strips, cut off any excess ends, and pinch a pretty, crimped border around the edge to join the two layers of dough. Brush crust with a glaze of beaten egg and water. Bake in a 350° oven for 45 minutes then strew with ½ cup of sugar and 2 tablespoons water. Bake another 10 or 15 minutes until the sugar forms a bubbled, crunchy topping and the entire crust is a handsome brown. Serve 1 hour out of the oven with thick cream.

Fresh Fig and Raspberry Trifle

SERVES 6 TO 8

½ cup sugar
⅔ cup water
1½ pounds fresh ripe figs, peeled and chopped

FOR THE CUSTARD

2 whole eggs and 4 egg yolks
½ cup confectioner's sugar
2 cups scalded milk
1 teaspoon vanilla

6 ladyfinger biscuits
Quality dry sherry
1 cup whipping cream
2 cups raspberries
2 ounces toasted, sliced almonds

Simmer ½ cup sugar and ⅔ cup water for 5 minutes to make a sugar syrup. Add figs and stew for 10 to 15 minutes or until soft. Strain. Purée into a thick jam in blender or food processor. Refrigerate.

Make a custard by beating the whole eggs, yolks and powdered sugar together. Slowly stir the milk into the eggs then return custard to heat. Whisk (but do not let boil) until thick. Strain, add vanilla, and chill.

Split the lady fingers in two. Sprinkle with sherry to taste. Arrange biscuits around bottom and sides of a glass bowl. When the custard is cold, whip the cream stiff. Spoon ⅓ of the figs onto the biscuits. Mix the rest lightly but not thoroughly with the custard. Fold cream, raspberries, and ½ the almonds into the custard. Again, don't blend as the trifle should be composed of variegated swirls and pockets of jam, fruit and cream. Pour onto the biscuits. Scatter the rest of the almonds on top and chill for 2 or 3 hours.

Sautéed Figs

3 or 4 large, fresh figs per person, peeled
Unsalted butter
Sugar
Cognac
Whipping cream

Slice figs in two crosswise. Flatten them gently and cut off the stems. Melt a generous amount of butter in a sauté pan and add figs, cut side up. When they have slightly browned on one side, turn them over and sprinkle a goodly quantity of sugar into the pan. As the sugar melts, add a dash of cognac and flame. Let figs fry until the syrup turns a pretty pale caramel. Shake pan occasionally to prevent sticking. Add a small amount of cream to form a coating sauce of medium consistency. Serve individual portions of lukewarm figs and caramelized cream.

Elderberry Fritters

SERVES 6

12 perfect, full, ripe elderberry flower clusters
1 recipe Fritter batter (see page 123) adding 1 teaspoon sugar
Vegetable oil for frying
Granulated sugar
Elderberry leaves for garnish

Pick the flower heads with 1 inch of stalk left on. Prepare batter, adding 1 teaspoon of sugar just before putting the batter to rest. Dip in the flowers. Fry in vegetable oil, stem end up. When fritters are golden, lift out by the stem and drain on absorbent toweling. Coat with granulated sugar and serve immediately, two to each plate. Garnish with a small spray of elderberry leaves.

Curious how evocative the peach is . . . how it rouses in so many writers thoughts of infant summers ". . . the very air of long summer afternoons–occasions tasting of ample leisure, still bookless, yet beginning to be bedless, or cribless; tasting of accessible garden peaches . . ." (Henry James)

. . . how it lingers primal in the memory . . . "I remember his showing me how to eat a peach by building a little white mountain of sugar and then dipping the peach into it." (Mary McCarthy)

. . . how its nectareous fragrance haunts from halcyon summers past ". . . summer was drunken. Among senses, smell was the strongest–smell of hot pine-woods and sweet-fern in the scorching summer noon; of new-mown hay; of ploughed earth; of box hedges; of peaches, lilacs, syringas." (Henry Adams)

Peaches Aswim in Rose Petals

SERVES 10

Petals from 10 highly scented roses
1 rose geranium leaf (optional)
1½ cups sugar
3 cups water
Juice of 1 lemon
½ vanilla bean or *1 teaspoon vanilla extract*
10 large, firm peaches
5 peach seeds
½ cup chilled raspberry purée, strained

FOR GARNISH
Peach seeds and pink rose petals

Depetal the roses. Tie petals (and the rose geranium leaf) loosely in a cheesecloth bag.

Make a syrup by combining 1½ cups sugar, 3 cups water and the petal bag. Simmer for 5 minutes. Add lemon juice and vanilla and allow the syrup to steep for 20 minutes. Mash down on the petal bag to intensify flavor, then remove it and the bean.

Peel the peaches by dropping them briefly in boiling water. The skins should strip off with ease after less than 1 minute. Cut peaches in half, remove stones, and crack 5 of them to free the almond-like seed. Add peach halves and seeds to the syrup and return to a simmer until the peaches are tender. (Test with a fork.) Allow them to cool in the syrup, then refrigerate until chilled.

With a slotted spoon, place the peaches in a pretty glass bowl. Spoon out the peach seeds and skin them. Mix the raspberry purée with the remaining syrup and pour over the peaches. Chop the seeds and sprinkle over the surface. Tear off the white portion (which is slightly bitter in taste) from the base of some pink rose petals. Scatter petals over the peaches.

Breaded Peach Pudding

SERVES 5 TO 7

12 slices firm, home style bread
1 stick unsalted butter, melted
1½ pounds peaches
⅓ cup sugar
½ teaspoon cinnamon
¼ cup dry breadcrumbs

Cut crusts from the bread and lightly brush both sides with butter. Put 4 slices in the bottom of a 12-inch pie dish. Cut 2 slices in half and place the half-slices around the sides.

Drop peaches in boiling water for 30 seconds. Remove them and peel off skin. Slice peaches into and over the breaded pie dish so no juice is lost. Sprinkle with sugar and cinnamon.

Place another 4 bread slices on top of the pie, adding half slices again at the sides. Sprinkle with breadcrumbs, dot with remaining butter and bake at 350° for 35 minutes. Excellent with a cold Sauterne.

Stuffed Peaches with Ginger and Almonds

SERVES 5

5 large firm peaches
5 slices crystallized ginger
½ cup Praline (see page 182)
¼ cup slivered almonds, lightly toasted
Unsalted butter
Whipping cream

Peel the peaches by dipping them briefly in boiling water. Cut in half and remove the stones.

Mince the ginger and mix evenly with the praline (this is easily done by putting both in blender or food processor). Put a few almonds in the hollow of each peach then fill with praline mixture. Put a thin scrape of butter on each half and bake for 20 minutes in a 350° oven.

Place 2 halves in each of 5 individual serving dishes. Spoon the buttery juices over the peaches and serve with a pitcher of cream on the side, if desired.

The remaining fruits, compotes and ices are nicely complemented and enhanced when served with a bit of crisp, unobtrusive pastry. These two sweets are particularly handy in the summer, for they can be composed, held, baked over a period of three or four weeks, and their oven time is brief.

Lemon Leaves

MAKES 8 DOZEN COOKIES

4 tablespoons butter
¼ cup sugar
⅔ cup honey
1 tablespoon fine-grated lemon zest
Juice of 1 lemon
1 teaspoon ground ginger
½ teaspoon salt
1 teaspoon baking soda
2 tablespoons boiling water
2¼ cups flour

Cream butter and sugar together. Add honey, zest, lemon juice, ginger and salt and stir well. Put baking soda in a small cup and add boiling water. Stir and add to batter. Mix in the flour and work the dough well with a heavy spoon. Cover and chill at least overnight.

Place a quarter of the dough on a lightly greased baking sheet. Moisten fingers with water (keep a cupful nearby) and pat the dough into an exceedingly thin circle around 13 inches in diameter. Bake in a 375° oven for about 6 minutes. The cookie should be dark gold but not too brown. Remove from oven and immediately press a leaf-shaped cutter over the thin wafer.

When cool, break out the design and divide the leftover crumbs with a small child. The cookies will stay crisp for a week in an airtight container. The dough can be shaped into rolls, covered tightly and frozen, and baked at intervals.

Rolled Cinnamon Pastries

MAKES ABOUT 5 DOZEN

1 recipe Rough Puff Pastry (see page 199)
½ cup brown sugar
½ cup granulated sugar
1 tablespoon cinnamon
4 to 5 tablespoons cognac

After the pastry has been given six turns and rested for ½ hour, roll the dough out into a 15-inch square. Mix the sugars and cinnamon and spread evenly over the dough. Hold a thumb over the mouth of the cognac bottle and sprinkle the sugar. Roll the pastry up, cut the roll in two, and cover each half first with plastic wrap then with aluminum foil. Refrigerate or freeze. (The cookies must be sliced when chilled but not frozen or they will crumble when cut. Bring frozen dough to refrigerator temperature before shaping.)

Cut the rough, uneven end from the roll and discard. Slice dough as thin as possible. Place on a pastry sheet and bake in a 375° oven for about 15 minutes. Turn the cookies over after 7 minutes. These pastries are best eaten within two days of baking.

A Macédoine in a Brandy Snifter

An inexpensive, 14-inch-tall brandy snifter intended as a terrarium is a good service piece investment. Lovely for layered salads of both vegetables and fruits, it can be filled half to two thirds full, depending on how many people are to be served. A glass tumbler placed in the bottom of the bowl lets the fruit volume be reduced while still allowing the sides to be built up in extravagant, patterned layers. The fruits used in this dessert are open to whim and fancy, but it takes a generous amount of fruit and juice to fill such a large container. Slice and peel all fruit over a bowl to catch the liquid. Squeeze peelings and cores to extract further juices.

SERVES 15 TO 20

1 cup sugar
1 cup water
Lemon juice
Bananas
Peaches
Purple plums
Strawberries
A pineapple
Apples or pears
Blueberries
Raspberries
Oranges and lemons for juice
Grand Marnier or *other favorite liqueur, to taste*

Make a sugar syrup by boiling 1 cup sugar and 1 cup water for 5 minutes. Squeeze some lemon juice into a small bowl.

Slice the bananas, dip in lemon juice and place them in the bottom of the snifter. Press the rounds against the glass to just the height where they can first be seen as an entire row. (Only the fruit against the glass must be carefully placed.) Fill with more banana slices to the top of the row.

Peel peaches by dropping in boiling water for 30 seconds to facilitate skin removal. Press a neat row of thin peach slices above the banana layer and fill center with peaches. Slice plums and layer them, dark skin-side out. Cut strawberries in half lengthwise and place cut side against the glass.

Cut a thick enough peel from the pineapple that the eyes are removed in the process. Slice the pineapple in two lengthwise, dig out the cores, and cut thin, half-round slices. Cut these slices in two and press them in a row against the glass. Continually fill to the top row with fruit as you go. (It will not matter if the fruit is mixed.) Add a final white row of apple or pear slices.

Make a thick ring of blueberries around the rim and heap raspberries in the center. Mix sugar syrup with orange and lemon juice, add liqueur to taste, and the reserved fruit juices. The juices must be slightly tart—add more lemon if necessary. Pour over the fruit to cover halfway. Leave to macerate 8 to 10 hours before serving.

Pineapple Compote in the Shell

SERVES 10 TO 12

2 large ripe pineapples
Purple grapes
1 quart strawberries
Green grapes
1 pint fresh or 1 pack frozen raspberries
Sugar
Lemon or pineapple sherbet
Wooden toothpicks

The first pineapple will be used to hold the sherbet. Cut a leafy cap from the top and set aside. Using a small, sharp knife and a spoon, first dig out the core (and discard) and then remove the flesh until the pineapple is empty. Try not to puncture the sides. Scrape down the inside with a spoon to smooth, and preserve all juices during the emptying process. Break some wooden toothpicks in two and stick the sharp ends in a neat row around the top of the pineapple. Impale dark, whole grapes, compactly and evenly spaced. Under them, form another row of toothpicks to hold small strawberries. Next, a row of green grapes, and last, another row of purple grapes. Refrigerate. (½ hour before serving, place in freezer.)

Cut the second pineapple lengthwise from the green crown down. Leave the leaves intact as much as possible. Dig out the core and discard, then spoon out pulp so 2 empty half shells remain. Refrigerate. (Place in freezer ½ hour before serving.)

Cut the pineapple flesh into bite-sized pieces and mix with the remaining strawberries and grapes (halved and seeded if need be). Put to chill.

Pass the raspberries through a sieve. Add the purée to the reserved pineapple juice. Add sugar to taste and place in the freezer.

To serve, mix fruit and juices. (It is nice if the juices have frozen to a slush.) Spoon fruit into 2 half shells. Scoop sherbet into the whole pineapple and replace cap. Center the pineapple on a silver tray and place the 2 cut shells at either side. Serves 10 to 12 if you refill once.

Cantaloupe and Cassis

½ cantaloupe per person
Black raspberries
Sugar
Creme de cassis or cassis syrup (black currant syrup available in food speciality shops)

Cut the cantaloupe in two. Remove seeds and cut a thin slice from the bottom so the melon will sit upright. With a dinner spoon, make seven or eight half moon cuts radiating from the center through the top flesh. Heap the cavity with berries, sprinkle with sugar and dribble on cassis to taste. Press down lightly on the berries to start their juices running. Refrigerate for at least 2 hours. At the end of this time, the dark liquid from the berries should have permeated the cuts, turning them into dark swirls against the pale orange flesh. A pretty breakfast presentation.

A Watermelon Snail

Use a round, dark-green melon rather than an elongated, two-toned one.

SERVES 10 TO 12

1 watermelon
1 honeydew melon
1 cantaloupe
⅔ cup sugar
⅔ cup water
Lemon juice
Blueberries

FOR GARNISH
Long mint sprigs

Draw the outline of a snail on the watermelon with a colored marking pen. Cut out the snail outline and clean out the interior so the melon can be used as a container. Make a spiraled shell design on the snail body by digging out a thin strip of peel with a lemon stripper or small knife. Make gentle zigzag cuts along the rim of the container for decoration.

Cut balls from scooped out watermelon, honeydew and cantaloupe, reserving juices in the process. Make a sugar syrup by gently boiling ⅔ cup sugar and ⅔ cup water for 5 minutes. Mix syrup, melon juice and lemon juice to taste, making sure the syrup is not too sweet. Ladle fruit into the snail, scatter blueberries on top, fill with syrup and chill. Garnish with trailing sprigs of mint.

For a splendid cheese and fruit platter, cut small watermelons in two in a lion-toothed (zigzag) pattern. Heap them in a large basket with bunches of purple grapes, apricots and strawberries. Serve cheeses on a grape leaf-covered basket with Grape Bread (see page 14) that breaks apart particularly well to accompany cheese.

Pears in Spiced Cherry Purée

SERVES 8

FOR THE SYRUP

2 cups sugar
2 cups water
¼ teaspoon each of cinnamon, ginger, allspice
1 teaspoon vanilla
Juice of ½ lemon

8 large firm pears
½ lemon
1½ pounds Bing cherries
Kirsch
Sugar
8 large mint or lemon balm leaves with small stems

Make a syrup with 2 cups sugar and 2 cups water. Simmer for 5 minutes. Add spices, vanilla and lemon juice. Steep for 20 minutes.

Peel the pears, leaving on the stems. Rub with lemon to prevent discoloration. Poach pears in syrup to cover at a gentle simmer until tender. Turn pears once during cooking. When done, remove from syrup with a slotted spoon and leave to drain.

Pit the cherries with a cherry stoner or by hand. Purée in a food processor or blender and press through a sieve. Sweeten the purée with spiced sugar syrup and add a dash of Kirsch to taste.

Moisten the rim of a glass serving bowl large enough to hold the pears upright. Roll the rim in sugar. Pour in the cherries and set the pears, stem up, in the purée. Refrigerate for up to 8 hours. Fifteen minutes before serving, press a small hole near each stem with a skewer and fit in the green mint leaves. Place bowl in freezer to frost.

Striped Oranges

1 large navel orange per person
Orange ice cream or sherbet
Strained, sweetened raspberry purée, frozen to slush

Hollow out the oranges over a large bowl. The easiest way is to use an apple corer. Plunge in the stem end, remove the cut-out circle, and continue cutting into and scraping out the orange flesh and seeds. Insert a finger into the orange and detach membranes from the pith if necessary. Rinse out the shells with water and drain upside down. Strain juice and reserve for breakfast.

Soften the orange ice cream. Using a small funnel, fill the oranges one-third full. Tap on a hard surface to settle the contents and place in the freezer to harden. When firm, funnel in enough raspberry purée to fill another third. Freeze until firm. Fill the final third with more orange ice cream. Tap to settle contents and fill to the very top. Freeze.

To serve, slice oranges in half lengthwise to reveal the raspberry forming a pretty ribboned stripe through the center. If the oranges are very hard, let them soften slightly before serving. Serve 2 halves per person in a dessert bowl.

Glacéed Orange Ice Cream

SERVES 10

Zest of 1 orange
1½ cups sugar
1 cup water
1 cup milk
3 egg yolks
Juice of 1 lemon, strained
Juice of 4 oranges, strained
6 leaves orange mint or *spearmint, minced*
2 cups whipping cream
1 tablespoon orange liqueur

Carefully remove the zest (the outer orange peel with no white attached) of 1 orange. Put the zest into 1 cup of the sugar, gently rubbing the peel over the sugar to flavor it with the volatile oil of orange. Remove zest and reserve this sugar for custard.

Put the zest into a small, heavy pan with the remaining ½ cup sugar and 1 cup water. Slowly cook until the sugar begins to caramelize. Remove from heat when a medium gold color and quickly spread the peel on a lightly greased cookie sheet. When it is hard and cool, grind in a blender or food processor.

Scald the milk and orange-flavored sugar together. Whisk the mixture slowly into the egg yolks, return custard to gentle heat and allow it to thicken. Under no circumstances should the mixture come near a boil. Off heat, add lemon juice, orange juice, and mint. Let cool.

Whip the cream until thick but not firm. Stir it into the cooled custard. Add caramelized zest and liqueur and freeze in an ice cream machine. Make this dessert a day before it is to be used as it firms slowly. Good with chocolate sauce.

Brown Sugar Ice Cream

SERVES 12

2 cups whipping cream
1 cup dark brown sugar, packed
Pinch salt
2 cups milk
4 egg yolks
1 teaspoon cinnamon
½ cup Praline *(see page 182)*

Place cream in freezer to chill.

Add sugar and salt to milk and scald. Whisk milk slowly into the egg yolks then place over gentle heat and stir constantly until slightly thickened. Do not allow to boil. Remove from heat and strain. Add cinnamon and praline and place in refrigerator. When the bottom of the pan is cool, whip the chilled cream until thickened but not firm. Fold into the custard and freeze in an ice cream machine.

Frozen Zabaglione

SERVES 6 TO 8

8 egg yolks
1 cup sugar
2 cups whipping cream, well chilled and half whipped
⅓ cup good quality Marsala wine (or to taste)

Combine yolks and sugar and beat with an electric mixer until thick and light in color. Keep beating until, when you take up a spoon of the mixture and feel it between the fingers, no grains of sugar are evident. Stir in the cream and put to chill thoroughly.

Freeze in an ice cream machine until the mixture thickens. Add the

Marsala and continue freezing. (This will be a longer process than for ice creams without alcohol.) For variation and in addition, Grand Marnier may be substituted for Marsala, and a half cup of chopped, toasted almonds and red and green candied cherries may be added with the alcohol to enliven color and consistency.

This is a cream (rather than an ice) and will not harden to the scoopable stage.

Chocolate Malted Ice Cream

12 TO 15 SERVINGS

3 cups whipping cream
2 cups milk
8 ounces semi-sweet chocolate
1 cup sugar
3 egg yolks
Pinch cinnamon
½ cup plain malt

Place cream in freezer to chill.

Combine milk, 6 ounces of the chocolate, and the sugar in a saucepan. Stir over low heat until the mixture is steaming. Gradually whisk a thin stream of the hot liquid into the egg yolks until eggs and milk are combined. Return custard to stove and allow to thicken slightly over medium heat. Stir constantly and do not let boil.

Add cinnamon and malt and stir until dissolved. Strain and cool. Grate the remaining 2 ounces of chocolate and add them to the mixture. Whip the cream until thickened but not firm, and stir into the custard. Freeze.

This ice cream is best a day after making, when it has had a chance to harden and develop its malted flavor.

Nectarine Cream

SERVES 10

2 pounds ripe nectarines
1 tablespoon lemon juice
½ to ⅔ cup sugar
1 tablespoon Grand Marnier
½ cup whipping cream

FOR THE MELBA SAUCE
2 cups fresh or frozen raspberries

Stone the nectarines and, working as rapidly as possible so they don't have time to discolor, purée them with the lemon juice in blender or food processor. Pass nectarines through a sieve, preferably a nylon drum sieve (*tamis*). Add sugar and liqueur. Beat the cream until firm and stir into the purée. Place in a stainless or pyrex bowl, cover with plastic wrap, and place in freezer. Stir from time to time.

About 4 hours later, the cream should be a thick and icy mush. This is the moment to eat it. Scrape into a crystal bowl and serve with crisp cookies and Melba sauce.

For the Melba sauce, purée raspberries in blender or food processor. Sieve out seeds and sweeten to taste.

Granités

EACH RECIPE WILL SERVE 6 TO 8

Frozen blocks of water ice (granités) are useful to have on hand in the freezer for emergency desserts. Each of the following ices maintains a distinct, elemental flavor which allows the palate to be refreshed in direct and forceful terms. A granité should be slightly tart, never edging into a sweet cloy. Because they are quick to melt, all due caution should be taken to serve them in chilled containers and only at the moment they are to be consumed. A traditional granité would be scraped down continually by hand as it freezes. The texture of these machine-beaten blocks will be different but no less interesting. Use within three weeks of freezing.

Grape Granité

1½ pounds sweet, seedless, green grapes
Juice of 1 lemon
2 tablespoons dry white wine
⅔ cup white grape juice
Instant dissolving (superfine) sugar

FOR GARNISH
Peeled grape halves

Purée grapes in blender or food processor. Add lemon juice and pass through a sieve. Add wine, grape juice and sugar to taste. Freeze. To serve, grate chunks in blender or food processor. Serve in tall goblets and garnish with a few peeled grape halves.

Rhubarb Granité

1½ pounds tender rhubarb
1 cup sugar
1 cup water
Juice of 1 lemon
1 pint small strawberries

Wash rhubarb and cut into 1-inch slices. Make a sugar syrup by simmering 1 cup sugar and 1 cup water for 5 minutes. Add rhubarb and stew until tender. Add lemon juice and a few strawberries for color and pass the entire lot through a sieve. Cool and taste for balance. Add more sugar if necessary. Freeze. This granité is a particularly lush shade of rose and deserves to be viewed through a transparent dish. Garnish with remaining unstemmed strawberries.

Tomato Granité

2 pounds ripe tomatoes
Pinch sugar
Juice of ½ lemon
Pinch salt

FOR GARNISH
Parsley sprigs

Stem and purée tomatoes and pass them through a sieve. Add sugar, lemon juice and salt. Freeze. Grate and serve in tall goblets with a parsley sprig for garnish. More of a between-course refresher than a dessert.

Preserving Summer

An open display of home-preserved foods is a handsome addition to any kitchen or dining room. I think particularly of the large, burled armoire sitting, with imposing presence, in Michel Guérard's Eugénie-les-bains restaurant. Placed with decorative care on the shelves is all the bounty of provincial Landes: cherries; olives; mixed *minceur* vegetables; peeled white asparagus spears arranged all on the same diagonal slant; conserves of truffles; large jars of ruby tomato pulp; green beans; a *confit* of duck; and paper-covered pots of thick jams and marmalades, each shining in jeweled relief against the dark wood, while tucked in the corners are amusing animal creatures formed from bread.

Preserving in grand manner takes much time and care, and, perhaps unfortunately, the necessity to put things by does not press upon us with the same intensity as it did upon generations past. In consequence, most busy lives hold few hours for this loving effort, and winter is the poorer for it. The following recipes are not too time consuming, and they should yield enough useful pickles and jam to fill a cupboard shelf and last a family through winter. The tomato curiosities are proffered as suggestions for dealing with bumper crops.

Cornichons are a traditional accompaniment to *pot au feu*, *pâtés*, and cold meats, and a fine-chopped addition to *gribiche* and *rémoulade* sauces. Though special varieties of cucumbers are grown in France for this pickle, it is possible to achieve satisfactory results using the smallest dilling cucumbers to be found on market. (If you grow your own, pick them while a still immature 2- to 2½-inches in length.) There are two methods used for preserving. The cold preparation yields pickles of excellent flavor but slightly yellowed color. Most commercial packers use the hot method, sacrificing flavor to maintain an intensely green product.

Cornichons by the Cold Method

Small, fresh-picked cucumbers
Salt
Garlic cloves, peeled
Small pickling onions, peeled
Thyme and tarragon sprigs
Bay leaves
Black and white peppercorns
Cloves
White wine vinegar

Cut off stems and rub cucumbers with a rough towel to remove spiky growth. Place them in a stainless or earthenware dish and sprinkle generously with salt. (A large bowl will require a good pound of salt.) Leave for 1 day to soak, but turn cucumbers frequently.

At the end of this time, the cucumbers will be totally limp and flexible. Wipe each one individually to remove salt. Rinse preserving jars with scalding hot water and turn upside down to drain. Place cucumbers in jars and add to each: garlic cloves, several pickling onions, a sprig of thyme and/or tarragon, 1 bay leaf, and a few whole peppercorns and cloves. Cover with vinegar, seal, and store 5 weeks before tasting. This method will produce strong, sharply acid pickles.

Cornichons by the Hot Method

Use the same ingredients as for the cold method. Stem, rub, salt, and wipe cucumbers clean. Fill a stainless pot half full of vinegar and heat. Just as it comes to a boil, add cucumbers. Stir until an actual boil breaks, then turn heat off. Continue stirring for another 3 minutes. Leave to steep for 3 days.

Place cornichons in clean hot glass jars, adding flavoring ingredients. Bring vinegar back to boil and fill jars. Can be eaten in a week.

Dilled Pickles

Pickling cucumbers, around 4 inches long
Powdered alum
Grape leaves
Dill flowers
Garlic cloves, peeled
Thin strips of red pepper (optional)
Cloves
Black peppercorns
Coriander seeds

FOR THE BRINE (PROPORTIONS TO BE MULTIPLIED AS NEEDED)

1 cup distilled vinegar
½ cup non-iodized salt
3 cups water

Scrub cucumbers and soak overnight in cold water. Sterilize Mason jars in very hot water. Turn upside down on paper towels to drain dry. Place ¼ teaspoon alum at the bottom of each jar. Dip grape leaves in steaming water and place 1 leaf over the alum. Drain and dry the cucumbers. Pack in jars and add 2 dill flowers, 2 garlic cloves and pepper strips, and several cloves, peppercorns and coriander seeds to each. Place another grape leaf on top. Bring brine to a boil and pour over cucumbers. Screw lids on loosely. When pickles have cooled to room temperature, tighten lids.

Tomato Figs

Halve this recipe.

Take six pounds of sugar, to one peck (or sixteen pounds) of ripe tomatoes—the pear shaped look best; put them over the fire (without peeling) in your preserving kettle, their own juice being sufficient without the addition of water; boil them until the sugar penetrates and they are clarified. They are then taken out, spread on dishes, flattened and dried in the sun, or in a brick oven after the bread is taken out. A small quantity of the syrup should be occasionally sprinkled over them whilst drying; after which, pack them down in jars, sprinkling each layer with powdered sugar. They retain surprisingly their flavor, which is agreeable and somewhat similar to the best figs.

from Elizabeth E. Lea's *Domestic Cookery* (1851)

Dried Sicilian Tomatoes

Though the following method for preserving tomatoes is common in southern Italy, I was first served this curious conserve in Venice's Il Forno Restaurant. The tomatoes were at the very bottom of an antipasto cart, and the waiter who served us was almost apologetic about them, perhaps because of their oddly withered appearance. They were, he said, made by his cousin who dried the tomatoes under his native Sicilian sun. The dish is not meant to stand alone, but it can be an interesting component in a selection of hors d'oeuvres.

Take a quantity of small tomatoes, no larger than 1½ inches in diameter. (Cherry tomatoes will work.) Stem them and cut in two crosswise. Salt and either place in the sun on drying pans protected with fine screening, or in a very low oven. (In a gas oven, they eventually dry with only pilot-generated heat.) Be careful not to darken, burn or crisp the tomatoes in any way. They should slowly dehydrate, shriveling to a thoroughly chewy morsel over a period of some time. Dip each dry half in white vinegar and shake off excess. Place in jars and cover with good Italian olive oil.

Note: In the south of France, tomatoes are cut in two and placed on screens in the sun. When almost dry, they are highly salted and strung up on plain cord then, throughout the winter, they are reconstituted into potent tomato sauces.

A Thick Confiture of Peaches

5½ pounds peaches
Juice of 1 lemon
5 pounds sugar plus ½ cup

Paraffin wax

Peel peaches by dropping them briefly in boiling water to facilitate skin removal. Dice them into and over a large bowl by chopping rapidly against the pit. Add lemon juice and 1 cup of sugar from time to time. When all are chopped, add remaining sugar and let peaches sit for 3 hours. Crack ten pits and extract their interior "almonds." Blanch them in boiling water. Slip off the skins, mince nuts, and add to fruit.

In a large stainless pot or preserving pan, bring peaches slowly to a boil. Skim continually to remove the frothy gray impurities which form on the surface. About the time the necessity to skim ends, there will be a subtle change in surface activity. From a large, bubbling boil, the jam settles into a seethe which can be heard as well as seen. Regulate heat so the turmoil remains constant but is in no danger of boiling over. Count an entire cooking time of about 50 minutes, or until the peaches look uniformly dark orange and a spoonful of the fruit placed on a plate runs slowly.

Place preserving jars in a large pot of warm water and heat slowly until steaming. Remove jars and drain upside down on paper toweling. Fill with thick peaches (not syrup). Sprinkle an extra tablespoon or two of sugar on top to make a deliciously sugary first bite, then close down the glass lids and leave to cool.

Melt paraffin and pour on a thin layer. When firm, add another light coating. Dip rubber in simmering water, place on lid and seal down. Strain and refrigerate remaining peach syrup to sweeten drinks or fruit compotes.

Blueberry Jam

MAKES ABOUT 4 PINTS

Use 3 pounds of sugar to 3 pounds of fruit. Rinse berries, drain, and stir in sugar. Mash fruit lightly to start a flow of juices. Let berries sit for 3 hours, then proceed as for the confiture of peaches, but the total cooking time will be closer to 30 minutes.

Red Fruit Preserves

MAKES ABOUT 4 PINTS

Many old-fashioned cookbooks prescribe this sun-preserved method for putting by cherries, strawberries, raspberries and currants—or a mixture of same.

Rinse and drain 3 pounds of perfect fruit. Place 3 pounds of sugar in a pan, add just enough water to moisten, and bring slowly to a boil, skimming off any impurities that form. Add fruit and boil for 3 minutes. Ladle out into shallow dishes and set in intense sun for 3 days. (The preserves should be brought in each night, or if there is a danger of rain.) The pans should be off the ground and covered with light screening. When preserves are thick and slide slowly from a spoon, they are ready to be canned. (This jam will remain more vividly red than if it had been cooked.)

Whole Raspberries in Compote

Make a measured weight of unblemished raspberries. For every pound of fruit, use 1½ cups sugar. Place berries and sugar in a heavy, stainless pan. Heat gently, all the while sweeping the pan bottom with slow strokes of a wooden spatula to prevent burning. When the sugar has finally dissolved and the syrup appears transparently clear, stop stirring and allow to heat until fruit threatens to boil. Ladle into hot, sterilized jars and seal at once.

Brandied Cherries

Choose large, firm, white-fleshed cherries rather than Bings. Rinse, drain, and cut off the stems at the half point. Make two pin pricks in each cherry.

Prepare a sugar syrup to cover the fruit. Add 2 cups sugar for every cup of water, bring to a boil and simmer for 5 minutes. Add cherries to warm syrup, cover, and steep for 24 hours. Strain and layer fruit into sterilized jars. Add a cinnamon stick to each. Pour in a mixture of good quality brandy and remaining sugar syrup in equal amounts. Seal. After 2 weeks the cherries are ready for use as an ice cream topping or an element in mixed fruit compotes.

Pears in Eau-de-vie

In spring, select an insect-free, double-blossomed branch on a pear tree. Pull leaves from branch and insert blossoms, still attached, into the mouth of a handsome decanter. Tie bottle firmly to the tree, and fasten a thin layer of cheesecloth over the neck opening so no large insects can enter. Allow pears to grow in the bottle. When fruit is just short of ripe and still slightly firm, pull out the branch, leaving the pears inside. Cover with pear brandy (*eau-de-vie de poires* or *birnengeist*), and top up the bottle whenever any is poured off. This feat is also possible with apricots (use *eau-de-vie d'abricots* or *aprikosengeist*), and plums (use *mirabelle* or *pflumli*).

A Simple Potpourri Base of Roses, Orange, and Cinnamon

For several months in winter, religiously peel thin strips of orange zest from the breakfast juice oranges. Lightly roll the strips in powdered orris root and cinnamon, and leave to dry in a low or pilot-lighted oven. (Keep a small spice tin of orris root and cinnamon in equal mixture. Label it ORRIS ROOT and keep separate from regular spices as orris root can sometimes cause a mild allergic reaction when in contact with skin or eyes.)

In June, collect masses of pink, red and yellow rose petals and spread them on newspapers to dry for three days. Then mix the petals with the orange peel and cinnamon sticks (bought in bulk). Throughout the year, add rose geranium leaves, dried buds and flowers, both cultivated and wild, bits of pretty moss, seed pods, whatever strikes the fancy. At Christmas, I buy a quality floral or spice potpourri and blend it half and half with the homemade collection. Some can be used to scent the house, some can be placed in glass containers or pretty sewn bags to be given as gifts.

As potpourri needs to be refreshed from time to time, keep at least two batches on hand, one sitting open to perfume a room, the other remaining (sprinkled with refreshing oil and tightly contained) in a dark closet to renew itself.

Caswell Massey (see Appendix) has an excellent floral potpourri as well as the best general refreshing oil I know.

On Growing Herbs

A serious cook will, sooner or later, find it necessary to cultivate herbs, if not in a garden, then at least in window boxes. It is becoming more and more fashionable to have a small plot of herbs at hand, but growers frequently do not use and preserve their herbs in all the myriad ways possible. A few sprigs are plucked for *bouquets garnis*, some leaves find their way into salads, but throughout the season, many are neglected, not picked in prime time, or simply ignored.

When I first started growing herbs, I had an inexperienced gardener's obsession to collect as many herbal varieties as possible. In time, I learned what I did not like and what was not needed or responsive to my care. Though my current garden is perhaps limited, it amply provides what is, to my way of thinking, useful. There is no more huge borage taking up room and proliferating seedlings. (I never have realized its famous cucumber taste, and even the tender leaves are offensively textured to my tongue.) No more comfry, or coriander or winter savory; no more decorative tansy and yarrows to draw scores of aphids, or mints (other than spearmint) to sap the soil of nutrients. But there *are* masses of thyme and oregano, enough so that large bunches can be spared to hang from kitchen rafters. There is a glut of basil to preserve as pesto and all the *fines herbes* to freeze for winter use.

My current small garden, consisting of a central, round bed surrounded by stony walks and four corner beds, is formal in layout but most informal in growth. Some perennial elements remain constant while around them grow plots and lines of tender lettuces, *mache*, rocquette, chard and radishes. Purslane weeds its way unhampered in the paths. Wherever there is an empty space, I drop a nasturtium seed. It is a busy person's garden that can be maintained, a bed at a time, in spare moments. Here is what it contains:

Basil: An annual, with young plants available at most nurseries in the spring, or grow it quickly from seed. (If buying plants, choose low branched ones rather than the tall, stalky numbers.) Place plants or seedlings a foot apart in richly manured soil. If you have limited space, grow only a plant or two, but force them into small bushes by pinching off the top two leaves. This will cause a double branching and these can again be topped off in time, and so on until a bush forms. On no account should the plant be allowed to flower. Pick off these formations as soon as you spot them. Late in the season, basil develops a harsh, anise edge. The plant should be cut down to 5 inches, and stripped and processed before it reaches this point. Some new growth can be expected from the cut base, but if more basil is desired, an August seeding will provide leaves and a plant or two to winter indoors. Choose common lettuce leaf basil as a single variety. If space permits, grow some dwarf bush basil and sprinkle the teardrop leaves on salads and vegetables.

Chives: Cheapest to start from healthy plants purchased in grocery produce departments. Remove (or cut) plant from plastic container. Run lukewarm water over the roots until clean, and untangle. Dig a long hole in the garden, fill it with water, and set in the plant. Sprinkle in dirt until roots are surrounded. (All transplants should be extended this same, gentle, water-in-hole courtesy.) Chives that are cut constantly for culinary use will remain a tender, pale green and never turn into the coarse, dark, decorative plants that one sees in show gardens. The plants can be cut three times during the season, but they should be regularly watered and fertilized with bone meal to help maintain their stable growth. The plants will flower in the second year. Allow blossoms to develop, then cut off their thick stems at the base. To use blossoms in salads or omelets (page 33) pull individual flowerets from the umbel, for an entire blossom is impossibly strong in the mouth. The entire flower may also be hung upside down by its stem until dry and added to a dried flower arrangement. Use the most tender leaves whole in a wild salad (page 89). In spring or fall, dig up the clumps and divide again into further plants if so desired. Cut the plant down before the first frost to preserve.

Chervil: Sow from seed in both spring and fall. In spring, I sow a crop between two bushes against the north side of the house. Chervil cannot stand full summer sun and too many growers fail to take this trait seriously. The seeds sprout, the plants gain hardly any growth before they start forming flower heads and turning reddish brown. In summer, chervil almost does better grown indoors. At the end of August, a sowing can be made in the garden proper. Use chervil in *fines herbes* or float whole leaves in soup (page 48). Try a chervil (instead of parsley) butter for fish or, if your crop is plentiful, make the herb sauce (page 164) using only chervil.

Dill: Seed annually in a patch well away from fennel. Dill, like lettuce, develops a long tap root as it grows and does not, therefore, transplant easily. In order to keep a supply of tender leaves for salads or vegetables (page 71) cut down half of the central stalks and do not allow them to flower. The remaining plants can provide flowers for pickling but will lose most of their foliage in consequence. Pull out the entire plant when it dies. It is very likely that dill will self-sow and a volunteer or two can be potted and brought inside for winter.

Fennel: Plant herb fennel (rather than the bulbous finocchio) at the opposite end of the garden from dill. It is too often mistaken for that similar plant, and the two can easily cross-breed. Start from seed, and soon a long-lasting perennial patch will establish itself. Cut central stems back often so the plant does not become leggy. Tall plants grown for seed will probably need staking to keep the heavy umbel flowers from dragging on the ground. Use fennel freely in rustic fish dishes and grills (page 141). It is possible to peel the thicker stalks and slice them into salad. Cut to the ground as winter approaches.

Hyssop: Hyssop forms a most agreeable and hearty hedge if one is needed in the garden. It grows rapidly from seed in a limed soil, and the shooting, second year growth is phenomenal. Plant seedlings one foot apart. As a member of the mint family, hyssop is highly aromatic and lightly touched with muted, medicinal peppermint. Lavender blue flowers grow in whorls along its tall stalks and these can be stripped back and scattered over any rough salad to its advantage. The plant should be cut back at the end of August so it can develop strong, non-sprawling branches. Use in wild salads, over grilled fish and on eggplant.

Lemon Balm or Lemon Verbena: It is good to have at least one plant of lemon leaning to draw upon. I would choose lemon verbena if I lived in a year-round temperate clime. The leaves are much more delicately flavored than those of balm, and the fragile white flowers can be used in drinks or desserts (page 198). The plant is deciduous, so it is a simple matter to strip all leaves at season's end and dry them. The plant will not winter-over north of Washington, so it must be placed in a green house or potted and brought inside.

Lemon balm is more practical in cold climates for it is a hardy perennial that cheerfully spreads and builds into a large shrub. It can be cut down in September and dried, and the fresh leaves can always be called upon to flavor drinks and desserts.

Lovage: Probably the most satisfying herb to grow, for its development is almost breathtakingly rapid. As purchased lovage seeds are not uniformly viable, it is best to buy a plant or beg a root cutting from a friend. One plant is enough for a family and it should be allowed a large growing area, for when it reaches full, four-year-old maturity, it will cover a good three square feet. (Keep the plant small by slicing off pieces of root, each with an eye or growing leaf. Pot up and give it to friends.) Cut off the flowering stalk as soon as it appears; cut away the outer leaves as often as needed but always leave the central heart intact. Lovage provides a combinative distillation of parsley, celery, anise and yeast, and one generous stalk added to stock will yield as much of these flavors as would a small amount of the actual ingredient. The full aromatic range is obvious in Lovage Soup (page 42).

Marjoram (Sweet, Knotted): Purchased plants are the easiest way to get a good crop quickly. In the north, marjoram will have to be treated as an annual, but in more temperate situations, it can perform as a tender perennial if planted in a secure place and protected by leaves and straw over winter. The herb should receive two cuttings, the first when clustered knots suddenly appear in June. Do not leave these to open into flowers but cut directly as they form. The second cutting should come in late August when the entire plant is trimmed to a height of four inches. Marjoram is a lovely herb with its slight edge of sweetness, but when used overabundantly it soon cloys. Use it especially with eggs (page 34). The plant tends to hug and spread on the ground, so special attention should be paid to rinsing the herb and particularly the knots, before drying.

Oregano (Wild Marjoram): Purchase plants or seeds of purple flowering *Origanum vulgare* rather than the white-flowered Greek marjoram which seems to me inferior. The plant layers easily, and in a limy soil one can soon have large holdings of the herb. To layer, press some side branches to the ground and fasten to the earth with heavy hairpins. Pack dirt over the pins and in six to eight weeks, a small root structure will form. In another month, the new plant can be severed from its parent.

Oregano should be picked in full-clustered, late July flower. Cut stems quite close to the ground and soon the plant will present a dense mat of green ready to flower up again the following spring. Garnish salads and grills with flower blossoms (page 89).

Parsley: If your garden area is limited and parsley easily available in stores, use space for other purposes. If parsley is grown, the Italian or flat-leafed variety is the most useful. Soak seed in lukewarm water for twenty-four hours before planting and even then expect a lengthy germination. It seems to me best to treat the biennial parsley as an annual, for its leaves are noticeably more tender the first year. Fertilize soil well with bone meal, manure and compost. Give each plant ten inches in which to grow and pick leaves frequently throughout the summer. Use leaves and tender stalks as a deep fried garnish (page 123). When seasoning a rustic dish, use roots as well as leaves. Dig up roots, scrape clean and mince, for therein lies the most potent essence of this herb.

Rose Geranium: Have a plant or two, if only in pots, of this fragrant geranium. Add leaves to finger bowls, to desserts (page 209), to drinks —anywhere a delicate hint of rose would be appreciated. Order plants from an herb grower or start a small stem cutting in the fall from a larger plant. The plants that are set outdoors should be stripped of all leaves before the first frost. Cut plant down to an eight-inch height, dig it up, shake dirt from its roots, and hang, root up, in the cellar. Set out again in warm weather.

Rosemary: South of Washington, D.C., it is possible to grow rosemary in a protected outdoor spot and preserve it through the winter. It is difficult to grow in the north unless one has a greenhouse or is willing to pot the plant up each year, bring it indoors, and coddle and mist it through the cold season. Start with as large a plant as is possible to buy. Plant it in light, limy soil. From the second year on, trim back the branches by a third each September. Throw dried branches on a grill fire; strip back the leaves from branches and use as brochette skewers; steep leaves in warm olive oil, strain, and use oil to fry chops of all kinds.

Sage: Though sage grows readily from seed, buy the bushiest plant available for a more rapid start. Sage is a perennial, and if correctly pruned, it will grow into a large shrub, one of which should be more than sufficient for a small family. Fertilize its full-sun growing spot with bone meal. As plant develops, pinch off the top double leaves and the growth will double branch until a large bush is formed. In the fall, cut plant back to eight inches above ground. Use fresh leaves under the skin of a chicken to flavor and protect the breast. Fry leaves until crisp (page 166) and serve over liver, gnocchi, pasta or veal chops. Make Focaccia (page 17).

Savories: Of the two varieties, summer is to be preferred to winter savory. While the latter is a hardy perennial that can be trained into a bushy shrub, the leaves are coarse and of an unrefined flavor. If space is limited, plant seed or purchase plants of annual summer savory only. When the herb produces a delicate, scattered flowering along the stem length, cut the whole plant at ground level and pull up the roots. (Second growth is so negligible that it is better to pull the plant and use the ground for other purposes.) Decorate soft goat banons and other cheeses with a sprig of savory (page 26), use tender leaves in salads and, of course, with beans (page 65).

Sorrel: An established patch of ten or so sorrel plants should take care of most needs. Start from seed and as soon as plants have formed six leaves, pick off the outer two. By continually concentrating growth in the center, plants should begin producing rapidly. Pick herb frequently and thoroughly, and on no account allow the tall seed stalks to push up to any height and flower. Use tender leaves in salad, larger leaves puréed with eggs (page 36), soup, or fish. Sorrel particularly complements oily fish such as shad. A few leaves of sorrel will curdle milk.

Spearmint: In limited space, a patch of spearmint would be my only mint choice. Any growing area should be thoughtfully allocated, for the spread of mint's underground root system is insidious. In a surprisingly short time, a large area can become overgrown, and mint so robs soil of mineral nutrients that it is impossible for other herbs to grow well in the vicinity. Contain mint either by sinking a tire rim into the bed or making a planting at some distance from the garden proper. (It loves to be up against a sunny wall.) Use in summer drinks, Tabbouleh Salad (page 101) or baked with artichokes in the Roman manner (page 102). Harvest just as plants break into flower.

Tarragon: There are two varieties of tarragon, French and Russian. French is the one to locate and grow. As this plant sets no seed, you must beg cuttings from a friend or purchase one from an herb farm. Russian tarragon grows tall, willowy stems with long, pale leaves. It is reputed to become more distinguished in flavor in succeeding years, but up against French tarragon it appears vulgar from the start, and the three-year-old plants I have tasted are little better than weeds. French tarragon has dark, thin, plentiful leaves, almost spiky in appearance. Leave plant alone through its first growing season. Harvest to the ground before frost, then sprinkle area with compost and, in the north, a light layering of straw. In spring the plant will double its area, with tender shoots sprouting up all around the original cutting from underground runners. A foresightful gardener might sink a tire rim in the ground to provide hidden limits to the plant's spread. Make two cuttings in following years.

Thyme: There should be more thyme in a garden than any other herb. In addition to standard *Thymus vulgaris,* I have three or four lemon thymes, and creeping red thyme is encouraged in the walks. The plants layer themselves each year, and as a result there are always new plants available for when the three-year-old specimens, grown woody with age, need tender replacements. Thyme thrives in light, limy soil, and it produces abundant growth sufficient for two cuttings each year. Pick first in June when the pale lavender flowers are newly open. The second cutting takes place in early September so the plants have opportunity to strengthen before winter. At neither cutting should the plants be trimmed back severely. Take one quarter of the growth, then wait a week before cutting another quarter. Scatter blossoms on grilled meat or Zucchini Salad (page 89). Place whole sprigs in mixed vegetable grills. Dry old woody plants and throw on grilling fires.

Some Good General Rules:

–Early in the season and immediately before a spring rain, add bone meal and lime to the garden.

–Add manure in the autumn.

–Make and use compost if possible.

Send a soil sample to the state agricultural department to be checked. Have a pH of around 7.5 to 8.0 for rosemary, thyme, oregano, chives, hyssop, and sage. 6.5 to 7.0 does for most other herbs.

–Keep herbs clean of weeds.

–Work in coffee grounds around chive and onion family plants.

–Soak egg shells in water. Water rosemary, thyme, savory, oregano and sage. Spade crumbled shells around plants.

–Do transplanting on warm, rainy evenings.

–Harvest herbs at 11:00 a.m. after two days of full sun.

On Preserving Herbs

The following suggestions for preserving present the most practical methods I know to keep herbs throughout the winter. They allow for no waste. What will result is a yield of salted basil, basil and tarragon vinegars, pesto sauce base, frozen *fines herbes,* dried lemon and mint tea, and frozen sorrel. Some herbs will be combined to form Mixed Herbs, a rough country mélange used to flavor provincial dishes. There will be a basket of individual bunches of marjoram, sage, thyme, etc., which can be used when a pure herb is wanted; also a basket of large and generous *bouquets garnis* (most cooks make them much too small).

Basil: Cut plant down to five inches before it becomes too strongly flavored. Strip leaves, rinse in cool water and dry impeccably. Make a jar of preserved basil in the Italian manner by placing a quarter inch of kosher salt in a crock, add a thin layer of basil leaves, then continue layering salt and basil until jar is filled. Seal, refrigerate, and use in rustic preparations throughout the winter.

Make basil vinegar. Stuff two leafy stalks into a glass decanter. Bring some quality white vinegar to a boil and pour into the bottle. Stopper when cool and leave to steep for three weeks before using.

Purée remaining leaves into a base for Pesto Sauce (page 28). Purée basil, whatever quantity of garlic it will support, salt, and just enough oil to smooth the way in blender or food processor. Freeze in realistic portions. To use, unfreeze and continue with olive oil and cheese additions.

Chervil: Make frozen *fines herbes.* The term *fines herbes* too frequently means only fresh parsley, but it should stand for the traditional *quatre fines herbes:* chervil, parsley, chives and tarragon. There is little sense in making a dried mixture as the whole point to *fines herbes* in a recipe is their last-minute addition wherein the fresh, fine-minced herbs contact with heat, release their delicate volatile oils, and provide a garnishing green at the same time. When chervil is in full leaf and just before it begins to flower, roughly chop the leaves and tender stems, add an equal amount of chopped chives and only a quarter the amount of tarragon. Place a tablespoon of the mixture in individual ice cube compartments. Fill with cold water and freeze. Turn cubes into a freezer container. This will help give an idea of quantity measurement. To use, defrost, pat dry, add fresh parsley, and chop fine.

Chives: The plant will die back in winter, so cut it off three inches from the ground before frost. Add as many chives as necessary to *fines herbes* (see chervil); then chop and freeze the rest in small portions, preferably in a rapid freezing unit.

Dill: Use flowers for pickling (page 228). Add any dried seed to a commercial bottle of same. I make a point of using all foliage fresh, but if I were to preserve some, I would freeze rather than dry it.

Fennel: When the plant is tall and the flowers have begun to open into blossom, cut stalks down in five-inch lengths. Dry in a single layer. (A large drum sieve or screen door placed up on bricks is good for drying and allows air to circulate around herbs. Turn the stalks over each day until they become brittly dry. Drying area should ideally be warm, airy and shaded. An oven with pilot light works well.) Gather into large bunches and tie together. Keep a pretty basket near the stove with these and other herb bundles in it.

Hyssop: I prefer other herbs for drying. When shrubs are cut back, dry the whole stalks and use on grilling fires or in the fireplace. It should be possible to have green hyssop year round in temperate climates.

Lemon Balm and Lemon Verbena: Cut both plants down to five-inch heights three weeks before the first frost threatens. Strip leaves and dry in a single layer. Crumble them slightly, add dried mint, and an equal amount of thin, dried lemon zest to form a pleasing tea. The verbena leaves could be added to a potpourri mixture.

Lovage: Dry for *bouquets garnis.* Use the outer stalks and dry only the top five inches. (Wash, string and blanch the lower stalks. Slice and braise, along with celery, for an interesting vegetable.) Place the tops on a cake rack. Place rack on baking sheet and dry for about an hour in a 175° oven. Keep the door ajar slightly. Preserve the tops of leeks by washing them and oven drying in the same manner. Dry some sprigs of thyme. Make large, generous bundles containing one bay leaf, a lovage stalk, several thyme branches, leek greens and parsley roots. Tie up and knot a loop on the end of the string for easy fishing out of stews. Keep *bouquets* in a basket. When needed, tuck in fresh parsley stalks.

Marjoram: This herb will need special washing as it trails the ground and its knots are frequently filled with dirt. Pick five- or six-inch lengths, wash well and pat dry. Give the sprigs six minutes in a 175° oven to assure their aridity, then dry on screening. Tie bunches together and place in the herb basket. When needed, crumble knots and leaves between fingers to provide the necessary amount.

Oregano: Cut stalks down in full flower to within three inches of the ground. Rinse if necessary and dry in a single layer on screening. Gather some stalks into bundles, tie up, and place in the herb basket for those occasions that call for pure oregano. Strip all remaining leaves and flowers from the stalks. Mix with equal amounts of dried thyme, add all the summer savory, three or four pulverized bay leaves, and a small quantity of pulverized rosemary. Crumble together and, wearing gardening gloves, hand rub the herbs through a sieve (a drum sieve is easiest) so they will be uniformly sized and mixed. Keep in a jar near the stove and throw some of these Mixed Herbs into rustic dishes.

Parsley: When treating parsley as an annual, dig out by the roots at season's end. Cut off the green leaves (add to *fines herbes* if desired), and clean and dry roots and stalks by the lovage method. Add to *bouquets garnis.*

Rose Geranium: Pick all leaves before first frost. Dry them on screening, and add to rose potpourri (page 233).

Rosemary: Strip leaves from cuttings and dry on screening. Rosemary must be pulverized, for it is offputtingly like having a pine needle in the mouth if left whole. Grind in a mortar. Add a cautious amount to Mixed Herbs (see Oregano) and preserve the rest in a jar.

Sage: Brush off any dirt. Tie several cuttings together and hang the bunch, upside down, in any airy place to dry. Keep in herb basket.

Summer Savory: Cut off entire plant at the ground. Rinse if necessary, dry with paper toweling, and hang plant upside down to dry in an airy place. Strip leaves and add to Mixed Herbs (see Oregano).

Sorrel: Wash and rib leaves. Cook in the water clinging to the leaves, with a tablespoon of butter and some salt. The sorrel will melt into a purée. When quite dry, freeze. Make several batches throughout the summer.

Spearmint: Cut just before flowers open. Dry like lemon balm and add to tea.

Tarragon: Make Tarragon vinegar in the manner of basil vinegar. Add to *fines herbes* (see Chervil).

Thyme: Cut when in flower. Dry whole stalks. Make a bunch or two for the herb basket. Add sprigs to *bouquets garnis* (see Lovage), and strip the rest for Mixed Herbs (see Oregano).

Three All-Purpose Herb Mixtures

Soup Herb Spirit

Of Lemon Thyme,
Winter Savory,
Sweet Marjoram,
Sweet Basil, —half an ounce of each
Lemon Peel grated, two drachms (grams)
Eschallots, the same,
Celery Seed, a drachm, avoidupois weight.

Infuse them in a pint of Brandy for ten days; they may also be infused in Wine, or Vinegar, but neither extract the flavor of the ingredients half so well as the spirit.

These preparations are valuable auxiliaries to immediately heighten the flavour and finish Soups, Sauces, Ragouts &c.—will save much time and trouble to the Cook and keep for twenty years.

The Cook's Oracle, LONDON: 1823

Soup-herb Powder, or Vegetable Relish

Dried Parsley,
Winter Savory,
Sweet Marjoram,
Lemon-thyme, of each two ounces;
Lemon-peel, cut very thin and dried and
Sweet Basil, an ounce of each

(Some add to the above, Bay-leaves and Celery Seed, a drachm of each.)

Dry them in a warm, but not too hot Dutch oven: when quite dried, pound them in a mortar, and pass them through a double hair sieve: put in a bottle closely stopped, they will retain their fragrance and flavor for several months.

The Cook's Oracle, LONDON: 1823

Herbed Salt

2½ cups coarse sea salt (sel gros)

Chives
Lemon thyme
Lovage leaves
Chervil or parsley
Tarragon

Spread half the salt in a pie pan. Add a thin layer of mixed fresh herbs to taste. Cover with remaining salt and bake in a very slow oven (175°) for about 1 hour, or until herbs are crisp and fragile. Grind in a mortar and keep in a tightly stoppered bottle. To be used in cooking.

For further reading, some practical and knowledgeable books on herbs are:

Foster, Gertrude B. *Herbs for Every Garden.* New York: E. P. Dutton & Co., 1966.

Hewer, D. G. and Kay N. Sanecki. *Practical Herb Growing.* London: G. Bell & Sons, 1969.

Loewenfeld, Claire. *Herb Gardening.* London: Faber and Faber, 1964.

Appendix:

MAIL ORDER SOURCES

Order herb seeds, plants and catalogues from any of these reliable nurseries:

Capriland's Herb Farm
Silver Street
Coventry, Connecticut
06238
(Plants and seeds)

Howe Hill Herbs
Camden
Maine, 04843
(Plants and seeds)

Nichols Garden Nursery
1190 North Pacific Hwy.
Albany, Oregon 97321

(Plants and imported garden seeds— Giant Italian Parsley, French Swiss Chard, Rocquette, Mache, Fava Beans, Pepperoncini Peppers, Elephant Garlic, Charantais Melons, etc.)

Well Sweep Herb Farm
317 Mount Bethel Road
Port Murry, New Jersey 07865
(Plants and seeds)

Taylor Herb Garden
Vista,
California 92083
Catalogue 25¢ (herb plants only)

FRENCH SEEDS: Vilmorin-Andrieux
4, Quai de la Mégisserie
Paris, 1er
France

DRIED HERBS: Aphrodisia
28 Carmine Street
New York, N.Y. 10014 Catalogue $1.50

POTPOURRI, FRAGRANT
OILS AND FIXATIVES: Caswell-Massey Co. Ltd.
Catalogue Department
320 West 13th St.
New York, N.Y. 10014 Catalogue $1

DRIED MORELS: Maison Glass
52 E. 58th Street
New York, N.Y. 10022 Catalogue $1

NATURAL SAUSAGE CASINGS: Wagner Products Division
E. R. Wagner Manufacturing Co.
331 Riverview Drive
P.O. Box 405
Hustisford, Wis. 53034

CONFECTIONER'S CHOCOLATE: Ten pound blocks of Peter's Chocolate Coating from:
Cherrydale Farms
922 Chestnut Street
Philadelphia, Pa. 19107

EQUIPMENT: Basic restaurant equipment (drum sieves, stainless bowls, cast iron baking sheets):
Cross Imports
210 Hanover Street
Boston, Mass. 02113 Catalogue 50¢

Pasta machines, terrines, trussing needles, pretty glass serving pieces, confectioner's chocolate:

Williams–Sonoma
Mail Order Dept.
P.O. Box 3792
San Francisco, Cal. 94119
$1 brings six catalogues throughout the year

A good selection of cooking equipment at reasonable prices:

Kitchen Bazaar
4455 Connecticut Avenue N.W.
Washington, D.C. 20008
Free Cook's Tour Catalog

COMPOST BINS: Rotocrop
50 Buttonwood Street
New Hope, Pa.
18938

Index

Adams, Henry, 208
Aïoli
  Chicken Legs with, 150
  Grand, 142–45
  Sauce, 145
Almonds
  Grissini with, 18
  Pastry of Orange and, 201
  Stuffed Peaches with Ginger and, 210
  Terrine of Salmon with, 55
Artichokes
  Baked in Mint and Garlic, 102
  with Gremolata, 62
  Lamb and Mustard Cream with, 172
  Sott'olio, with Mushrooms and Olives, 60
Asparagus
  Fritters, 63
  Stew of Lettuce and, 64
  Quiche, 28
  Sauce, 64

Basil
  Basque Pipérade with, 38
  Growing, 235
  Pesto Sauce, 28
  Potato Salad with Cream of, 99
  Potato Soup with, 45
  Preserving, 243
  Rigatoni with Eggplant and, 112
  Rolled Omelets with Chicken Livers and, 161
  Salted, 243
  Zucchini Gratin with, 87
Basque Pipérade with Basil, 38
Batter
  Dumpling, 84
  Fritter, 123
Beans
  Roasted *Ceci* (Chick peas), 21
  Salad of Green, with Shrimp, 92
  Sautéed, with Savory, 65
  Soup of Green, with Pesto, 46
Beef
  Roast of, with Sauce Rémoulade, 169
  Salad of Leftover, 109
  Steak Grilled, à l'Oriental, 170
Beets, Grated with Greens, 66
Berry Turnover, 204
Beurre blanc, 121
Bing Cherry Flan, 202
Bittersweet Chocolate Tart, 196
Blackberry Pudding with Suet Crust, 205
Blueberry
  Crusted Cake of, 178
  Jam, 231
Boned, Roasted Chicken with Country Pâté, 156
Boning
  Chicken Legs, 151
  Whole Chicken, 158
Bouquets Garni. See Lovage
Bourride, 147
Braised Shank of Veal with Turnip Purée, 164
Bread, 10–18
  Filigreed Designs, 13
  Focaccia with Sage, 17

Bread (*continued*)
  Focaccia with White Wine and Olives, 16
  Grape Loaf, 14
  Ligurian Focaccia with Marjoram, 17
  Picnic Loaf, 15
  Pretzel Bread, 14
Breaded Peach Pudding, 210
Breadsticks (Almond Grissini), 18
Brandied Cherries, 232
Brik, 22
Brioche, Sausage in Herbed, 23
Brochettes
  of Mackerel with Saffron Sauce, 136
  of Shrimp with Lemon and Dill Sauce, 122
Brown Sugar Ice Cream, 221
Butter, Clarified, 63
Butter Cream, 182

Café Brûlot and Cream, 190
Cakes,
  Chilled Chocolate Framboise, 182
  Choux, with Almond Cream, 184
  Crusted Blueberry and Cream, 178
  Lemon "Terrine," 179
  Neapolitan Potato, with Sausage, 167
  Peach, 175
  Red and Green Soufflé, 31
Cantaloupe and Cassis, 215
Caramel Soufflé, 195
Cassis, Cantaloupe and, 215
Ceci, Roasted (Chick peas), 21
Celery
  Braised, with Grilled Fish, 141
  and Watercress Purée, 66
Champagne Jelly with Raspberries, 193
Chapons, grilled, with Wild Greens, 89
Chard
  Gratin of, 68
  Paupiettes of, 68
Cheese, Herbed, 26
Cherries
  Brandied, 232
  Flan of Bing, 202
  Pears in Spiced Purée of, 218
Chervil
  Growing, 236
  Preserving, 243
Chicken, 150–162
  Boned, Roasted, with Country Pâté, 156
  and Cucumbers, 152
  Herbed and Jellied, 160
  Legs, with Aïoli, 150
  Livers and Basil, Rolled in Omelets, 161
  Livers, in Molded Mousse, 58
  Pressed Lemon, 155
  Salad of Leftover, 108
  in Sorrel Cream, 153
  Stuffed "Cutlets," 151
  Vinegared, with Tomatoes and Croutons, 159
Chick peas. *See Ceci.*
Chives
  Growing, 235
  Omelet of Blossoms, 33
  Preserving, 243
Chocolate
  Bittersweet Tart, 196
  Confectioner's (source), 250
  Framboise Cakes, 182
  Malted Ice Cream, 222
  Sauce, 189
  and Vanilla Pudding with Pears, 188
Choux Cake with Almond Cream and Strawberries, 184
Cinnamon
  Potpourri of Roses, Orange and, 233
  Rolled Pastries, 212
Clarified Butter, 63
Compote
  Pineapple, in Shell, 214
  Whole Raspberries in, 232
Confiture of Peaches, 230
Consommé, Iced Seafood, 48
Corn, Grated Pudding of, 70
Cornichons
  by Cold Method, 227
  by Hot Method, 228
Crab and Onions in a Crumb Crust, 125
Cream, Sour, with Cymling Squash, 86
Crisp Sage and Liver, 166
Crumb Crust, 125
Crusted Blueberry and Cream Cake, 178

Crusted Eggplant, 107
Cucumbers
  Chicken with, 152
  Dilled Custard of, 71
  Dilled Pickles, 228
  Salad of Pickled, 105
  Stuffed, with Tomato Cream, 70
Custard
  Dilled Cucumber, 71
  Eggs in an Orange Nest, 186
  Technique, 185
Cutlets, Stuffed Chicken, 151
Cymling Squash in Sour Cream, 86

Delicacies in Grape Leaves, 78
Desserts, 175–225. *See also* Cakes; Custards; Fruits; Ice Creams; Pastries
  Berry Turnover, 204
  Café Brûlot and Cream, 190
  Champagne Jelly with Raspberries, 193
  Chocolate and Vanilla Pudding with Pears, 188
  Eggs in an Orange Nest, 186
  Raspberry "Pâté," 180
Dill
  Cucumber Custard with, 71
  Growing, 236
  Pickles, 228
  Preserving, 244
  Shrimp Brochettes, with Sauce of Lemon and, 122
Dough
  Brioche, 24
  Pasta, 113
  Pizza, 168
Dried Sicilian Tomatoes, 230
Dumplings, Herbed, with Vegetable Stew, 84

Egg(s) 33–41
  As Big As Twenty, 41
  Baked in Peppers, 39
  Basque Pipérade with Basil, 38
  Chive Blossom Omelet, 33
  with Cressed Mayonnaise, 41
  Flowered Green Frittata, 34
  Fritatta Niçoise, 35
  Lemon Soufflé Omelet, 194
  in an Orange Nest, 186
  Quick Baked, 40
  Roulade with Spinach and Sorrel, 35
  Scrambled, with Sorrel, 36
  Terrine of Salmon with, 55
Elderberry Fritters, 208
Elegant Showpieces, 7
Eggplant
  Crusted, 107
  Rigatoni with Basil and, 112
  Soufflés of, 72
Eugénie-les-bains, 226

Fast, Easy Dishes, 8
Fennel
  Growing, 237
  Preserving, 244
Fig(s)
  Raspberry and, Trifle, 206
  Sautéed, 207
  Tomato, 229
Fines Herbes, 243
Fish
  Bourride, 147
  Grilled, with Braised Celery, 141
  Kathleen Taylor's Stewed Flounder, 135
  Mackerel Brochettes with Saffron Sauce, 136
  Poached, 49
  Small, à l'Orientale, 56
  Terrine of Salmon with Eggs and Almonds, 55
  Three-layered Terrine, 52
  Whole "Soufflé" of, 139
Flemish Tart, 198
Flounder
  Fishing, 134
  Kathleen Taylor's Stewed, 135
  Paupiettes of Salmon and, 138
Flower Blossom Salad with Herbed Vinaigrette, 91
Flower Garden Soup, 43
Flowered Green Fritatta, 34
Focaccia
  Ligurian, with Marjoram, 17
  with Olives and White Wine, 16
  with Sage, 17

Forcemeats
on Mousseline, Technique, 51
Scallop Mousseline, with Watercress Sauce, 130
Shrimp Mousseline with Sauce Américaine, 128
Foster, Gertrude, 248
Fritatta
Flowered Green, 34
Niçoise, 35
Fritters
Asparagus, 63
Elderberry, 208
Shrimp and Zucchini, 123
Fruit
Berry Turnover, 204
Bing Cherry Flan, 202
Blackberry Pudding with Suet Crust, 205
Cantaloupe and Cassis, 215
Cherries, Brandied, 232
Elderberry Fritters, 208
Fig and Raspberry Trifle, 206
Figs, Sautéed, 209
Macédoine in a Brandy Snifter, 213
Nectarine Cream, 223
Oranges, Striped, 219
Peaches Aswim in Rose Petals, 209
Peaches with Ginger and Almonds, 210
Peach Pudding, Breaded, 210
Pears in Eau-de-vie, 233
Pears in Spiced Cherry Purée, 218
Pineapple Compote in the Shell, 214
Preserves of Red, 232
Raspberry "Pâté," 180
Watermelon Snail, 216
Fumet, 49

Garlic
in Aïoli, 145
Baked Artichokes in Mint and, 102
Potatoes, 82
Garnishing, for Poached Fish, 51
Génoise, 175
Ginger, Stuffed Peaches with, and Almonds, 210
Glacéed Orange Ice Cream, 220
Grand Aïoli, 142
Recipe for, 144
Appropriate wine with, 144
Granités
of Grape, 224
of Rhubarb, 224
of Tomato, 225
Grape Granité, 224
Grape Leaves, Delicacies in, 78
Grape Loaf, 14
Grated Beets and Greens, 66
Grated Corn Pudding, 70
Gratin
of Chard, 68
of Mushrooms, Provençal, 78
of Shredded Turnips, 83
of Zucchini and Basil, 87
Green Bean
and Shrimp Salad, 92
Soup, with Swirled Pesto, 46
Green Green Pasta, 113
Green Olive Paste, 21
Greens, Rough and Wild, with Walnut Sauce, 89
Gremolata, Artichokes with, 62
Grills
Breast of Lamb Riblets with Artichokes and Mustard Cream, 172
Chapons, with Wild Greens, 89
Delicacies in Grape Leaves, 78
listed, 9
Pepper Salad, 106
Smoked Fish with Braised Celery, 141
Steak and Vegetables à l'Orientale, 170
Zucchini Salad with Herb Flowers, 89
Grissini, Almond, 18
Guérard, Michel, 226

Hardboiled Eggs
an Egg As Big As Twenty, 41
Eggs with Cressed Mayonnaise, 41
Herbed Brioche, Sausage in, 24
Herbed Cheese, 26
Herbed Dumplings, Vegetable Stew with, 84
Herbed and Jellied Chicken, 160
Herbed Jelly, Spring Vegetables in, 94
Herbed Salt, 248

Herbs 234–248
  Grilled Zucchini Salad with Flowers of, 89
  Growing, 234–242
  Mixed Provincial. *See* Oregano
  Preserving, 242–248
  Sources, 249
  Vinaigrette of, 91
Herb Sauce, with Veal Chops, 164
Herb and Scallop Pie, 132
Herb Soup Powder or Vegetable Relish, 247
Herb Soup Spirit, 246
Herb Stock, 42
Hewer, D. G., 248
Hors d'oeuvres 21–26
  Brik, 22
  Green Olive Paste, 21
  Herbed Cheese, 26
  Roasted *Ceci,* 21
  Sausage in Herbed Brioche, 24
  Toasted Pan Bagnat, 23
  Toulonnais Pizzas, 22
Hyssop
  Growing, 237
  Preserving, 244

Ice Creams, 220–223
  Brown Sugar, 221
  Frozen Zabaglione, 221
  Glacéed Orange, 220
  Malted Chocolate, 222
  Nectarine Cream, 223
Iced Seafood Consommé, 48

Jack Heerick's Dutch Potato Salad, 98
Jam
  Blueberry, 231
  Quick Tart of, 203
James, Henry, 208
Jelly, Spring Vegetables in, 94

Kathleen Taylor's Stewed Flounder, 135
Kneading Bread, 12

Lamb
  Leg of, in a Crust, 173
  Riblets with Mustard Cream, 172
  Salad of Leftover, 109
La Tour d'Argent, 191
Leftovers
  Salad of Beef, 109
  Salad of Chicken, 108
  Salad of Lamb, 109
Lemon
  Leaves, 211
  Omelet Soufflé, 194
  Pressed Chicken with, 155
  Salad of Squash and, 88
  "Terrine," 179
Lemon Balm
  Growing, 237
  Preserving, 244
Lemon Verbena
  Growing, 237
  Preserving, 244
Lettuce
  with Asparagus Stew, 64
  Tabbouleh Rolled in Bibb, 101
Ligurian Focaccia with Marjoram, 17
Liver
  Chicken, with Basil, 161
  Chicken, in Molded Mousse, 58
  Crisp Sage with, 166
Loaf, Vitello Tonnato, 163
Lobster
  à l'Américaine, 126
  to kill a live, 126
Loewenfeld, Claire, 248
Lovage
  Growing, 237
  Preserving (Bouquets Garni), 244
  Soup, 42
Low-Calorie Dishes, 8

Macédoine
  in a Brandy Snifter, 213
  of Grated Vegetables, 96
Machine Pesto Sauce, 28
Mackerel Brochettes with Saffron Sauce, 136
Mail Order Sources, 249
Marinade, for Chicken, 150
Marjoram
  Ligurian Focaccia with, 17
  Growing, 238
  Preserving, 245

Mayonnaise
  Aïoli, 145
  Eggs with Cressed, 41
McCarthy, Mary, 208
Meat. *See* Beef; Chicken; Lamb; Liver; Veal
Melba Sauce, 223
Menus, 7
Mint
  Baked Artichokes in, and Garlic, 102
  Growing, 241
  Preserving, 246
Mirepoix, 92
Molds
  of Chicken Liver Mousse, 58
  of *Risotto alla Primavera,* 110
  of Spring Vegetables in Herbed Jelly, 94
Morels
  Hunting, 74
  Sausage of, Fresh, 75
  Source of Dried, 250
Mousse, Molded Chicken Liver, 58
Mousseline Forcemeats
  Scallop, with Watercress Sauce, 130
  Shrimp, with Sauce Américaine, 128
  Technique, 51
Mushrooms
  with Artichokes and Olives, *Sott'-olio,* 60
  Hunting, 74
  Morel Sausage, 75
  Provençal Gratin, 78
  Quiche, 29

Nasturtium, Rolled Stuffed Salad of Leaves, 102
Neapolitan Potato Cake with Sausage, 167
Nectarine Cream, 223
Niçoise, Frittata, 35

Olive(s)
  Focaccia with White Wine and, 16
  Paste of Green, 21
  Quiche, 30
  Sott'olio, with Artichokes and Mushrooms, 60
Omelets
  Chive Blossom, 33
  Flowered Green Fritatta, 34
  Fritatta Niçoise, 35
  Lemon Soufflé, 194
  Rolled, Stuffed, with Chicken Livers and Basil, 161
One-Dish Meals, 9
Onion
  Flowers, with Pine Nuts, 104
  Thin Tart of, 80
Orange
  and Almond Pastry, 201
  Eggs in a Nest of, 186
  Ice cream, Glacéed, 220
  Potpourri Base of, with Roses and Cinnamon, 233
  Striped, 219
Oregano
  Growing, 238
  Preserving, 245
Oriental Salad Plate, 97

Pan Bagnat, Toasted, 23
Parsley
  Growing, 239
  Preserving, 245
Participation Dishes, 6
Pasta
  Green Green, 113
  Rigatoni with Eggplant and Basil, 112
  with Scallops, à la Provençal, 116
Paste, Green Olive, 21
Pastry
  Berry Turnover, 204
  Brik, 22
  Lemon Leaves, 211
  Orange and Almond, 201
  Prebaked Pie shells, 200
  Rolled Cinnamon, 212
  Rough Puff (technique), 199
  Suet Crust, 205
Pâté
  Raspberry, 180
  Rough Country, in Boned Chicken, 156
Patty Pan Squash. *See* Cymling Squash
Paupiettes
  of Chard, 68

Paupiettes (*continued*)
of Salmon and Flounder, 138
Peach (es)
Aswim in Rose Petals, 209
Breaded Pudding, 210
Cake, 175
Confiture of, 230
Stuffed with Ginger and Almonds, 210
Pears
in Eau-de-vie, 233
Poached, with Chocolate and Vanilla Pudding, 188
in Spiced Cherry Purée, 218
Peppers
Eggs Baked in, 39
Grilled Salad of, 106
Persillade, 85
Pesto
Green Bean Soup with Swirled, 46
Sauce, 28
Tomato Tart with, 27
Pickled Cucumber Salad, 105
Pickles
Cornichons, Hot Method, 227
Cornichons, Cold Method, 228
Dilled, 228
Picnic Food, 6
Picnic Loaf, 15
Pie, Scallop and Herb, 132
Pineapple Compote in the Shell, 214
Pine Nuts, Onion Flowers with, 104
Pipérade with Basil, 38
Pizza
Elegant Shrimp, 116
Stuffed, 167
Toulonnais, 22
Poached Fish, 49
Poaching, technique, 50
Polenta Tart, 81
Potato (es),
Cake, Neapolitan, with Sausage, 167
Garlic, 82
Salad, in Basil Cream, 99
Salad, Jack Heerick's Dutch, 98
Soup, with Swirled Tomato and Basil, 45
Potpourri Base of Roses, Orange and Cinnamon, 233
Potpourri Oils and Fixatives, source, 250
Praline, 182
Prebaked Pie Shell (technique), 200
Preserves
Blueberry Jam, 231
Cherries, Brandied, 232
Peaches, Thick Confiture of, 230
Pears in Eau-de-vie, 233
Potpourri Base, 233
Raspberries, Whole in Compote, 232
of Red Fruit, 232
Tomatoes, Dried Sicilian, 230
Tomato Figs, 229
Pressed Lemon Chicken, 155
Pretzel Bread, 14
Provençal Mushroom Gratin, 78
Pudding
Blackberry, with Suet Crust, 205
Chocolate and Vanilla, with Poached Pears, 188
Corn, Grated, 70
Peach, Breaded, 210
Purées
of Celery and Watercress, 66
of Shrimp with Watercress Cream, 47
of Spiced Cherries with Pears, 218

Quiche
Asparagus, 28
Crab and Onions in a Crumb Crust, 125
Mushroom, 29
Olive, 30
Quick Baked Eggs, 40

Raspberries
Champagne Jelly with, 193
in Compote, 232
"Pâté," 180
Trifle, with Fresh Figs, 206
Ratatouille Terrine, 72
Red Fruit Preserves, 232
Red and Green Soufflé Cakes, 31
Rhubarb Granité, 224
Rice
Molded *Risotto alla Primavera*, 110
Salad of Wild, 100

Rigatoni with Eggplant and Basil, 112
Risotto, Molded, *alla Primavera*, 110
Roast of Beef with Sauce Rémoulade, 169
Roasted *Ceci* (Chick peas), 21
Rolled Cinnamon Pastries, 212
Rolled, Stuffed Omelets with Chicken Livers and Basil, 161
Rose Geranium
  Growing, 239
  Preserving, 245
Rosemary
  Growing, 239
  Preserving, 245
Rose Petals, Peaches Aswim in, 209
Roses, Potpourri Base of, with Orange and Cinnamon, 233
Rough Puff Pastry, 199
Rough and Wild Greens with Grilled Chapons and Walnut Sauce, 89
Roulade with Spinach and Sorrel, 35

Sage
  Focaccia with, 17
  Growing, 240
  Liver and Crisp, 166
  Preserving, 245
Salad Dressings
  Herbed Vinaigrette, 91
  Walnut Sauce, 89
Salads 88–109
  Artichokes, Mushrooms and Olives *Sott'olio*, 60
  Flower Blossom, with Herbed Vinaigrette, 91
  Green Bean and Shrimp, 92
  Grilled Pepper, 106
  Grilled Zucchini, with Herb Flowers, 89
  Jack Heerick's Dutch Potato, 98
  Leftover Beef, 109
  Leftover Chicken, 108
  Leftover Lamb, 109
  Macédoine of Grated Vegetables, 96
  Molded Spring Vegetables in Jelly, 94
  Oriental Plate, 97
  Rough Greens with Walnut Sauce and Grilled Chapons, 89
  Pickled Cucumber, 105
  Potato, in Basil Cream, 99
  Squash and Lemon, 88
  Stuffed Nasturtium Leaves, 102
  Tabbouleh Rolled in Bibb Lettuce, 101
  Wild Rice, 100
Salmon
  Paupiettes of Flounder and, 138
  Terrine of, with Eggs and Almonds, 55
Salt, Herbed, 248
Sanecki, Kay N., 248
Sauce
  Aïoli, 145
  Américaine, 126
  Asparagus, 64
  Beurre Blanc, 121
  Chocolate, 189
  Herb, with Veal Chops, 164
  Lemon and Dill, with Shrimp Brochettes, 122
  Machine Pesto, 28
  Mayonnaise, 145
  Melba, 223
  Pesto, 28
  Reduced Cream Sauce, 120
  Reduced "Stock" Sauce, 120
  Reduced Tomato Sauce, 120
  Rémoulade, 169
  Saffron, 136
  Simple Summer, 120
  Tomato, 39
  Watercress, 132
Sausage
  Casings (source), 250
  Fresh Morel, 75
  in Herbed Brioche, 24
  Neapolitan Potato Cake with, 167
Sautéed Beans with Savory, 65
Sautéed Figs, 207
Sautéed Vegetables with Persillade, 85
Savory (summer and winter)
  Growing, 240
  Preserving, 246
  Sautéed Beans with, 65
Scallops
  Mousseline of, with Watercress Sauce, 130

Scallops (*continued*)
Pasta with, 116
Pie of Herbs and, 132
Scrambled Eggs
Basque Pipérade with Basil, 38
with Sorrel and Croûtons, 36
Seafood
Crab and Onions in a Crumb Crust, 125
Iced Seafood Consommé, 48
Lobster à l'Américaine, 126
Pasta with Scallops à la Provençal, 116
Scallop and Herb Pie, 132
Scallop Mousseline with Watercress Sauce, 130
Shrimp on a Bed of Spinach, 119
Shrimp Brochettes with Lemon and Dill Sauce, 122
Shrimp Mousseline with Sauce Américaine, 128
Shrimp "Pizza," 116
Shrimp Purée with Watercress Cream, 47
Shredded Turnip Gratin, 83
Shrimp on a Bed of Spinach, 119
Brochettes with Lemon and Dill Sauce, 122
Fritters of Zucchini and, 123
Mousseline with Sauce Américaine, 128
"Pizza," 116
Purée, with Watercress Cream, 47
Salad of, with Green Beans, 92
Small Fish à l'Orientale, 56
Sorrel
Chicken in Cream of, 153
Growing, 240
Preserving, 246
Purée of, 246
Roulade with Spinach and, 35
Scrambled Eggs with, 36
Soufflés
Cold Caramel, 195
Eggplant, 72
Lemon Omelet, 194
Red and Green Cakes, 31
of Whole Fish, 139
Soup-herb Powder, or Vegetable Relish, 247
Soup Herb Spirit, 246
Soups 42–49
Bourride, 147
Flower Garden, 43
Green Bean with Pesto, 46
Iced Seafood Consommé, 48
Lovage, 42
Potato, with Tomato and Basil, 45
Purée of Shrimp with Watercress Cream, 47
Spinach,
Roulade with Sorrel and, 35
Shrimp on a Bed of, 119
Squash
Cymling in Sour Cream, 86
Salad of Lemon and, 88
Zucchini and Basil Gratin, 87
Zucchini Salad with Herb Flowers, 89
Steak, Grilled with Vegetables à l'Orientale, 170
Stew
of Lettuce and Asparagus, 64
of Vegetables with Herbed Dumplings, 84
Stock
Fish, 148
Herb, 42
Strawberries, Choux Cake with Almond Cream and, 184
Striped Oranges, 219
Stuffed Chicken "Cutlets," 151
Stuffed Cucumbers with Tomato Cream, 70
Stuffed Nasturtium Leaves, 102
Stuffed Pizza, 167
Stuffed Tomato Tart with Pesto, 27
Suet Crust, 205
Summer Bread, 11
Summer Menus (general thoughts), 5
Swift, Jonathan, 63
Swirled Soups
Green Bean, with Pesto, 46
Potato with Tomato and Basil, 45
Purée of Shrimp with Watercress Cream, 47

Tabbouleh Rolled in Bibb Lettuce, 101
Tarragon
  Growing, 241
  Preserving, 246
Tarts
  Bing Cherry Flan, 202
  Bittersweet Chocolate, 196
  Flemish, 198
  Onion, 80
  Polenta, 81
  Quick Jam, 203
  Stuffed Tomato, 27
Terrail, Claude, 192
Terrine
  Lemon, 179
  Ratatouille, 72
  Salmon, with Eggs and Almonds, 55
  Three-layered Fish, 52
Thin Onion Tart, 80
Three-layered Fish Terrine, 52
Thyme
  Growing, 241
  Preserving, 246
Toasted Pan Bagnat, 23
Tomato (es)
  Dried Sicilian, 230
  Figs, 229
  Granité, 225
  Potato Soup with, and Basil, 45
  Sauce, 39
  Tart of, with Pesto, 27
Toulonnais Pizzas, 22
Trifle, Fresh Fig and Raspberry, 206
Turnip
  Purée with Spring Vegetables and Veal, 164
  Shredded Gratin of, 83

Veal
  Braised Shank of, with Spring Vegetables and Turnip Purée, 164
  Chops, with Herb Sauce, 164
  Vitello Tonnato Loaf, 163
Vegetable (s) 60–87
  Artichokes with Gremolata, 62
  Artichokes, Mushrooms and Olives *Sott'olio*, 60
  Asparagus Fritters, 63
  Asparagus Quiche, 28
  Beans, Sautéed with Savory, 65
  Beets and Greens, Grated, 66
  Corn Pudding, Grated, 70
  Cucumber Custard, Dilled, 71
  Cucumbers with Tomato Cream, 70
  Delicacies in Grape Leaves, 78
  Eggplant, Crusted, 107
  Lettuce and Asparagus Stew, 64
  Macédoine of, Grated, 96
  Molded, in Herbed Jelly, 94
  Mushroom Quiche, 29
  Potatoes, Garlic, 82
  Sautéed, with Persillade, 85
  Stew, with Herbed Dumplings, 84
  Tomato Tart with Pesto, 27
  Turnip Gratin, Shredded, 83
  Turnip Purée and Spring, with Braised Veal, 164
Vinaigrette, Herbed, 91
Vinegared Chicken with Tomatoes and Croutons, 159
Vitello Tonnato Loaf, 163

Walnut Sauce, with Wild Salad, 89
Watercress
  Eggs with Cressed Mayonnaise, 41
  Purée of Celery and, 66
  Purée of Shrimp with Cream of, 47
  Scallop Mousseline with Sauce of, 130
Watermelon Snail, 216
White Wine, Foccacia of, Olives, 16
Whole Fish "Souffle," 139
Wild Rice Salad, 100

Zabaglione, Frozen, 221
Zucchini
  Fritters of Shrimp and, 123
  Gratin of, and Basil, 87
  Salad of Grilled, with Herb Flowers, 89

Judith Olney

Judith Olney has kept a home and cooked on three continents. She received her professional training as an apprentice at the Westminster Catering School, the Connaught Hotel and the Belgian Pâtisserie in London, and at Avignon with her brother-in-law, Richard Olney. She now conducts regular cooking classes in Durham, North Carolina, where she lives, as well as in various schools and kitchens throughout the country.